London 1849

London 1849

A VICTORIAN MURDER STORY

Michael Alpert

Harlow, England • London • New York • Boston • San Francisco • Toronto
Sydney • Singapore • Hong Kong • Tokyo • Seoul • Taipei • New Delhi
Cape Town • Madrid • Mexico City • Amsterdam • Munich • Paris • Milan

PEARSON EDUCATION LIMITED

Edinburgh Gate
Harlow CM20 2JE
Tel: +44 (0)1279 623623
Fax: +44 (0)1279 431059
Website: www.pearsoned.co.uk

_____

First edition published in Great Britain in 2004

© Pearson Education Limited 2004

The right of Michael Alpert to be identified as author of this work has been
asserted by him in accordance with the Copyright, Designs and Patents Act 1988.

ISBN 0 582 77290 7

British Library Cataloguing in Publication Data
A CIP catalogue record for this book can be obtained from the British Library

Library of Congress Cataloging in Publication Data
A CIP catalog record for this book can be obtained from the Library of Congress

10   9   8   7   6   5   4   3   2   1

Set by 35 in 9.5/14pt Melior
Printed and bound in China
GCC/01

The Publishers' policy is to use paper manufactured from sustainable forests.

Contents

Acknowledgements   viii

Introduction   1

1   'Orrible murder in Bermondsey   4

2   'An extremely fine woman'   25

3   What they ate and what they wore   43

4   In sickness and in health   69

5   Money, housing and class   87

6   Learning, literature and liturgy   110

7   'A burst of applause that made the building ring'   132

8   Outsiders   155

9   Communications   176

10   Crime and punishment   197

Epilogue   219

Bibliography   221

Index   229

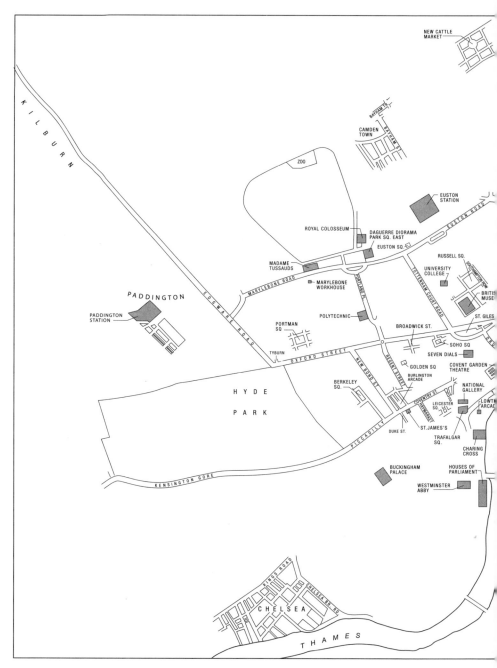

London at mid-century

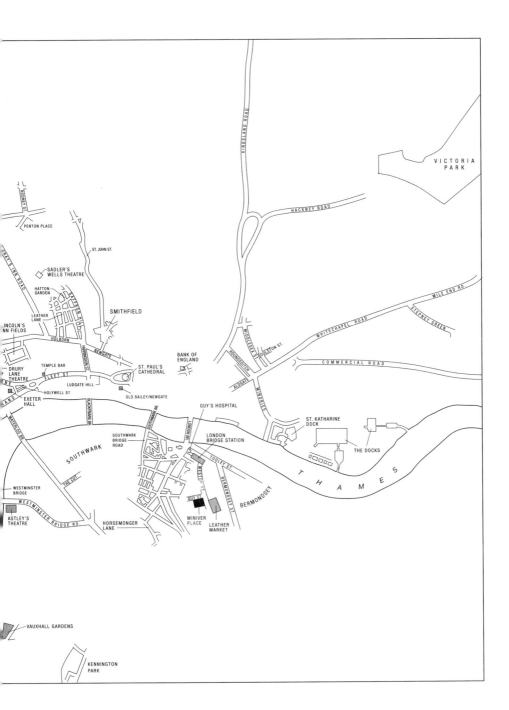

Acknowledgements

The publishers would like to thank the following for permission to reproduce copyright material:

Bodleian Library, University of Oxford for plates 1, 2, 3, 4, 5, 11, 12, 13, 15, 16, 19, 20, 25, 26, 27, 28, 30, 31, 32, 34, 35, 36, 38, 44, 45, 46, 47.

London Transport Museum for plates 42, 43.

Mary Evans Picture Library for plates 9, 10, 24, 33.

Southwark Local Studies Library for plate 21.

Westminster Local Archives (photographer Geremy Butler) for plate 8.

In some instances we have been unable to trace the owners of copyright material, and we would appreciate any information that would enable us to do so.

Introduction

The murder of Patrick O'Connor by Maria and Frederick Manning, their trial and subsequent execution have already been written about, notably by Albert Borowitz, but no book has used the affair, as Heather McCallum, my editor at Pearson Education, suggested, as a background to a picture of life in London in the particular year of the crime: 1849.

1849 came between the great revolutionary scare of 1848, at the end of the 'Hungry Forties', when London was shaken by the threat of Chartism and seemed to be under invasion by Continental revolutionaries, and the high noon of the century: the Great Exhibition of 1851. 1849 was also the year of the great cholera epidemic, of a rash of women murderers and of the threat – as yet on the other side of the Atlantic – of Mrs Amelia Bloomer's perceived brand of feminism. In many ways, 1849 lay on the cusp of brilliant new technical developments. The omnibus, the railway, the penny post, anaesthetics and the telegraph were either becoming familiar or just coming into use, while contraception, antiseptics and employment for women, other than as sweated labour or governesses, were imminent.

The murder of Patrick O'Connor by the Mannings occupies part of the first chapter of this book, and their trial and execution are described in the last part of the final chapter. In between, I find myself continually referring to Maria and Frederick Manning – what did they do and what might they have done? – in my accounts of food, clothes, medicine, entertainment, communications and the multifarious picture which I have tried to draw of ordinary people's lives in London at mid-century. Very often valuable information about the details of life are to be found, almost by accident and by the way, in the evidence presented in the investigation and trial of the Manning murder; at other times, a range of sources, together with the press and the very geography of the city, allow me to speculate on how the Mannings lived and what they did.

I have used the rich resources of the London Library and University College London. My friend and ex-colleague Professor Donald Hawes has lent me books, encouraged me and shared his extensive knowledge of Victorian life and literature. Francis McFarland has devoted his intense powers of concentration to listening to me read my raw chapters aloud, spotting inconsistencies, repetitions and awkward phrases. Philip Bagwell supplied important railway information. Brenda Weeden, archivist of the University of Westminster, found useful material for me on the mid-nineteenth-century Polytechnic. Dr Barry Hoffbrand read the chapter on medical matters and saved me from making howlers. Dr Gordon Higgott gave me valuable advice on Victorian housing in London. The Southwark Local Studies Library came up with the photograph of No.3 Miniver Place, just before it was demolished over a century after the murder had been committed, while the archivist at Westminster City Archives has helpfully found and provided me with a copy of the Mannings' marriage entry with its useful information.

I owe much thanks to my patient wife. She has had to cope with a husband who, besides his normal tendency to absent-mindedness, must have seemed for the last few months to be living in 1849.

Note on money

It may be helpful to explain how sums of money were expressed before the currency was decimalised in 1971. The change was not merely a question of arithmetic, but also of the vocabulary and even of the oral expression with which people described how much something cost.

In 1849 relatively few people ever handled a pound (also called a sovereign) or even a half-sovereign. The pound was divided into twenty shillings (a 'guinea' was not a coin but the sum of 21 shillings). Each shilling had twelve pence. There were quarter-pence ('farthings') and halfpence, referred to as ha'pence (pronounced 'hay-pence'). Pence were abbreviated as d (the Latin *denarius*), so one wrote, for example, 10d but said 'tenpence' with the stress on the first syllable. Shillings were abbreviated as s or /-. Thus one pound and five shillings would be written as £1 5s, £1.5/-, 25s or 25/-. One usually said 'twenty-five shillings'. When shillings and pence were quoted together the sum would be expressed, for example, as 7/6, or 7s 6d, that is seven shillings and sixpence or, colloquially, 'seven and six'.

So, something might cost £1 5s $4\frac{1}{2}$d, or one pound, five shillings and four and one-half pence. People would say 'one pound, five and fourpence ha'penny' or 'twenty-five and fourpence ha'penny'.

Twopence was pronounced 'tuppence' and threepence 'thruppence'. Sixpence was referred to as 'a tanner', a shilling as 'a bob' and 2s 6d as 'half a crown'.

The table below shows equivalent values for pre- and post-decimal British coinage (these are approximate for amounts under 6d).

Table of equivalences

'Old' money	Decimalised
1d	$\frac{1}{2}$p
$2\frac{1}{2}$d	1p
6d	$2\frac{1}{2}$p
1/-	5p
2/-	10p
2/6	$12\frac{1}{2}$p
5/-	25p
7/6	$37\frac{1}{2}$p
10/-	50p
15/-	75p

CHAPTER 1

'Orrible murder in Bermondsey[1]

Cross over London Bridge from the north to the south side of the River Thames and turn immediately left into Tooley Street; walk along a few yards, leaving London Bridge Station on your right. A little further on, cross the road, dodging the traffic, and walk under the railway tracks which now, as in 1849, run south-east on a series of arches towards Greenwich. The road under the tracks, still dark and dank, is Weston Street, and when it emerges on the other side it continues southwards through the part of London known as Bermondsey. Its narrow streets were once busy with people, mostly of the poorer class, whose children played noisily in the streets, which were lined with stalls and noisy with the rattling of wooden and metal wheels on the cobblestones, the cries of the coalman, the milkman and the people who made a living from what they could sell or the services they could provide. Only on Sunday did a hush fall, punctuated by the bells of the many churches. At night, especially in the winter, the streets were dark. Shop fronts were shuttered, as were house windows. The few gas lamps cast a dim, yellowish light under which a patrolling police constable stopped to consult his watch. But the gin palaces and public houses brought a riot of sudden noise and light when their doors opened and their carousing customers poured out, bidding each other noisy farewells before dispersing to their dark, cold homes.

Today, the streets are eerily silent. Nobody may cause an obstruction in them with a stall or bawl his wares. Cars drive through but children play elsewhere. The streets are dotted with expensive restaurants. The old pubs and gin palaces are now fashionable bars, and the people lunching in them wear smart suits, speak into mobile phones and rush out to feed the meter with coins to allow them to park expensive cars in the gutter where shabby men and worn-out women used to offer a few cheap goods for sale. The area has been colonised by the public relations consultants, the lawyers and the property men, while the older inhabitants are corralled away from the street into public housing. They do their shopping in distant malls rather than in the neighbouring market whose fancy cheeses and organic produce suit neither their taste nor their pockets.

Further down Weston Street you come into the area which used to be the centre of the Bermondsey leather-tanning trade. Many of these smelly alleys were bombed in the Second World War or later demolished for slum clearance, and were replaced by patches of grass. There is no longer any trace of the tanning trade except the late nineteenth-century leather-market building itself, now partitioned into offices.

Just off on the right is Guy Street, where a century and a half ago, in 1849, close by the corner stood a row of newish two-storey villas. Street names were not standardised; the terrace was called Minver or Miniver Place.[2]

In nineteenth-century London people rented their homes. Contracts used to begin on what were called quarter days. On Lady Day (25 March) 1849, a couple called Frederick and Maria Manning took a year's tenancy of 3 Miniver Place. Frederick was about 30 and Maria 28 years old. The rent, probably about £22 a year, plus the extra charges called the Poor Rate and the Church Rate, were beyond their means, so they invited Patrick O'Connor, a tall Irishman of about 50, who had been Maria's lover before her marriage and still maintained relations with her, to be their subtenant. He agreed but then went back on his word when the couple had already signed the lease, so they had to take a different tenant, a medical student called William Massey from the nearby Guy's Hospital.

Although the Mannings owned some capital, they had difficulties in ensuring a regular income for themselves. O'Connor, in contrast, was a well-off moneylender who had shares in French railway companies. Maria bore a grudge against him for not marrying her, and also suspected that he was having affairs with other women.

The Mannings conspired to murder the Irishman and rob him of his cash and shares. On 25 July 1849, Frederick bought a crowbar; on the 26th the couple ordered a bushel of quicklime for 6d (plus 1½d for a boy to bring it); on the 28th they told the lodger to go, saying that they intended to spend some time out of London; Maria bought a shovel in Tooley Street on the morning of Thursday 9 August.

The Mannings had invited O'Connor to dine that same evening at five. Somewhat earlier, two acquaintances saw him crossing London Bridge on his way to 3 Miniver Place. Only his murderers saw him alive after that.

The afternoon was still hot when O'Connor arrived. Maria suggested that he might like to have a cooling wash in the basement kitchen. She led him over a hole, where they had lifted a flagstone to dig a pit for his corpse, and told him that it had been excavated for some work which was needed on the drains. As he bent over the sink to cool his head and neck, one of the couple, probably Maria, shot him through the back of the head with a pistol which Frederick had recently bought at a gunsmith's. O'Connor fell. According to the confession that Frederick Manning wrote in the death cell, the Irishman was still breathing stertorously. Frederick, now at last able to discharge the hatred he felt towards his wife's lover, raised the crowbar high above his head and finished the dying O'Connor off in a paroxysm of anger – the police surgeon estimated that O'Connor had suffered seventeen savage blows to the head with the crowbar. Then the Mannings stripped their victim, bent his legs up behind him, bound them to his trunk with strong cord and manhandled the corpse into the pit under the stone-flagged floor, covering it with the quicklime which at once began to eat O'Connor's body away. Then they relaid the flagstone and plastered it with new mortar. Some journalists later wrote that the couple then sat down calmly to eat the goose that Maria had cooked for the three of them to enjoy.

Later on that evening, Maria went to O'Connor's lodgings, crossing London Bridge and turning east through Aldgate and busy Whitechapel to Mile End, where the Irishman had a bedroom and a sitting room over a shop on the corner of Greenwood Street. If she took a cab it was never traced. Given the crowded streets and the slow pace of omnibuses, the police calculated that it would not have taken her much longer to walk than to ride the two miles. O'Connor's landlady, Ann Armes, told the court that her tenant had instructed her to allow Maria into his rooms even when he was not there. Maria rifled his possessions, taking all the cash she could find and a number of share certificates.

Strangely enough, the Mannings were in no great hurry to run away, nor do they seem to have laid their plans with care. O'Connor's workmates reported him as missing when he did not appear either the next day or the day after at the docks, where he worked as a 'gauger' or inspector of ships' cargoes in the excise duty department. Since O'Connor had met one of his colleagues as he was crossing London Bridge on his way to dinner at the Mannings, his workmates asked the police to go with them to 3 Miniver Place. Here Mrs Manning denied any knowledge of the Irishman's whereabouts. She insisted that O'Connor had not dined there, which was suspicious since he had been seen on the way. On the following Monday, 13 August, a policeman again visited the house and questioned Maria more closely. He noticed that she seemed nervous but still insisted that O'Connor had not come to dinner. He might well have been seen on his way, she said, but he was a man who often changed his mind at the last moment.

O'Connor's friend, William Flynn, was nothing if not persistent. On the Monday, he visited O'Connor's rooms, discovering that Maria had been there and that the moneylender's cashbox had been looted. Then he learned that, on that same afternoon, 13 August, Maria had left 3 Miniver Place in a hansom cab with several large trunks and boxes. The next day he also discovered that the house was empty of furniture. A search made late on the Tuesday found little in the house, except signs of a hasty departure. The next morning a second-hand dealer called Bainbridge came to pick up the furniture, which Frederick Manning had sold him for £13. Bainbridge told the police that Manning had been staying with him and had just left.

As yet, there was no reason to suspect foul play. O'Connor might have left his lodgings hurriedly and arranged to meet the Mannings, or perhaps just Maria, somewhere else. But two days later, on Friday 17 August, already eight days after the murder, two police constables were sent to Miniver Place to make a thorough investigation. They dug fruitlessly in the garden and then went into the house. In the basement kitchen, they noticed that everything was much more neat and tidy than in the rest of the house. One of the flagstones appeared to have dampish mortar around it. One police constable checked with his pocket knife. The mortar gave easily. It seemed new. Borrowing tools from some labourers working nearby, the policemen lifted the flagstone. Under it was a bed of damp mortar and a layer of hurriedly gathered earth. A little way down they found a human toe and then the rest of the gruesome corpse, almost unrecognisable after more than a week under its coat of quicklime.

A local surgeon, closely observed by an eager journalist, lifted the skull away and found several fractures in it. Reaching into the repellent relic, in which the brain had already decomposed, he removed a set of false teeth. Just behind the right frontal bone of the skull, the police surgeon, who had now arrived, discovered the bullet that had been fired into O'Connor's head. Shortly after, the dentist who had made the false teeth identified them as O'Connor's.

Hue and cry

The hunt was on. Where were the Mannings? An emigrant ship, the *Victoria*, had been lying in London docks, due to sail that same Friday, 17 August. An acute reporter questioned the baggage-master, who told him that there was luggage on board marked with the name Manning. Messages flashed to and fro on the recently invented telegraph, and late that evening, Admiral Capel, in command of the naval base at Portsmouth and acting on a request from the police and the Home Office, ordered a fast frigate, the *Fire Queen*, commanded by Captain Allen, to catch and stop the *Victoria*. At 1.45 a.m. on the Saturday the *Victoria* was boarded, but the most respectable and American Mrs Manning, who was on board with her daughter, was named Rebecca, not Maria.

Maria, in fact, had been seen leaving 3 Miniver Place the previous Monday afternoon, 13 August, in a cab. Where had she gone? The police eventually tracked down the cab driver, William Kirk, who said that he had taken 'a female of very respectable exterior' (this sounds like the police description rather than the words the cab driver would have used) with some large boxes and trunks. She had told him to go to London Bridge Station but on the way she had stopped him at a stationer's and bought some labels. Asking for a pen and ink, she had inscribed on the labels the lines: 'Mrs Smith, Passenger to Paris. To be left till called for.' At the station she had told a porter to fix the labels on the boxes and had deposited them in the left-luggage office. The police opened and searched the trunks and found Maria's clothes. Even though these were only a small part of her wardrobe, the police inventory covered four foolscap sheets.

But where was Maria? Perhaps she did intend to go to Paris at some time, which was probably a wise thing to do, especially if she continued on to her native Switzerland. British consuls in the French Channel ports were asked to keep their eyes open for her. A police inspector and a sergeant went to Paris, where the French police searched hotels for the Mannings and kept a watch on the railway stations. Could Maria have been extradited if she had been arrested in France? In theory, there was an Anglo-French agreement on extradition, but Britain had refused to hand over most of the offenders demanded by the French authorities in the previous few years, so it doesn't seem likely that the French would have handed over even obvious murder suspects like the Mannings.[3]

It would have taken longer to trace Maria had she not re-engaged William Kirk's cab to drive her from London Bridge Station to Euston Square Station, as it was still called. Here she appears to have stayed all night, perhaps taking a room at the Adelaide or the Victoria Hotel, both of which stood until 1963 when the station was rebuilt. She left at 6.15 the next morning in a first-class carriage for Edinburgh, paying an excess charge for the several trunks she instructed the porter to place in the luggage van. In the Scottish capital Maria took rooms but she aroused suspicion by trying to sell the share certificates which she had removed from O'Connor's lodgings. A canny Scots stockbroker to whom she tried to sell some shares noted her foreign accent, though she said her father's name was Robertson and lived in Glasgow. The stockbrokers were soon made aware by circular letter that certain railway share certificates had been stolen in London and were not to be handled. This aroused their suspicions and they went to the Edinburgh police, who had already been wired from London via the newly introduced telegraph to look out for Maria. She had given the stockbrokers a note of the address where she had taken a room, so the police had no difficulty in finding her. As she sat trying to compose herself with the aid of a glass or two of wine, the police searched her luggage and found seventy-three gold sovereigns, a bank-note for fifty pounds, a five pound note and six ten pound notes: £188 in total, though it turned out that more than a third of this belonged to the

Mannings themselves. Maria also had O'Connor's French railway shares and some that he was holding for her. The police then arrested her for the murder of Patrick O'Connor.

It was Maria's chattering that had trapped her so soon. She could not resist telling fanciful accounts to the stockbrokers, which only attracted their attention. As for Frederick, his addiction to the brandy bottle also led him to behave boastfully, to quarrel and ultimately to draw attention to himself. He left No. 3 Miniver Place on Tuesday 14 August. The house was now empty, probably without even a bed, so Frederick slept at the Bainbridges', the dealer to whom he had sold the furniture. In any case, to sleep alone in the house where O'Connor's body was rotting away under the flagstones in the basement kitchen would have been hard for even a stronger-minded man than Frederick Manning. On the Wednesday he left the Bainbridge house. He travelled to Southampton from the nearby and recently opened Waterloo Station, stayed at a pub for a few hours, and took the midnight crossing to the Channel Island of Jersey. Apparently unable to control his tongue, he started a conversation with a man on board ship and took a room with him in St Helier, capital of the island. Foolishly he attracted everybody's attention in the hotel by his overbearing behaviour and heavy drinking. He talked about going to France, a destination which the police were already investigating, but changed his mind for some unknown reason. Did he know where Maria was? Had they made plans to meet when the hue and cry died down? It doesn't look like it. Maria seems to have abandoned her husband. No message to him from her was ever discovered.

Incomprehensibly, Manning attracted everybody's notice in the bar of the hotel in St Helier, where he put away large amounts of brandy while claiming to be a salesman for a gin company. It was almost as though, consumed with guilt for his horrendous crime, he was subconsciously wanting to be found. Yet, when he met a man who knew him from his home town, Taunton in the county of Somerset, Manning decided it would be better to leave St Helier and take a room in a rural cottage with fewer people around. In any case, despite his loud boasting about how much money he had and what he intended to do with it, his funds must have been running low by now, because he had left London with no more than the thirteen pounds that Mr Bainbridge had paid for the furniture. Maria had taken their seventy-odd pounds of savings with her.

Meanwhile, the police traced the cab that Manning had taken from the Bainbridges'. The driver remembered Frederick's odd instructions to go the long way around to Waterloo Station, rather than straight along the New Cut, which would have taken him direct from Bermondsey to Waterloo. Manning, however, proved difficult to trace and the police were led on several wild-goose chases up and down the London and South Western Railway line. But soon they received a report that Manning had been seen on a steamer sailing to the Channel Islands by a woman who had recognised him from when he had once stayed on Guernsey.

The police now concentrated their attention on Jersey. By now the local police, warned from London, were looking for Frederick, who was quietly drinking himself into a stupor in a remote house called Prospect Cottage, where a couple named Berteau rented him a room for four shillings a week. In the close society of the island, where news of the murder had by now arrived, suspicions were aroused. Manning's excessive drinking and his rude behaviour drew attention to him. The police went to the cottage. Late on Monday 27 August Detective-Sergeant Langley and Constable Lockyer from London, and Monsieur Chevalier, Head of the Jersey police, arrested Manning as he lay in bed. Two and a half weeks after the murder, the Mannings were in custody.

Among Frederick's first words were, 'Is the wretch taken?' (That was what the newspapers reported, though he might well have said 'the bitch'.) When told that Maria had indeed been arrested, Manning said, 'Thank God: I am glad of it; that will save my life. She is the guilty party; I am as innocent as a lamb.' Of course, he was not at all innocent, for even if Maria had fired the shot, it was never disputed that Frederick had struck the blows which finally killed O'Connor. Frederick talked freely, accusing Maria. What he said would be read out at the trial as part of the police evidence. It would prejudice Maria's defence even though the judge said that the jury should ignore Frederick's words because, in law, what he said was inadmissible evidence against his wife.

Early on Friday 31 August, Frederick, nonchalantly smoking a cigar, walked half a mile with the detectives through the streets of St Helier to the harbour to board the steamer to the English mainland. On the crossing he continued to chatter nervously. From Southampton he was taken by train to London. The police took him off the train down the line from Waterloo, at Vauxhall, probably to avoid the press of curious sightseers who had met Maria when she was brought back from Edinburgh to London. At Stone's End police station in Southwark, Frederick Manning was charged with the murder of Patrick O'Connor.

On Thursday 25 and Friday 26 October 1849 the Mannings stood trial at the Old Bailey amid intense public interest. *The Times* carried, in all, 72 stories about the trial. The public was fascinated by Maria. She was foreign, attractive, well dressed, and resolute if not arrogant, and she provided a frisson of sexual interest.

Hanged by the neck . . .

Both Mannings were found guilty of murder and hanged three weeks later at Horsemonger Lane Gaol, Southwark, close to the scene of their crime, at nine in the morning of Tuesday 13 November 1849. They were buried in the precincts of the prison. Nothing remains of them save the carved stones which noted the place of their interment. Perhaps the waxwork model that Madame Tussaud displayed of Maria Manning until 1971 still exists in some remote place of storage. But the London in which they lived, the streets where they walked, are still there, though much changed.

'The largest, richest, most populous and refined city in the world'

As you stroll eastwards along the wide path on the north bank of the Thames today, from London Bridge to the Tower of London, you are actually walking along some of the most bustling of the nineteenth-century wharves and quays. Until 1800, the City of London, which had jurisdiction almost as far up the river as the tide rose, allowed ships to unload their cargoes only on that short stretch of the north bank. Most ships had to unload and load from barges at their moorings in the river. All imports had to be cleared at the Custom House, which had been built in 1814–17 and collected nearly one-half of the duties paid in the country. Newly cleaned, it still stands imposingly beside the Bridge. Sailing ships and their attendant lighters and barges negotiated the river amid a torrent of shouting and cursing, whistles and hooters; stevedores and foul-mouthed coal-whippers strove and sweated to unload the colliers which brought a huge amount of coal from north-east England for London's consumption, while others manhandled boxes, crates and casks out of the holds of the tall sailing ships with their cargoes of sugar, rum, wine, tobacco, cocoa, coffee, indigo, India rubber and raw materials that came from all over the world to feed the burgeoning British economy.

As the import and export trade of London grew in the boom years after the defeat of Napoleon in 1815, so the Pool of London, as that stretch of the Thames is called, suffered ever greater congestion. In the end, over £5 million was spent to build new wharves lower down the river. The West India, London, Surrey, East India and St Katherine's docks were constructed over the next thirty years. By mid-century, as many as six hundred ships could be moored at the quaysides of the Port of London. Every day over one hundred vessels came into the docks, not counting the steam tugs, which pulled the great sailing ships into place, and the river passenger steamers.

Even after the new docks had been opened, from a distance the ranks of masts still crowding the Pool of London looked like a forest to travellers as they sailed up the Thames Estuary. In 1852, Baron Dupin, who had represented France at the Great Exhibition in the Crystal Palace in Hyde Park the previous year, said at the Paris Conservatoire des Arts et Métiers:

> *Imagine the ships of all countries lying in order at anchor from the last of the bridges [Tower Bridge had not yet been built], arrayed [. . .] in transversal ranks, succeeding each other almost without interval for a league in length [. . .] Imagine five groups of floating docks [. . .] a surface of water always available, never subject to the rise and fall of tides [. . .] Imagine around these docks an establishment of warehouses and workshops for the rigging and armament of ships of commerce and of war.*[4]

And Hippolyte Taine, the French historian, left this more dramatic, if exaggerated, description after visiting London in the 1860s.

> *If you get on a height, you see vessels in the distance by hundreds and thousands, fixed as if on the land: their masts all in a line, their slender rigging, make a spider's web which girdles the horizon. Yet, on the river itself [. . .] we see an inextricable forest of masts, yards and cables [. . .]*[5]

So, despite the new docks, ships were anchored in the Pool of London two or three abreast in two tiers as far downriver as the eye could see, and steamboats, barges and wherries navigated their way between the long lines of vessels just arrived from Africa or the Pacific, laden with palm oil and ivory, or awaiting the perspiring, shouting dockers as they lowered cases full of Birmingham metalware into the hold, or cotton goods from Manchester bound for exotic places. What a sight as you walked across London Bridge or glanced at the river from the top of an omnibus!

Smuggling, despite precautions, was rife, and it meant severe loss for the national revenue, given that in 1849 the Customs and Excise duties were the largest source of Government income. They were worth nearly £38 million in comparison with the £10 million that came from taxes on income and on property. Duty on tobacco was three shillings per pound, probably a very high proportion of the retail price paid by the smoker, just like today. Hardly surprisingly, people smuggled, even though 2,187 tobacco smugglers were convicted between 1843 and 1845 in England alone.[6] On 13 November 1843, *The Times* thundered against the draconian powers of customs officers and the courts, rather like the powers that today's customs officers had, until recently, to confiscate people's cars if they thought they were bringing in more cigarettes from a day trip to the Continent than they needed for personal use. Yet at the same time the Customs and Excise itself had suffered scandalous frauds and was a hotbed of corruption. Patrick O'Connor, the Mannings' victim, was involved in lucrative smuggling from his position in the Customs and Excise Department, which he had secured through pulling influential strings.

A clever and a lucky man, O'Connor was one of the 26,000 inhabitants of London, only about one in a hundred, who enjoyed an official position, and one of the 2,228 attached to the London Customs and Excise Department.[7] Originating from the Irish Catholic middle class, O'Connor had arrived in England in 1832 armed with a letter of introduction from his brother, the principal of Thurles College in Tipperary, addressed to an Irish barrister at the London Inns of Court, who in turn gave him a note of recommendation for Commissioner Richard Mayne of the Metropolitan Police. Probably because the Commissioner had no vacant high-level appointments, and because the pay and conditions of an ordinary police constable were poor, O'Connor did not continue his attempt to join the police, but went in for tobacco smuggling instead, using a position he had acquired in the Customs and Excise service.

Technically he was known as a tidewaiter, that is a man who waited for ships, boarded and inspected them. Soon he became a gauger, one who estimated the contents of casks and other containers. How he obtained these posts was not clarified at the Mannings' trial, but there was some suspicion that he had got in with a group of Protestants who were proselytising among the Irish Catholic dockers and had ways of placing their favourites. Whatever the truth of this, O'Connor enjoyed a far better life than the Irish dockers of the Port of London, who lived on a daily plate of mashed potatoes with a herring, occupying one room and being swindled out of their half a crown ($12\frac{1}{2}$p) a day wages by being paid in vouchers for the company store or 'tommy shop'.

By the end of his first year in London, O'Connor had entrusted the large sum of £184 to his barrister friend, who avoided enquiring too closely into his protégé's source of income. When Maria Manning looted O'Connor's rooms at 21 Greenwood Street, off the Mile End Road, a very respectable area far from the rowdiness of the dock slums, she found a bank passbook showing that O'Connor had over £3,000 deposited. No wonder she had set her cap at the older Irishman when they had first met on a Channel crossing late at night in the ship's saloon, when she was still an ambitious lady's maid.

On the fatal Thursday 9 August 1849, O'Connor, whose apparently undemanding job allowed him to sign off at 4.30 p.m., although he did not start work until 8 a.m., was last seen on London Bridge walking south towards the Mannings' house in Bermondsey.

The new bridge had been built to replace the one demolished in 1831, and by now 100,000 pedestrians crossed it daily. As the Irishman walked across the river, dodging the hurrying people and the traffic, he would have glanced downstream at the serried rows of ships in the Pool, and upstream towards Southwark Bridge. The weather was hot; people were lighting fires only for cooking, not heating, and perhaps for once this, the largest city in the world, was not covered by the permanent haze of smoke that characterised it.

In 1861, the investigative journalist Henry Mayhew took a balloon flight over London. Below him, he wrote,

. . . lay the Leviathan Metropolis, with a dense canopy of smoke hanging over it, and reminding one of the fog of vapour that is so often seen steaming out of the fields at early morning. It was impossible to tell where the monster city began or ended, for the buildings stretched, not only to the horizon on either side, but far away into the distance, where, owing to the coming shades of evening and the dense fumes from the million chimneys, the town seemed to blend into the sky, so that there was no distinguishing earth from heaven.[8]

London was a universe. It stretched nine miles from Fulham in the west to Poplar in the east, and seven miles from Highbury in the north to Camberwell in the south, with great continents of suburbia such as Paddington and Lambeth. It was twice the size of Paris, four times Vienna and six times Berlin. No city in the British Isles approached it.

Despite its size, parts of London were even more congested than today. And it was ugly, despite some new and attractive buildings such as the Bank of England, the British Museum and the Gothic mass of the new Houses of Parliament, which was rising beside Westminster Bridge to replace the old Palace of Westminster, which burnt down in 1834.

London had not been redesigned when it was rebuilt after the Great Fire of 1666, so its streets were narrow and winding, particularly in the City, but also behind the great avenues of Regent Street, Oxford Street and the Strand. It had spread as far as the New Road, today the Marylebone and Euston Roads, opened in the late eighteenth century between Paddington and Battle Bridge (today's King's Cross) in order to bypass the City. London was spilling over the New Road into the slum of Agar Town, which would soon become railway goods yards and where the new British Library stands today. And from the top of Tottenham Court Road London had stretched as far as Camden Town and was beginning to move up the hill towards Hampstead. The sheds, stables and warehouses of the London and North Western Railway stretched for over a mile up the line from Euston, as far as the engine shed known as the Round House and the opening of the Primrose Hill tunnel.

London was a huge concentrated market for goods. It pulled merchandise into its huge maw by sea, canal and increasingly over the previous decade by rail. Even though London had no staple manufacturing base like the northern cities, it employed 15 per cent of the workers engaged in manufacturing in England and Wales. There were hundreds of little factories and workshops, mostly in the City and the inner suburbs, making clothing in Stepney and Bethnal Green, furniture in the Tottenham Court Road, and scientific instruments and clocks in Clerkenwell. Along the river flourished the trades associated with shipping, such as sugar-refining, soap, rubber, chemicals, paint, and tobacco-blending. Southwark and specifically the area of Bermondsey, where the Mannings lived, was a centre of tanning, brewing and flour-milling. Downriver there were still shipbuilding firms in Limehouse, Millwall and Rotherhithe. Like other big cities in later epochs, London's building industry was a magnet for skilled and unskilled men, a population calculated in 1861 at 91,000, and it drew people into employment in government, medicine, the law, education, banking and insurance, together with a huge population of 168,701 domestic servants.

The post-war boom, following the still-living Duke of Wellington's victory at Waterloo, had stimulated the growth of London's population. Up to the late 1830s the city had been growing at the rate of a quarter of a million each decade, but with the arrival of the railways in the 1830s, the population had surged. With its 2,363,141 people (as counted in the census of 1851), London had between one-fifth and one-sixth of the total population of England and Wales. Frederick and Maria were two of these new Londoners.

They had come from Taunton to a London where some major rebuilding had taken place. The inns, churches, ancient houses and Olde Curiosity Shoppes of Charles Dickens's early novels were now being swept away or overshadowed by railway tracks, sidings, stations and viaducts, and by the terraces and villas of suburbia. Trafalgar Square had been laid out in 1844 with the new National Gallery on its north side. The 17 foot high statue of Nelson was displayed at Charing Cross in 1842, where 10,000 people admired it over a period of two days. Shortly afterwards, the 145 foot high column itself was reared in Trafalgar Square to commemorate Nelson's great victory over the French and Spanish fleets on 21 October 1805, off the Spanish coast. Just after the Manning case, the relief depicting the death of Nelson was inserted on its south face. The Hungerford Market, where Charing Cross Station is now, had been rebuilt, along with a footbridge across the river. Liverpool Street had been remodelled and New Oxford Street had just been driven through the fetid and criminal slums – the so-called 'rookery', because people seemed to disappear into holes in the walls and ground just like rooks – of St Giles. All of London was now lit by gas. Maria and Frederick Manning were young; had they not died on the scaffold they might have lived to see Shaftesbury Avenue and Charing Cross Road driven, 35 years later, through a rabbit warren of filthy slums. But in 1849 there were as yet no purpose-built flats, no Victoria Embankment, no Tower Bridge and no new Royal Courts of Justice in the Strand.

Thousands of people had been dislodged to build the railway lines leading into Euston, Waterloo and London Bridge Stations, and for the rebuilding of main streets, but no arrangements had been made for rehousing them, so the existing slums became even more overcrowded. Men had to live close to where they worked if they wanted to be first in the queue for whatever jobs were available at six in the morning when work started in the docks and on building sites. The fast and cheap Metropolitan Railway would not come until the 1860s. Omnibuses were slow and expensive, and the narrow roads were crammed with carts and solid masses of moving humanity. So most people walked. Even the well-off O'Connor did not take a cab to go to dine with the Mannings that fateful Thursday 9 August 1849.

London was chaotically administered. Except for the Metropolitan Police, established in 1829, no single body covered all of London and none would until the Metropolitan Board of Works began to rebuild London's inadequate sewers in 1855. That vast mass of people had only eighteen Members of Parliament to represent them, one for every 131,285 people, though only 6,870 had the right to vote even after the Reform Bill of 1832 had extended the suffrage. The City of London itself, the financial centre, was run by the Court of Common Council and the age-old Guilds. It was a self-perpetuating, tightly-knit oligarchy of ratepayers which excluded the non-taxpaying residents, who were the majority, and resented interference. Outside the City, London was governed by parish councils and about two hundred other bodies, which had responsibility for paving, cleansing and lighting the streets, the relief of the poor and the draining of streets and houses, though a chaotic web of individual Acts of Parliament controlled these activities. The parish of St Pancras, for instance (there were no borough councils until the 1880s), had eighteen separate paving trusts in its four square miles.[9] Secrecy and corruption reigned.

All attempts at intervention clashed with local interests. London's administration was totally inadequate for its huge extent and its immense population.

Central London's noise and gloom struck most observers. The sky was dull; the rattle of wooden and iron wheels across cobbled streets was ceaseless and was now, in some areas, punctuated by the puffing, whistling and rattling of the railway. Even in semi-rural Chelsea, where Jane Carlyle and her husband, the writer Thomas Carlyle, took a house in 1834, there was constant noise, 'of men, women, children, omnibuses, carriages . . . steeple bells, door bells, gentleman raps, twopenny post raps, footmen showers-of-raps . . .'[10]

Mud, gloom and starvation

According to the season, the carts, cabs and omnibuses sent up fountains of dirty water, mud and horsedung or whirlwinds of dust, straw and dry dung. In the autumn and winter a dense and permanent canopy of gloom hung over the city, and every now and then there came a 'London particular', a fog brought about by low cloud, still air and the rising mass of sulphurous smoke. London was foul, noisy and stinking. Its narrow streets squelched with mud and dung ('the mud lay thick upon the stones,' writes Dickens in *Oliver Twist*) and even the flaring gas lights did not always manage to penetrate the gloom created by the three and a half million tons of coal burnt every year, pouring smoke out of the multi-chimneyed roofs that even today rise, though unused, from the skyline of London's Victorian suburbs. Those streets which were not cobblestoned were poorly paved and their surfaces were easily broken up by the traffic. Ladies delicately lifted their skirts to cross the road and gave a coin to the ragged boys employed as crossing-sweepers, who brushed away just some of the dung and dust. Near the meat market and slaughterhouses of Smithfield they whisked away blood and flies and, as in many areas of London, human excrement. And, like Jo in Dickens's *Bleak House*, who had no parents and no friends, who had never been to school and lived in the rookery (which Dickens called 'Tom All-Alone's'), the poor and the destitute, the starving, the sick and the freezing were everywhere.

Henry Colman, an American visitor, wrote to his Bostonian friends in 1849:

In the midst of the most extraordinary abundance, here and there
men, women and children are dying of starvation, and running
alongside of the splendid chariot, with its gilded equipages, its silken
linings and its liveried footmen, are poor, forlorn, friendless, almost
naked wretches . . .[11]

Colman had a parlour and bedroom in a London hotel for 30 shillings
a week, including breakfast and tea. He paid extra for coal and candles,
one shilling to have his boots cleaned and a tip for the chambermaid.
He could have had as good a place on the unfashionable south side of
the river for only a pound. But such prices were far beyond the means of
the poor, who thought in pence and rarely saw a golden pound or even a
half-sovereign. Colman thought that Londoners were very civil, but this
was perhaps because he had been given introductions to polite society.
He also thought it was very clean, contrary to every other visitor's
impression. He wrote that he had scarcely seen a smoker. He probably
hadn't seen anybody chewing tobacco and spitting out the juice, as the
disgusted English journalist and rising novelist Charles Dickens saw in
the United States. But Colman also said that he had not heard a profane
word or a risqué story. He must have meant among high society, for he
certainly visited the slums. Yet, despite his praise for the general public
order of London, Colman contrasts the French fishing port of Boulogne,
where people were neatly dressed and well fed, with the hunger, squalor
and drunkenness of London.[12]

Rookeries

A visitor could hardly help but notice the street urchins, the barefoot
and ragged crossing sweepers, the men who ran for miles behind the
cab to earn a few pennies for unloading luggage, the children turning
cartwheels in the mud for coins, sleeping in the streets, eating when and
where they could, the mudlarks of the river, ragged, filthy, starved and
prematurely active sexually, illiterate and probably bound for gaol. They
were among the perhaps 150,000 who lived in London's rookeries, where
the houses were high and narrow and the largest possible number were
crowded together in a given space. Some areas had become rookeries as
soon as they were built, such as Agar Town just north of the New Road,

a district which disappeared when the railways arrived. A speculative builder might design his houses for middle-class people, then find that he could not, for one reason or another, attract them. To maintain his cash flow he would have to let the houses cheaply, in flats, which were soon subdivided into rooms. The district became poor and rowdy, and would remain like that until the slums were finally demolished, sometimes not until a century later. Other rookeries were the abandoned houses of prosperous folk who had moved away. In 1849 one of the worst of the rookeries was St Giles, where New Oxford Street meets Shaftesbury Avenue today. Occupied by poverty-stricken Irish immigrants, or labourers, vagrants and a criminal class, St Giles housed up to eight people living and sleeping literally cheek by jowl in the same room, often sleeping on the floor or on some straw. Here is the description of it that the journalist George Augustus Sala wrote some years later:

From a hundred foul lanes and alleys have debouched on to the spick and span new promenade, unheard-of human horrors. Gibbering forms of men and women in filthy rags, with fiery heads of shock hair, the roots beginning an inch from their eyebrows, with the eyes themselves bleared and gummy, with gashes filled with yellow fangs for teeth, with rough holes punched in the nasal cartilage for nostrils, with sprawling hands and splay feet, tessellated with dirt – awful deformities, with horrifying malformations of the limbs and running sores ostentatiously displayed [. . .] They hang around your feet like reptiles, or crawl round you like loathsome vermin, and in a demoniac whine beg charity from you. One can bear the men; ferocious and repulsive as they are, a penny and a threat will send them cowering and cursing to their noisome dens again. One cannot bear the women without a shudder and a feeling of infinite sorrow and humiliation. They are so horrible to look upon, so thoroughly unsexed, shameless. Heaven-abandoned and forlorn, with their bare liver-coloured feet beating the devil's tattoo on the pavement, their lean shoulders shrugged up to their sallow cheeks, over which falls hair either wildly dishevelled or filthily matted, and their gaunt hands clutching at the tattered remnant of a shawl, which but sorrily veils the lamentable fact that they have no gown – that a ragged petticoat and a more ragged undergarment are all they have to cover themselves [. . .] Look at the lanes themselves,with the filthy rags flaunting from poles in the windows in bitter mockery of being hung out to dry after washing; with their belching doorways, the threshold littered with wallowing infants, and revealing beyond a Dantean perspective of infected back yard and cloacal staircase. Peer as well as you may through the dirt-obscured window-panes, and see the dens of wretchedness where people dwell – the sick and infirm, often the dying, sometimes the dead, lying on the bare floor, or, at best, covered with some tattered scraps of blanketing or matting: the shivering aged crouching over fireless grates, and drunken husbands bursting through the rotten doors to seize their gaunt wives by the hair, and bruise their already swollen faces, because they have pawned what few rags remain to purchase gin [. . .][13]

The novelist Mrs Gaskell's description in *Mary Barton* (1848) of a Manchester slum could easily apply in London also:

[The street] was unpaved; and down the middle a gutter forced its way, every now and then forming pools in the holes with which the street abounded. Never was the old Edinburgh cry of 'Gardez l'eau!' more necessary than in this street. As they passed, women from their doors tossed household slops of every description into the gutter; they ran into the next pool, which overflowed and stagnated. Heaps of ashes were the stepping-stones, on which the passer-by, who cared in the least for cleanliness, took care not to put his foot.

The 'slops of *every* description' (italics in the original) and the 'heaps of ashes' are euphemisms for excrement.[14]

Quite a lot of money could be made from letting rooms in these rookeries, even for a few pence a week. There was one – Calmel Buildings off Portman Square, close to some of the most elegant property in the city – which consisted of a courtyard 22 feet wide surrounded by 26 three-roomed houses. A malodorous open sewer ran down the middle. In the houses lived 426 males and 518 females, an average of 36 people per house. Each house brought its owner £20 to £30 per year.[15] Even though the Metropolitan Association for Improving the Dwellings of the Industrious Classes, founded in 1845, put up the Albert Family Dwellings in Stepney in 1849, with flats containing a kitchen, scullery, two bedrooms, mains water and a water closet, at the rents of 3/6 and 4/- a week, which were required to make them financially feasible, they were beyond slum-dwellers' ability to pay. Victorian manuals of household economy reckoned 10 per cent of income should be spent on the rent. But even a skilled man earning as much as £2 a week might have to pay 5/- to 7/6. A 15/- labourer might be paying 2/6 a week, one-sixth of his meagre income, for a room for his wife and family.

Punch, serious for a moment, wrote on 1 September 1849:

> At this moment, refined civilized, philanthropic London reeks with the foulness of the Bermondsey murder . . .

Given the slums, the cholera which was raging at the time and the statistics for premature death, *Punch*'s reaction seems exaggerated. For, even if the Mannings needed a subtenant to help them pay the rent of their house in Bermondsey, one of sixty thousand built between 1839 and 1851, they were a great deal better off than the inhabitants of the rookeries. But it didn't take much – an illness, unemployment, a large family – to bring a person down to the lowest level in the London of 1849.

Notes

1 For details of the murder, the capture and trial of the Mannings, as well as much of the information that is to be found in the trial record and the police files, I have relied on the excellent book by Eugene Borowitz; see Borowitz, E., *The Bermondsey Horror* (London: Robson Books, 1989).

2 It does not appear on any street map. Most reports call it 'Minver' but the court transcript of the trial always termed it 'Miniver'.

3 Porter, B., *The Refugee Question in Mid-Victorian Politics* (Cambridge: Cambridge University Press, 1979), pp. 143–4 and note 69.

4 Dodd, G., *The Food of London* (London: Longman, Brown, 1856), pp. 127–8.

5 Taine, H., *Notes on England* (1872).

6 Porter, G.R., *The Progress of the Nation* (London: John Murray, 1847), p. 575.

7 *Murray's Handbook to London* (London: John Murray, 1851), p. 49.

8 Mayhew, H. and Binney, J., *The Criminal Prisons of London and Scenes of Prison Life*, first published 1862 (London: Frank Cass, 1968).

9 Sheppard, F., *London 1808–1870: the Infernal Wen* (Berkeley: University of California Press, 1971), p. 26.

10 Holme, T., *The Carlyles at Home*, first published 1965 (London: Persephone Books, 2002), p. 4.

11 Colman, H., *European Life and Manners in Familiar Letters to Friends*, 2 volumes (Boston and London, 1850), vol. 1, p. 165.

12 Ibid., vol. 2, p. 117.

13 Sala, G.A., *Twice Round the Clock*, first published 1859 (Leicester: Leicester University Press, 1971), pp. 351–2. It had first appeared as essays in magazines in the 1840s.

14 Quoted in Sutherland, J., *Is Heathcliff a Murderer? Puzzles in 19th-Century Fiction* (Oxford: Oxford University Press, 1996), p. 95.

15 Mottram, R.H., 'Town Life', in G.M. Young (ed.) *Early Victorian England 1830–1865*, 2 volumes (Oxford University Press, 1934), vol. 1, pp. 155–223.

CHAPTER 2

. . . .

'An extremely fine woman'[1]

Popular rumour rendered Maria Manning both scarlet in her immorality and black in her cruelty. The press called her 'Lady Macbeth' and 'Jezebel'. By the power of the newspapers and the street balladeers, this woman, accused of murder but ordinary in every other way, became larger than life. Her French-accented voice, her elegant neatness, her stillness, aplomb, silence and apparent cold arrogance contributed to weaving a legend about her.

She was born Marie de Roux in a village near Lausanne where her father was postmaster.[2] Her Swiss origin led Londoners who read about the murder to think not so much of cuckoo clocks and picturesque chalets as of the notorious Swiss manservant François Courvoisier, who had cut his employer's throat and was hanged outside Newgate on 6 July 1840. Some of the press even put about the baseless rumour that Maria was related to him.

Maria was described as being thirty years old, though reports varied slightly. She was five feet seven inches tall, which was a good height for a woman at the time. She was well built, with a fresh complexion and long dark hair. The expression 'a fine figure of a woman' would have been very fitting.

The sensationalist accounts which were published at the time of the trial make it difficult to sort out fact from fiction, especially when they discussed Maria's early life and tried to show that even then she had displayed the qualities expected of a savage yet seductive murderess. Robert Huish was the author of the longest and best known of these accounts: *The Progress of Crime, or, The Authentic Memoirs of Maria Manning,* which was a collection of penny chapters written and hawked in the streets during the trial. Huish narrated the probably apocryphal story that Marie, which was her real name, was engaged by an Irish couple who were touring Switzerland. The lady was impressed by Marie's ability to dress her hair and sew, while the gentleman was attracted by the Swiss girl's beauty. Back in Ireland, the lady caught her husband and Marie *in flagrante delicto*. Marie was immediately dismissed. The gentleman offered to set her up as his mistress in a home of her own, but Marie made off for London to collect a legacy. Here Huish linked his fictional account with the truth, for Marie had been contacted by a London solicitor in connection with her inheritance.

What is certain, however, is that, in about 1842, Marie, now in her early twenties, was taken on as personal maid to Lady Palk, whose husband, Sir Lawrence, was a Member of Parliament. Lady Palk was an invalid and when she died in 1846, Marie was engaged as personal maid to Lady Evelyn Blantyre, daughter of Harriet, Duchess of Sutherland. The Duchess was a stately woman, of great beauty and nobility. She was Mistress of the Royal Robes, so Marie may have been summoned to help out, perhaps at Windsor Palace, with her dressmaking skills.

Marie, as she still called herself, was competent and energetic, ambitious and self-confident. She was well suited to her occupation. Ladies' maids were high up in the pecking order of servants, enjoying roughly the same social status as the butler and the cook.

As a personal maid, Marie would accompany Lady Blantyre everywhere she went. Most reports said that Marie met Patrick O'Connor on a cross-Channel steamer in 1846 during one of Lady Blantyre's trips to some Continental spa or other resort. O'Connor was on leave from his post in the customs service. This was another indication of how much of a sinecure the job was, for few enjoyed the right to annual leave in those times. O'Connor was tall and well-spoken, though over twenty years older than Marie. Journalists at the time speculated wildly, but one may imagine that the Irishman relaxed in Marie's company and perhaps had a glass or so too many in the ship's saloon. A bachelor of sober habits and over fifty years of age, O'Connor did not often get the chance to talk to respectable and attractive young ladies, especially one with a fascinating French accent, which, he said, reminded him of Madame Celeste, an actress of the time. Marie made up her mind. She was not going to remain a lady's maid all her life. She was realistic enough to know that she wasn't going to marry much higher than herself in the social scale. O'Connor was, despite the difference in age, a good catch.

The Irishman was an ardent suitor and followed Marie to London. Marie assumed that they were engaged but he was slow in suggesting a date for the wedding. Marie complained about this in letters which O'Connor unchivalrously showed to his friends, which is how the newspapers got to know about their contents. 'Of what good is it to continue our correspondence?' wrote Marie, 'You never speak of marriage.'

Whether Marie and O'Connor were lovers in the sexual sense was never revealed at the trial, though the judge strongly hinted at it. However, later on, after her unhappy marriage to Frederick Manning in May 1847, Maria ran away and lived with O'Connor as 'Mr and Mrs Johnson'. It is not unlikely, then, that they were intimate before Marie's marriage.

As a lady's maid, nothing, however private, would have been hidden from Marie. She would have been aware of, and perhaps even a party to, the infidelities and adulteries that took place in high society. She certainly would have learned from the examples she observed. When a lady's maid helped her mistress to undress at night, the complications of wrongly united buttons and buttonholes and hooks and eyes would reveal if milady had dressed herself without aid after a secret tryst with a lover during the day. 1849 was only twelve years into Queen Victoria's long reign, and the looseness of morals of the later Regency period had not yet been overwhelmed by Victorian austerity. Society drawing rooms still echoed with the scandal of Mr Norton's legal action in the summer of 1836 against the Prime Minister, Lord Melbourne, whom he sued for 'crim.con.' or adultery with his wife Caroline, a society beauty. Maria's knowledge of love affairs in the circles in which her employers moved gave her a sense of power and responsibility, for there was no deeper level of disgrace for a lady than for her husband to sue another man for crim.con. with her. In such a case the journalists would have a field day, leaving a disgraced adulteress irrevocably finished in society.

'Ah, Marie! You have acted cruelly'

Disappointed and doubtful whether O'Connor really wanted to wed her, Marie now made her first big mistake and married Frederick George

Manning. He came from Taunton, where his recently deceased father had kept a public house called the Bear. Frederick himself was a guard on what became the Great Western Railway. Rumour had it that Marie had caught his eye on one of her trips with Lady Palk up to London. Before his face acquired the puffiness that struck the newspaper sketchers when they saw him in court, Frederick Manning was quite a good-looking young man, very close to Marie in age. He had expectations of a legacy of several hundred pounds when his mother died, a factor which is likely to have attracted the ambitious lady's maid. Yet despite his smart railway guard's uniform, Frederick's wage was only eighteen shillings a week. It was a reliable income but it was hardly enough for setting up house in any respectable way.

Marie does not seem to have been as greatly attracted by Frederick as she was by O'Connor, an older man with an Irish brogue who knew how to turn a pretty compliment which moved even the hard-headed Marie. Still, O'Connor delayed so long in proposing marriage that Marie despaired and, when Frederick Manning made her an offer, she accepted. Although Lady Blantyre must have been sorry to lose her personal maid, she did well by Marie. In the middle of the London society season, on 27 May 1847, the lady's maid and the railway guard were married at the elegant and fashionable St James's, Piccadilly, parish church of the Royal Academy. When she signed the register, Marie anglicised her name to Maria, pronounced Ma-rye-ah. Both signatures were literate; Frederick's was bold and obviously one he frequently used, while Maria's was sloping and crabbed. Frederick described himself as a 'clerk on the railway', which was stretching a point, for he was only a guard. He wrote that his father was 'a gentleman', which at the time meant a man who lived off income from investments or rents and did not work. It certainly could not describe an innkeeper, however highly respected he was in his native Taunton. Maria said that her father was 'postmaster at Geneva' but left the space for her profession blank. She could hardly lie if she was with Lady Blantyre, but she would not want a permanent record of her calling as a lady's maid. Perhaps she was already egging Frederick on to describe himself as more than he was. Or perhaps she had told Lady Blantyre that Frederick was a clerk rather than a mere guard. As the police inventory of her possessions would later reveal, Maria certainly had the external equipment to look like a grand lady, for Lady Blantyre gave her an amazing quantity of clothes, underwear and household linen, most of which would be described at inordinate length in the police inventory of the possessions that Maria deposited in the left-luggage room at London Bridge Station or took with her to Edinburgh.

The newly-weds moved to Taunton. But before she left London, Maria arranged a meeting with O'Connor. The Irishman was taken aback to hear that she had married. The day after their meeting, 11 June, he wrote a sad letter claiming that he had been saving up for their marriage, that he had arranged his leave and had planned to spend their honeymoon at Boulogne. 'Ah, Marie! You have acted cruelly to me,' he lamented. However, he wished the new couple well and even invited them to come and see the exotic Chinese junk then moored in the docks and open to the public, not far from where O'Connor worked.

Frederick Manning's respectable and stable job on the railway did not last long. Gold in the guard's care, sent from London's Paddington Station to Bristol on 10 January 1848, was missing on the train's arrival. It had probably been taken by a gang occupying the neighbouring carriage. Manning was never charged with the theft, but his friend and the co-executor of his will, Henry Poole, was found guilty of bold thefts from trains on that same line a year later. Bills of exchange, parcels of banknotes and other valuables were taken from trains on the up and the down lines on the night of 1 January 1849. While Frederick Manning knew Henry Poole well, his part in the thefts was uncertain, but the railway decided in any case to dismiss him. He and Maria next opened a public house in Taunton, the White Hart.

Eighteen months into the marriage, whatever harmony there had been had faded. There were reports of furious rows. Maria fled with the takings from the inn and went to live with O'Connor in London, in Bermondsey, paradoxically, in view of her later move to that ill-omened part of the capital.

Maria's absconding with the money ruined the White Hart, and the liquidators moved in. Frederick followed Maria to London in the spring of 1849. For a brief period the Mannings lived with O'Connor in his rooms at 21 Greenwood Street off the Mile End Road, perhaps in a *ménage à trois*. Then Frederick and Maria decided to try tavern-keeping again, and opened a beerhouse, the King John's Head, in Kingsland Road, Hackney.

Charles Dickens preached in his journalism, that 'drunkenness is the inseparable companion of ignorance'.[3] Spirits were drunk at an average of a gallon per head per year. Frederick drank brandy, perhaps at home, but, given his public house background, he may have sought shelter from Maria's bitter tongue in the pub or the gin palace. In the latter, the brilliance of the gas lights, sharpened and magnified by huge cut glass mirrors, contrasted with the streets, and massive chandeliers reflected waves of heat over the sweaty, unwashed crowds as the gas hissed and buzzed. The gin palace could hardly avoid attracting a labourer from his chilly room and nagging wife, to have a tot of gin, a friendly word and perhaps a singsong for the cost of a few pence.

The King John's Head was a beerhouse rather than a public house. Less beer was being drunk, which worried the powerful brewing pressure groups. The beerhouse Act of 1830 was aimed at encouraging beer sales by relaxing the strict licensing laws. Little shops and even the front rooms of dwelling houses might now, for the cost of an excise licence, be converted into beershops, and 45,000 of them were opened in the next eight years.[4] Competition with licensed premises led to a price war. By 1850 beershops such as the King John's Head were selling porter – a kind of stout – at $1\frac{1}{2}$d per pint rather than the usual 2d, and making up the shortfall by selling the beer as a loss leader and drawing their profits from spirits. Alternatively, they diluted the beer and concealed its weakness by adulterating it with the poisonous *cocculus indicus*, a berry grown in Malabar and Ceylon which had the effect of increasing the intoxicating power of the brew. Competition, allied to the squabbles between Maria and Frederick, may have been the reason for the failure of the King John's Head.

'No hope of anything better'

The Manning household was far from reflecting the Victorian ideal. Frederick was no worthy, hardworking paterfamilias, but a railway guard sacked from his job and unable to make a go of a pub where the landlord, at least, ought to have remained sober. Maria, for her part, was determined and ambitious, a woman who certainly would not have been satisfied with Charlotte Brontë's contemporary description of the female lot in her novel *Shirley*, published in 1849:

[Women had] no earthly employment but household work and sewing; no earthly pleasure but an unprofitable visiting, and no hope, in all their life to come, of anything better.[5]

By 1849, rectitude, chastity and seriousness (a Victorian vogue word) were replacing the easier-going sexual attitudes of the Regency period. Besides, women's legal status was entirely dependent on their husbands. It was particularly relevant for the Mannings that Frederick could not be a witness in court against his wife, nor she against him. Except in cases of high treason or murder, as the Attorney-General was to emphasise at the beginning of the Mannings' trial for murder, the law presumed that Frederick's wife acted under his direction unless it could be convinced that this was not the case. If it had been put to Frederick that the law assumed Maria acted under his direction, he might have replied, like Charles Dickens's hen-pecked Mr Bumble in *Oliver Twist*, that the law was an ass. The fact was, however, that a wife could not be an agent, trustee or executor without her husband's consent. She had no independent legal existence. Her property was his unless settled by trust on her. Her earnings, if she had any, belonged to him. If Frederick had wanted to divorce Maria, he would have had to bring an action against O'Connor for 'crim.con.', or adulterous intercourse. He would have asked for damages and then instituted a suit in a Church court for a divorce *a mensa et thoro* – 'from table and bed' – and then in the House of Lords for divorce *a vinculo* – from the bond of marriage. It would have cost a great deal.[6] There were only 7,321 divorces in England and Wales in the thirty years after divorce was made possible by the Matrimonial Causes Act of 1857, an average of only 244 a year.[7] Divorce, of course, would have made Maria a marked woman, especially if Frederick had divorced her for adultery. She could, of course, have countered that he had consented but this would have left them open to an accusation of collusion, which would have made the divorce impossible. In the 1840s, however, for all practical purposes, Maria and Frederick were married in perpetuity and, as the marriage service said, till death did them part.

'Left on the shelf'

Marriage to Frederick might not have been the best alternative for Maria, but it was better than staying single. In 1851, the census reported that there were more than 1.4 million unmarried women of her age. By the time she married, Maria was already having to compete for a husband with the 45 per cent of women in England and Wales who were unmarried. She risked becoming, as the phrase cruelly put it, 'left on the shelf' and 'an old maid'. What would happen to her if she did not marry? Apart from never having a home of her own, if she ever lost her job it would be difficult to get another one when she got older.

In the mid-nineteenth-century view, social order relied on sexual stability. So the predominant atmosphere of piety, evangelism and social discipline took an ascetic view of sex. A 'serious' person was not only faithful to his or her spouse, but also self-controlled or Malthusian, that is aware of the demographic consequences of over-indulgent copulation. The serious middle class required society to be protected against the rampant sexuality of the mob. This would be done first by requiring the aristocracy to show an example, and then by removing the ignorance and squalor in which the lower classes lived. The earnest or evangelical stance was not hostile to love or marriage. Quite the contrary: celibate Roman Catholic priests in particular were suspected of furtive sexual indecency. The purity of young love was a reflection of religious faith. The angelic wife was a form of domestic saviour, which was all the more reason for the horror felt towards hard-as-nails Maria Manning.

Maria did not reflect the Victorian concept of the wife as the angel of the hearth dedicated to preserving the home as a refuge from the abrasive outside world. She was not fragile, but nevertheless the legal and social situation of women made her dependent on Frederick, who ought to have been the strong male breadwinner. Maria's adultery with O'Connor, and of course her French accent, also gave the impression that she did not fit the ideal of the Victorian wife, who was thought to lack sexual passion, though to be so frightened of it that she preferred never to be naked in front of her husband.[8] The famous Dr William Acton's much reprinted *Functions and Disorders of the Reproductive Organs* of 1857 laid down that:

> *The best mothers, wives and managers of households, know little or nothing of sexual indulgences [. . .] As a general rule, a modest woman seldom desires any sexual gratification for herself.*[9]

What Acton was really saying was that women who liked sex were immodest. A liberal view of sex was impossible for most Victorians because it was associated with atheism and revolutionary extremism in an England which, in the general view, had escaped by good fortune the excesses of the French Revolution and of the social and political uprisings in Continental Europe in 1848.

A woman's place?

Fear of defeminisation was widespread. Two years later, in 1851, there was a violent reaction to the campaign to relieve women of their cumbersome clothing. The garments devised by Mrs Amelia Bloomer, editor of an American temperance journal, were based on Turkish trousers gathered at the ankle and worn beneath a calf-length skirt. There was nothing immodest about them except that the trousers suggested the presence of legs beneath the skirt. Mrs Bloomer, dressed in her 'rational' clothes, walked along Piccadilly on 11 September 1851 distributing handbills. When she reached St James's Park, threats to duck her in the lake made her take to her heels, a flight facilitated by her clothes. Not discouraged, she held meetings all over town. But it would be forty years before her 'bloomers' were adopted for women who took up cycling. In 1851 they provoked masses of articles and cartoons revealing profound anxiety about the advance of the movement for women's rights. Saintly feminine purity was seen as the protection against the depravity of the squalid lives of the male mob. Sexual decency and self-restraint were the guardians of respectable society. Charles Dickens asked:

> [. . .] should we love our Julia better, if she were a Member of Parliament, a Parochial Guardian, a High Sheriff, a Grand Juror, or a woman distinguished for her able conduct in the chair? Do we not, on the contrary, rather seek in the society of our Julia, a haven of refuge from Members of Parliament, Parochial Guardians, High Sheriffs, Grand Jurors and able Chairmen?[10]

Nor was the prolific family of Victorian times reflected in the Manning household. Maria and Frederick's marriage was childless, though by the time of their murder of O'Connor they had been together for over two years. Robert Huish, the inventive writer of the longest account of Maria's early life, claimed that she was a Catholic. He had no evidence of this. She owned a French translation of the Psalms, an item more likely to be possessed by a Protestant, and indeed she came from the Protestant part of Switzerland. Perhaps more importantly, no rosary or crucifix was found among Maria's personal jewellery. If Maria had not had sexual relations with O'Connor before her marriage, it wasn't her religion that had stopped her. She certainly was his mistress after her marriage.

Sex and contraception

So, was Maria or were both her partners infertile, or was she determined and clever enough to avoid becoming pregnant?

Contraception in those days consisted usually of withdrawal before the man climaxed, known as *coitus interruptus*. Once a woman was pregnant, abortion was common enough. There is no evidence that Maria ever aborted a child, though products which could bring about abortions were widely, if euphemistically, advertised as 'restoring female regularity', and indeed until 1837 abortion had not even been criminal when carried out by the woman herself, at least not before the foetus 'quickened' or began to stir. The law was not tightened up until the 1861 Offences against the Person Act. Women used all sorts of dangerous preparations, usually with the aim of producing violent spasms with the aid of an explosive mixture of gin and gunpowder, or with emetics, cantharides, mercury, or purgatives such as aloes, juniper or ergot. Sophisticated contraceptive methods such as a sponge soaked in spermicide or the condom were recommended in pamphlets such as Richard Carlile's *Every Woman's Book or What is Love?* But these devices were quite difficult to get hold of even if a woman had heard of them. The Goodyear vulcanization process developed in the USA in 1843 was copied a year later in England. It was to open the way for the spread of the rubber sheath, but though the expression 'French letter' was common currency in the 1840s,[11] it was too associated with prostitutes to make it acceptable for married people. The so-called Dutch cap, actually devised in Germany in 1838, was not widely known either. Charles Knowlton's *Fruits of Philosophy* (1834) recommended douching, which was probably the most frequently used contraceptive method after withdrawal. Knowlton's book, however, sold poorly for forty years. Sales took off only after the 1877 prosecution of the freethinkers Charles Bradlaugh and Annie Besant for republishing the pamphlet.[12]

Maria, however, was intelligent and determined. She wasn't the sort of woman to let O'Connor or Manning make her pregnant. Had she lived, she might well have developed into one of those women who, from the 1860s onward, began to alter the statistics in the direction of smaller families.

'Dark and exotic'

The Manning case had prurient elements about it which made for obsessive public interest. Maria and her victim had had an illicit relationship to which her husband had consented. She was foreign and, though Swiss, she had a French accent with all the sexual immorality it suggested. She was carefully dressed, reserved, dignified, dark and thus mysterious, or at least she could be made so by the press, which harped on the faint flush which reporters claimed to note in her pale cheeks, and on her slightly jutting and red lower lip, both taken as signs of passionate sexuality. And Maria really was foreign; her accent was genuine, unlike the other scandalous woman of the time, the dancer and singer known as Lola Montes.

Lola[13] was one of the great adventuresses of the nineteenth century. She was born Eliza Gilbert in Ireland in 1820, the daughter of an army officer. Beautiful and musically talented, she eloped to India at the age of seventeen with Lieutenant Thomas James. Her marriage broke up and soon she was in England again, living it up on money given to her by her generous stepfather and driving matched ponies and a glittering phaeton in Hyde Park in the company of several male friends including Lieutenant George Lennox. In time her money ran out. Disgraced when Lennox admitted crim.con. and paid James a token £100 to settle his action, Eliza went to Andalusia to study Spanish dance. She adopted the name of Maria Dolores (Lola for short). Meanwhile, on 15 December 1842 James obtained a separation at the ecclesiastical court. It was not a divorce, so any subsequent marriage was forbidden. Under her stage name of Lola Montes, Eliza became the toast of Paris, where she combined her undoubted talents with daringly erotic movements and the minimum of clothing, especially in her famous Spider Dance in which she pretended to search in her clothes and intimate parts of her body for a spider which had crawled in there.

In London, however, she tried to attract the attention of the press by going to the Princess Theatre in Oxford Street wearing a revealing crimson dress, a colour which identified prostitutes. Her gamble for notoriety failed. People looked away. Lola was ostracised, but this would be no more than a temporary hiccup in her career.

She was spotted by Ludwig I of Bavaria, a sovereign in his sixties, a mediocre poet and builder of neoclassical edifices. He was irresistibly smitten by the exotic Lola, whom he made Countess of Landsfeld. Here, on her estates and in the capital, Munich, she behaved like a modern spoiled pop idol, beating her servants, breaking windows, refusing to pay her bills and finally having the local university closed to suppress student protest at Ludwig's excessive spending on her. Lola became involved in so much political intrigue that Ludwig was eventually forced to abdicate.

Carrying a fortune in jewels that the doting king had given to her, Lola returned to London and took an expensive ten-roomed apartment at 27 Half-Moon Street, off Piccadilly. A production about her Bavarian adventure was so scandalous that the Lord Chamberlain, who censured plays, banned it. Snubbed by high society, she nevertheless caused a general sensation. Everybody talked about her. Women copied her hair and her clothes, while tradesmen put her picture on fans and snuffboxes. She married the eligible bachelor George Stafford Heald at the fashionable St George's, Hanover Square, on 19 July 1849. Soon afterwards, as she returned from her honeymoon, she was arrested for bigamy.

Lola claimed that she had been granted a legal disolution of her early runaway marriage to Captain James, and insisted that she was unaware that she was not allowed to remarry. On 6 August, as Maria and Frederick Manning were planning the murder of Patrick O'Connor, Lola and Mr Heald appeared amid great public interest at the magistrates' court in Great Marlborough Street, in London's West End. *The Times*'s reporter wrote, somewhat ungallantly, that Lola claimed to be 24 years old, as indeed she was, but looked thirty and was 'quite unembarrassed' by her predicament. Anticipating the great interest that would be shown in Maria Manning's clothes, readers were informed that Lola wore black silk, a close-fitting black velvet jacket and a white straw bonnet trimmed with blue. She was plump, with prominent cheekbones and large blue eyes framed with long black lashes. Heald had a turned-up nose, which gave him a look of 'great simplicity'. He was only 21. The charge of bigamy had been laid by his maiden aunt, concerned that Lola the adventuress had her hooks into his income of six or seven thousand pounds a year.

Lola and Heald were granted bail in the huge sum of £2,000, but preferred not to appear in court and slipped over the Channel. Their marriage soon failed. Lola continued her dancing career on the Continent, in the United States and in Australia. Finally she decided on a new life in the United States, where she married twice more. The rest of her life was a decline into nostalgia for her past. In the end, she became religious and expressed regret for her earlier conduct. Always a heavy smoker, a habit she had picked up while studying dance in Spain, she suffered a series of strokes and died on 17 January 1861. She was just over 40 years old.

'The fouled hindquarters of English life'

Lola's was a short life, but fun while it lasted. Other young women, however, brought up in conditions of filth, drunkenness, immodesty and foul language, or single working girls, particularly in the abysmally low-paid dressmaking trade, might begin like her, or perhaps as rich young bachelors' girlfriends, lower-class women with whom they could amuse themselves before they were ready to marry in society. She would enjoy the high life for a short time, but when he married and dumped her, or if she had one of the 42,000 illegitimate children born in 1851, many of whom ended up drowned in the river or farmed out, she would have already lost her reputation and might have to go on the streets in the higher class of trade in St James's, or prowl the theatre bars at Drury Lane and Covent Garden.[14] The Haymarket and Lower Regent Street were not yet separated by Piccadilly Circus from the streets of the north side of Coventry Street, such as Lisle, Wardour and Windmill Streets. All were perambulated by prostitutes, their pimps and their customers from early evening onwards. Instead of driving down Regent Street in a glossy carriage, stopping to finger expensive materials behind the brightly lit plate glass, she might walk the Haymarket and the pavement of the Colonnade where Regent Street curves into Piccadilly. When the Colonnade was demolished in the early 1840s the high-class whores had to move to

Burlington Arcade, which was frequented by men about town. City clerks would go there to cut a dash, to fantasise and ogle the expensive tarts as they perambulated, awaiting a sign from similarly strolling gentlemen, after which prostitute and client would meet upstairs. Rooms above milliners' and trinket shops in this still most exclusive and expensive shopping arcade were known to be devoted to prostitution. Because dressmakers were paid so poorly to sew garments that they could only yearn to own themselves, they were exposed to irresistible temptation by the promise of fine clothes, and attracted to 'gay' living (the term implied not homosexuality as now but general sexual looseness) and financial independence in the anonymity of the big city. The police rarely intervened. There were only 9,409 arrests of prostitutes, mostly of the lowest class, in London in 1841.[15]

As powder and paint became less effective in concealing the effect of passing years, the London whore's earnings might drop from the £20 to £30 that these heavy spenders were reputed to be able to demand at the height of their success. She might move to Portland Place and join its voluble French detachment of ladies of the town, or to the top of the Haymarket and the little streets around. Later she would look for trade in Vauxhall and Cremorne Pleasure Gardens, then in Edgware Road, and finally she would tumble to the rough end of the vice trade. The very worst part of London was Dockland, where pox-marked whores known as 'Lushing Lou' 'Cocoa Bet', 'China Emma' and 'Black Sarah'' paraded half-dressed in cheap second-hand finery from pub to pub along the Ratcliff Highway and fought other women who muscled in on their trade among the sailors who were spending their accumulated pay. The men who used her services would decline in behaviour and fastidiousness until she reached the bottom, when she could be had up against the wall for the price of a glass of gin or a bed for the night, like the Whitechapel prostitutes who became Jack the Ripper's victims forty years later. For the wretched, gin-soaked slattern, her ill-clad body at the mercy of wind and rain, her careworn, emaciated face bedaubed with rouge, it was a toss-up whether she died of a beating-up, of alcoholism or of syphilis.

Hippolyte Taine reported that in the 1860s you couldn't walk one hundred yards down the Haymarket or the Strand without being accosted for gin or money to pay the rent. 'It seemed as if I was watching a march-past of dead women. Here is a festering sore, the real sore on the body of English society,' he wrote.[16]

Prostitutes swarmed in the Haymarket. A police magistrate said, 'About this town, within our present district of Westminster, or halfway down the Strand towards Temple Bar, there would every night be found above five hundred or one thousand of that description of wretches; how they can gain any profit from their prostitution one can hardly conceive.'[17]

Mothers brought their 12-year-old daughters for sale, since until 1875 that was the legal age of consent. The customer was assured that he was the girl's first man, an important point because sex with a virgin was commonly thought to cure venereal disease. But, in any case, teenage girls were often outside parental care. Promiscuity was frequent among the delinquent or semi-criminal class of young people who lived in the lodging houses of London's rookeries.

The lowest figures for London prostitutes, omitting many clandestine and part-time whores, were the Metropolitan Police statistics of around 10,000. The press exaggerated the figure to upwards of 100,000. On 8 January 1858 *The Times* proclaimed that in no other European capital city was there 'daily and nightly such a shameless display of prostitution as in London.'[18] Many of the streets of the West End were clamorous with the soliciting of prostitutes. Fleet Street, the Strand, the Haymarket and Regent Street as far as Portland Place were their thoroughfares. In 1848 the shopkeepers of Regent Street went as far as getting Nash's arcade in the Quadrant demolished because prostitutes sheltered under it. One correspondent to *The Times* protested strongly, appealing to Londoners to say if they had ever been annoyed by the 'helpless creatures' who now had nowhere to shelter.[19] Nevertheless, respectable ladies on shopping expeditions in Piccadilly or Regent Street might well find themselves insulted by whores who thought they were competitors or, perhaps even worse, they might be solicited by the equivalent of modern 'kerb-crawlers'. And, in some ways prefiguring the contemporary polemic of whether or not women should be advised to dress modestly, ladies were warned to wear poke-bonnets, thus hiding their faces except to the onlooker from the front, and to avoid wearing red, which, as Lola Montes perhaps innocently discovered, was the uniform of ladies of the town.

'Beauty for Ever'

In the decade after the Mannings' execution, ladies whose faces were their fortune would patronise Madame Rachael's establishment in Bond Street, the heart of fashionable London, where they could have their hair dyed and their wrinkles concealed by what was known as 'enamelling', together with dozens of other treatments, none costing less than one guinea and many of which – toothpastes, shampoos and eye-shadow – are quite familiar today, as are some others which were no more than water and common druggists' items, all described in Madame Rachael's promotional brochure entitled 'Beauty for Ever'. This slogan echoed, somewhat grotesquely, Coventry Patmore's 1860 poem 'Faithful for Ever', later incorporated into his poem 'The Angel in the House', which was an idealisation of the Victorian married woman.[20] Madame Rachael's advertising was carried vividly by women parading in pairs in the street. First came the beauty and then another, whose faked ugliness was meant to indicate how the beauteous one had looked before putting herself in Madame Rachael's hands. Madame Rachael had once owned a fish shop in Clare Market, a slum standing where the London School of Economics does now, and had worked Drury Lane Theatre as a procuress. In the end, she was tried at the Old Bailey and gaoled for obtaining money under false pretences. She had extracted £7,000 from a widow by forging amorous letters to her from a lusty young viscount, which encouraged the ageing lady to buy Madame Rachael's full range of rejuvenating treatments.[21] Madame Rachael's was also known as a place where married women could meet their lovers, for, despite the advance of piety and Victorian respectability, London had a bubbling underworld of high-class sexual vice, reflected in the flourishing market in pornography, centred in Holywell Street off the Strand, where in 1851 William Dugdale's shop was raided by the police who removed 822 books, 3,870 prints and a huge mass of other material.[22]

It was not, however, necessary to read pornography to obtain information about what people got up to, because the newspapers offered accounts of salacious sex crimes and actions for crim.con., even before the Divorce Act of 1857 gave them much more opportunities to report fashionable adultery – 'in the public interest', of course.

As Victoria's reign advanced, high-class sexual impropriety ceased to be a light-hearted matter as it had been in the Regency period. Lord Palmerston, the Home Secretary, familiarly known as 'Pam', found this out in 1840 when he was discovered in the bedroom of one of Queen Victoria's ladies-in-waiting. The Queen's long-lasting hostility towards him stemmed from this escapade.[23]

Thus, when the Mannings appeared in the magistrates' court that late August of 1849, the public was already morbidly excited and primed with information and rumour about Maria Manning. As the press portrayed her, Mrs Manning hardly fitted the cult of purity and moral inspiration personified in these lines from Coventry Patmore's classic expression of home-loving idealism, his poem 'The Angel in the House', which would go on to sell a quarter of a million copies:[24]

The best things that the best believe,
Are in her face so kindly writ,
The faithless, seeing her, conceive
Not only Heaven, but hope of it.

Quite the contrary, Maria Manning was the foreign woman, Lady Macbeth, Jezebel, an adulteress and the murderer of her lover.

Notes

1 For personal details of the Mannings and O'Connor I have relied on Borowitz, E., *The Bermondsey Horror* (London: Robson Books, 1989).

2 Huish, R., *The Progress of Crime: or, Authentic Memoirs of Maria Manning (a Romance)* (London: Huish, 1849) was the first to provide the details.

3 Dickens, C., *Dickens's Journalism*, ed. M. Slater, 4 volumes (London: Dent, 1996), vol. 2 'The Amusements of the People and Other Papers 1834–1851', p. 166.

4 Burnett, J., *Plenty and Want: A Social History of Diet in England from 1815 to the Present Day*, first published 1966 (London: Scolar Press, 1979), p. 113.

5 Quoted by Hoppen, K.T., *The Mid-Victorian Generation 1846–1886* (Oxford: Oxford University Press, 1998), p. 319.

6 Stanley, M.L., *Marriage and the Law in Victorian England 1850–1895* (London: I.B. Tauris, 1989), p. 37.

7 Pearsall, R., *The Worm in the Bud: The World of Victorian Sexuality*, first published 1969 (Harmondsworth: Penguin, 1971), p. 19.

8 Trudgill, E., *Madonnas and Magdalens* (London: Heinemann, 1976), p. 4.

9 Quoted in Ibid., p. 56.

10 See Slater, M., *An Intelligent Person's Guide to Dickens* (London: Duckworth, 1999), p. 138, quoting Dickens in his magazine *Household Words*, 8 November 1851.

11 Chesney, K., *The Victorian Underworld* (London: Temple Smith, 1970), p. 357 note.

12 Perkin, J., *Women and Marriage in Nineteenth Century England* (London: Routledge, 1989), p. 128; *History Workshop Magazine*, no. 4 (1977), pp. 57–60, 71; Greer, G., *Sex and Destiny* (London: Secker and Warburg, 1984), p. 133.

13 Seymour, B., *Lola Montez* (sic) (New Haven: Yale University Press, 1996).

14 On London prostitution, see Chesney, K., *The Victorian Underworld* (London: Temple Smith, 1970), pp. 307–65.

15 Pearsall, R., *The Worm in the Bud: The World of Victorian Sexuality*, first published 1969 (Harmondsworth: Penguin, 1971), p. 313.

16 Taine, H., *Notes on England* (1872), quoted in Laver, J., *Manners and Morals in the Age of Optimism 1848–1914* (London: Weidenfeld & Nicolson, 1966), p. 36.

17 Weinreb, B. and Hibbert, C., *The London Encyclopaedia* (London: Macmillan, 1983), under 'Crime'.

18 Quoted in Trudgill, E., *Madonnas and Magdalens* (London: Heinemann, 1976), p. 107.

19 Ibid.

20 Altick, R., *The Presence of the Present: Topics of the Day in the Victorian Novel* (Columbus: Ohio State University Press, 1991), p. 542 note.

21 Ibid., pp. 540–4.

22 Trudgill, E., *Madonnas and Magdalens* (London: Heinemann, 1976), p. 132. On Madame Rachael, see Chesney, K., *The Victorian Underworld* (London: Temple Smith, 1970), pp. 239–45.

23 Trudgill, E., *Madonnas and Magdalens* (London: Heinemann, 1976), p. 176.

24 Ibid., pp. 28, 76.

. . . .

CHAPTER 3

What they ate and what they wore

When did they eat?

Maria Manning invited Patrick O'Connor to dine at 5.30 p.m. on Thursday 9 August 1849. The time when people ate their evening meal was a clear marker of their social class. 5.30 had been the usual upper-class time in the eighteenth century, but by a couple of generations later, dinner for high society had been put off until 7.30. For the 'middle' middle class, dinner was served at 6 p.m. As corresponded exactly to their position at the lower end of the middle class, the Mannings dined half an hour earlier than this.[1]

It was smart, however, to dine even later. The thousands of readers of George Reynolds's very successful serial *The Mysteries of London* (1846) read that:

> The banquet was served up at seven precisely. Mr. Greenwood had
> gradually made his dinner an hour later as he had risen in the world;
> and he was determined that if ever he became a baronet he would
> never have that repast put on the table till half past eight o'clock.[2]

'Dinner' had stayed at its original midday time for ordinary working people. At night, men did not finish work until eight or even later. They took time off for their 'tea' at about four in the afternoon and had a meal called 'supper' much later. Well after dark the children of the poor would be sent out for an ounce of ham and a few pieces of cheese for dad's supper. They could be observed selecting 'the most savoury piece of plaice or flounder from the oleaginous pile in the fried-fish shop'. Chips, however, were not yet a familiar accompaniment to fried fish.

The working man's supper time could be as late as 11 p.m., wrote the Victorian journalist George Augustus Sala. He added, perhaps with tongue in cheek:

> . . . when, by the steady and industrious mechanic, the final calumet
> is smoked, the borrowed newspaper read, the topics of the day, the
> prospects of the coming week, discussed with the cheery and
> hardworking helpmeet who sits by the side of her horny-handed lord,
> fills his pipe, pours out his beer and darns the little children's hose.[3]

What did they eat? What did it cost?

While the Mannings probably ate their meals at home, there were lots of takeaways, as we would call them today, to be had from a shop or a stall: puddings, pies, baked potatoes with butter and salt, hot eels and pea soup. The poor, who ate whenever they had money, and who possessed few cooking facilities, pots and pans, or plates, had no well-provided table to look forward to at home, so they bought when and where they could, and ate what they fancied. One Whitechapel trader told the investigative journalist Henry Mayhew that he could sell 300 penny pies a day, mostly to boys. 'Is it just up?' they would ask, 'I likes it 'ot.'[4]

The fictional David Copperfield's account of his early life reflects Charles Dickens's memories of the time when, as a ten-year-old boy, he worked putting paper labels on bottles at Warren's factory near Hungerford Bridge. In the novel, David's lodgings at the Micawbers are paid for, but every penny of the six to seven shillings he earns weekly goes on his food. He breakfasts on a penny loaf and a pennyworth of milk. He sups on another penny loaf and a piece of cheese. If the cheese costs a penny that would be fourpence a day or two shillings and fourpence per week, leaving him about four shillings a week for his main meal. Sometimes he is so hungry that he cannot wait for his (midday) dinner and buys some of the stale pastry put outside the bakeries at half price. Then he goes without a proper dinner and buys:

*a stout, pale pudding, heavy and flabby, and with great, flat raisins in it,
stuck in whole at wide distances apart. It came up hot at about my time
every day, and many a day did I dine off it.*

When he saves his money until dinner time, David has a saveloy and a
penny loaf, or a fourpenny plate of beef, or bread and cheese and a glass
of beer.

'Tea' is a pint of coffee and a slice of bread and butter. The older
David, looking back at his childhood, recalls that, not surprisingly for a
ten-year-old boy who worked from morning till night and walked about
three miles each way from Camden Town to Charing Cross, he was
hungry all the time and bought food with any extra money he could get.
His breakfast and supper were monotonous and nutritionally poor. This
would not have mattered so much had he eaten a properly balanced
dinner during the day. Yet how many London working children did not
even have David's six or seven shillings for their week's food?

The staff of life

For all but the wealthiest, food was the most important item in family
expenditure, and bread was the largest item in the weekly food bill. Maria
Manning, who had known the tasty products of Swiss bakeries in her
youth, had by now probably grown accustomed to the stodgy, soggy,
greyish-coloured English quartern loaf, which weighed about $4\frac{1}{2}$ pounds
and cost $8\frac{1}{2}$d in 1846.[5] When the Corn Laws were repealed in that year
to allow the import of cheap wheat, the price of the loaf fell slightly,
though not till the development of railways in the USA and Russia, and
the cheapening of sea freight by the widespread use of steampower for
ships, did the poor of London benefit from the vast production of the
wheatfields of those still distant lands.[6]

A 'nice cuppa'

Given her years as a lady's maid, Maria would have striven to imitate the
habits of the English aristocracy. She had doubtless schooled herself to
get used to English tea, unless she was one of the few who drank coffee.
Prior to 1833 the East India Company had enjoyed a monopoly of tea

importing, which kept the price high. Tea was also heavily taxed. With the duty, tea in the 1840s cost a substantial three shillings a pound, so consumption was still quite low.[7] The high cost led people to brew their tea very weak and watery. However, as in so many aspects of life, the Mannings lived on the brink of widespread change. In 1853, the duty on tea was reduced, while new sources in India and Ceylon were steadily being developed. Tea consumption, consequently, began to rise.

Milk was not drunk very much. In any case, Maria had no way of keeping it fresh, especially in the summer, so she bought a small jugful every day from a milkmaid who had milked a backyard cow and carried two heavy tubs of the fluid round the local streets suspended from a yoke over her shoulders. Weak tea with little or no milk was made more palatable with sugar, which had fallen in price to fivepence a pound. The huge amount of 36 pounds of sugar per head per year was consumed in England and Wales, with all that would mean for the history of dental decay among people who were unfamiliar with a toothbrush.[8]

The type of food one ate, as well as the quantity, depended on one's income. Bacon was considered cheap at eightpence per pound. It was easy to slice and cook over an open fire, but economy-minded housewives who had some skill in cooking, and time for it, could buy coarse cuts of offal for fourpence a pound or less. Best butcher's meat was expensive and could not be so carefully eked out, nor so easily cooked as bacon.

Another consideration, for poorer people at least, was the facilities they had for preparing food. Many did not even have a hearth of their own, or possess more than a frying pan. And if women as well as men worked hard all day, perhaps sewing shirts for a pittance, the time it took to prepare food to be cooked was ill-affordable. The manicured vegetables and fruit sold in today's supermarkets, the meat tailored to the needs of quick cooking, and the profusion of prepared meals that require mere heating on today's reliable and fast cookers, tend to make us forget that it was not too long ago that the greengrocer offered the London housewife, particularly in the winter, a few earth-covered and battered potatoes, some tired looking cabbages and wormy apples, while a chicken, which the housewife had to draw and pluck herself, was a luxury. Life is incomparably easier in this respect than anything even the wealthy could have enjoyed in 1849.

What one ate also depended upon the time of year. To be able to have any vegetable or fruit one wants in the middle of the winter is a very recent development. Throughout most of the London winter one would not have much of a choice. There were greens, but these were not much eaten, potatoes which were beginning to get old, and some root vegetables, but litle else.

Family budgets

The London labourer on fifteen shillings a week, with a family to keep, had little choice of food. If his wife was really economical and a skilled manager and housewife, she could buy for her husband, herself and their three children the following basket of food:

	s	d
Five 4-pound loaves at $8\frac{1}{2}$d	3	$6\frac{1}{2}$
5 pounds of meat at 5d	2	1
7 pints of porter at 2d	1	2
Half hundredweight (56 pounds) of coal		$9\frac{1}{2}$
40 pounds of potatoes	1	4
3 ounces of tea, 1 pound of sugar	1	6
1 pound of butter		9
Total	11	2

Three-quarters of that family's income went on food and coal. The remainder of the fifteen shillings went on rent for their one room, and on soap, candles and sundries. There was nothing left for clothes, shoes, medicine or for any emergency or pleasure at all.

This diet was not, however, ideal. The amount of protein obtained from the meat was not inconsiderable, but there were hardly any fats save the pound of butter to be shared between the five people. They drank no milk. Bread and potatoes provided the required bulk. Father had to have his daily pint of beer while the children's sweet tooth seems to have been well provided for by the pound of sugar consumed every week. But no greens and no fruit came home in this family's shopping basket.

A better paid workman, earning perhaps 25 shillings a week, and especially if he was in regular employment, could eat meat daily, and add bacon and cheese to his diet, but when times were hard, in the winter, for example, if he was in the building trade, meat might disappear from the table and be replaced by the appetite-satisfying bread and potatoes, with or without butter or dripping. Margarine had not yet been invented to provide a cheap source of fats. At the lowest level, hunger could be assuaged only by bread, potatoes and gruel, this last a staple in prisons and workhouses, like the one where Dickens's Oliver Twist was so hungry that he asked for more. At the bottom of the heap, the desperate Irish immigrant subsisted on potatoes alone.

At a higher level, the man on £250 a year, with two or three children and a live-in servant, had a weekly diet, according to Mrs Rundell's *New System of Domestic Economy* (1825), of $3\frac{1}{2}$ pounds of butter, that is over half a pound for each person, a quarter of a pound each of cheese and a staggering $4\frac{1}{2}$ pounds of sugar, which was approaching a pound each. They ate eighteen pounds of meat, but only sixpence worth per person of vegetables and fruit.[9]

Families on a still higher income ate more meat and more butter. Thomas Carlyle, the author of the famous history of the French Revolution, his wife and their servant, living in Cheyne Walk, Chelsea, with an income from writing and land, ate 10 pounds of potatoes and $2\frac{1}{2}$ pounds of butter between them every week, but still consumed little if any fresh fruit. Yet Carlyle lived till the age of 86. His diet does not seem to have done him much harm.

How they cooked

The butcher would have killed the goose that Maria bought to entertain O'Connor on that hot August evening. It would have eased her task considerably if he had drawn it and plucked it as well. If, however, she bought it from a drover who had chivvied a few head of poultry to the market, she might have had to carry out those unpleasant and time-consuming jobs herself. She did not go to work, or take in sewing, so she did have time, if she wanted, to prepare soups, stews and puddings, or in this case cook the goose, which other women could not when they had children hanging round their skirts while they tried to earn a few shillings.

We can only speculate about how Maria cooked. Was it in the Continental manner with garlic – if she could have found any – and sauces, which Frederick would probably not have liked, or did she follow the recommendations of the popular cookbooks? In our day, when Indian or Chinese food is commonplace, it is interesting to see that the best-selling recipe book of the 1840s, Eliza Acton's *Modern Cookery for Private Families*, devoted only 15 of its 650 pages to foreign cookery.

Advertisements from families and agencies asked for 'a good, plain cook'. She would be expected to provide straightforward English food, such as this weekly menu.

SUNDAY: Roast beef, Yorkshire pudding, potatoes and greens.
MONDAY: Hashed beef and potatoes.
TUESDAY: Broiled beef and vegetables.
WEDNESDAY: Fish, chops and vegetables.
THURSDAY: Boiled pork, pease pudding, greens.
FRIDAY: Pea soup, pork.
SATURDAY: Stewed steak and suet dumplings.[10]

Maria's few books did not include any volumes of instruction in housewifely skills but, had she not been in prison, she would have certainly heard of the instant success of the book in which the above menu appeared. It was by Alexis Soyer, the famous French chef at the Reform Club, who had fled the 1830 Paris revolution, and repaid English hospitality by setting up soup kitchens in Leicester Square during a period of high unemployment, as well as in Ireland in 1847 during the Great Famine. In 1853 he would go out to the Crimea to help Florence Nightingale improve the diet of soldiers lying sick and wounded in the military hospital at Scutari. Soyer's menu appeared in his *The Modern Housewife or Ménagère*, published that same year, 1849. The book sold so well that it was reprinted after the first fortnight, and by 1851 it had sold 21,000 copies.[11] So well known was Soyer's book that the humorous weekly *Punch* published a piece on 15 September 1849 in which two married women, 'Mary A.' and 'Eliza B.', complain about how much more demanding their husbands have been since the work appeared.

Soyer did at least include greens in two of his daily menus, whereas they were absent from the favourite lower middle-class and better-off working-class meals of boiled leg of mutton with carrots, turnips and dumplings, or black pudding, pig's trotters or a sheep's head with tripe and patties.[12]

How the food arrived:
shopping in London

In 1849 the railways were not yet bringing in the huge amounts of food that London required for its vast population of over 2 million. Every day, in the light of early summer dawn or still in winter darkness, hundreds of horses plodded in from the fields of Essex, Middlesex and Surrey, and women walked long distances carrying produce from the market gardens of Hammersmith, Fulham or Deptford, to supply Covent Garden and London's other large markets. The wholesalers bought produce from the market gardeners at between five and seven in the morning, and one of the specialities of poor immigrant Irishwomen was to buy small quantities of vegetables and carry them in baskets to all parts of London.[13] One hundred thousand head of cattle and 3 million sheep were driven annually to Smithfield meat market, while the main roads into the capital were thronged with people driving ducks and geese, one of which ended up on Maria's cooking fire.

All the same, the railway was beginning to make a difference. By 1853, seven railway companies were bringing over 1 million head of live cattle annually to London. A striking example of how railways could reduce prices came from St Thomas's Hospital. For years St Thomas's had bought milk for its patients from local dairies at the cost of a shilling a gallon. From 1854 onwards, however, the hospital could buy milk 25 per cent cheaper from an Essex farmer and have it brought in by rail. The Eastern Counties Railway brought in 750,000 gallons that year, or 2,000 gallons daily to London.[14] Fruit and vegetables, not yet a major component of diet, dropped in price once they could be bought from cheaper producers abroad, discharged at Southampton and brought to London by railway. Jane Carlyle, however, thought fruit was of no use; all it did was give you the colic.[15] Even the exotic West Indian pineapples were beginning to appear in local markets. Charles Dickens had seen them in the main market of Covent Garden as early as the late 1830s.[16] They were very expensive, however. The Carlyles' servant, Bessy Barnet, was rumoured to have a wealthy grand-uncle who thought nothing or paying £2 10s for a pineapple.[17]

It would be the invention of refrigeration, and its use on cargo ships, that would finally cut the price of imported foodstuffs so greatly that the economy of much of English agriculture collapsed. Had they not been hanged at about the age of thirty, Maria and Frederick would have had a good chance of living another forty years and enjoying that era of falling food prices.

Maria was fastidious about what she ate, so did she restrict her custom to established shops or the ancient Borough Market in Southwark? Did her dignity allow her to shop on Saturday nights in the bustling markets of Bermondsey or in the New Cut off the Waterloo Road? Walking daintily to avoid getting too much mud on her white cotton stockings, on her merino wool dress and her dark blue or black shawl, ignoring the vulgar repartee of the stallholders as she passed, did she stoop to buy a shilling's worth of mackerel, a plateful of sprats or a quart of mussels? Did she point disdainfully with gloved forefinger at the piles of earth-covered potatoes, carrots and other vegetables? Surely she would not have deigned to buy from the 'baked tater' man, or a penny mutton pie or a penny's worth (a 'penn'orth' in London speech) of the cockney favourite, stewed eels, sold in little metal dishes. Did she worry about how much of the food sold in London was adulterated?

Publican: Looks like rain
Drinker: Yes, I thought it wasn't beer

Whether there was much real mutton in the pie sold by the 'flying pieman', as one famous purveyor of this delicacy styled himself, might be doubted. There was virtually no control save competition over the genuineness of what one was being offered, and food was widely adulterated. This is known, curiously enough, because about this time books were published which, in due course, led to something being done about the scandal. In 1848, for example, John Mitchell published his *Treatise on the Falsifications of Food and the Chemical Means used to detect Them*. Greed was not the only cause of adulteration. There was great competition to reduce costs, particularly of bread and beer, as well as heavily taxed products like tea. Bakers ground up potatoes and beans into the flour, or mixed alum, chalk, ashes and powdered bones into their product, already falsified by the stone dust which millers added to their flour. Brewers and publicans were among the worst culprits, using not only the toxic *cocculus indicus* but also another poisonous berry from the East Indies, *nux vomica*, together with the pungent capsicum and coriander, as substitutes for malt or hops, by which diluted beer was given false strength and flavour. New beer could be rapidly matured with sulphuric acid; oyster shells could restore old sour beer, while iron sulphate allowed diluted beer to froth. Gin contained sulphuric acid and white arsenic.

As for grocers, they sold loose 'tea' well mixed with ash, sloe or elder leaves. Used and old, dried tea leaves were coloured with chemicals and mixed with the genuine article. Copper was added to give colour to pickles; red lead and pepper dust were added to cheese rind, as deceitfully, if more dangerously, than today's practice of placing tired meat under bright light to suggest a falsely exaggerated freshness.[18] On 25 August 1849, *Punch* quipped that the anti-diarrhoeic chalk mixture prescribed during the current cholera epidemic could easily be provided from the heavily adulterated milk that people bought. Let the milkman advertise his 'Genuine Chalk Mixture' and he would make his fortune.

Attitudes towards official interference, even for the benefit of the public in controlling the adulteration of food and drink, as well as the purity of the water supply, were seen as intolerable Continental-style snooping on the individual citizen. It is hard to understand why the uniformed French inspectors who checked the weight of Parisian bakers' loaves were held up as examples of the police state that might come about in this country if people were not vigilant, until one sees how unpopular even the idea of a patrolling uniformed police force was. However, here, as in so much else, the Mannings lived on the brink of change. Opinion, echoed as ever by Dickens, was coming round to the view that traditional authorities were not up to the job of running a modern and pulsating city. If Parisian cabbies were better governed than their foul-mouthed, cheating, London opposite numbers, because they were centrally controlled, then let us have 'centralisation' (the then current bogey word), said Dickens.[19] His plea might have been cheered by the twenty guests who were taken ill at a public banquet in Nottingham in the 1850s. They had eaten blancmange, the green colour of which had been intensified by the addition of arsenite of copper. Fortunately, only one died.[20]

'Let's eat out'

There were only a few hotel dining rooms open to the public in London. The best restaurants, according to *Murray's Handbook to London* of 1851, were Verrey's in Regent Street, Bertolini's and Giraud's, off Leicester Square, and Mouflet's in Knightsbridge. 'Restaurants' had been opened in London during the French Revolution by the unemployed chefs of guillotined aristocrats. The word 'restaurant' still had French connotations and was probably pronounced as in French. All these restaurants served 'French' dinners, advised the *Handbook*. Ladies are said not to have eaten alone in such places. Yet, when Jane Carlyle was being driven to despair by the builders, who seemed never to be going to finish the repairs and alterations to her Chelsea house, she had her 'dinner' – that is lunch – at Verrey's. Jane ordered a mutton chop and a glass of bitter ale. It cost only 1s 5d. On another day she ate in a restaurant in the Strand. Her dish was half a roast chicken, a large slice of ham and three new potatoes, all for one shilling. She noted that there were other respectable-looking ladies eating out besides herself.[21] This was as early as 1852, so times were evidently changing.

Where you ate was firmly marked by your class, or perhaps it was the other way round. There were grimy eating houses, like our contemporary 'greasy spoons', for working men, where house painters and carpenters, a cut above mere labourers or navvies, sat in their white paper hats and paint-stained corduroy trousers. Men in suits ate in 'dining rooms' at partitioned-off tables. Today still, in rows of shops in gloomy Victorian inner London suburbs awaiting the demolition men, the fascia board can still be seen of a long-closed shop carrying the sign 'Dining Rooms'. Here, the diners in their black coats sat in enclosed wooden booths, hanging their hats on the corner of the partition and eating their meat and potatoes as they read their newspaper propped up against the cruets. In the City there were 'chop houses' where the man of affairs could enjoy his steaming mutton chop or his plate of boiled beef, accompanied perhaps by a potato or two. At a higher level still, unmarried men and retired officers, like Thackeray's Major Pendennis, ate at their clubs cheaply and well. You could have a well-served dinner at the Athenaeum for 2s 10d, which was good value if compared with what three Dickensian law clerks ate when they had a meal out.

Phiz's illustration in Chapter XX of *Bleak House* shows Mr Jobling, Mr Guppy and young Bart Smallweed sharing a booth in the type of eating house known, Dickens tells us, as a 'slap-bang', probably because of the unceremonious way the meal was served. The clerks push the boat out. Smallweed reckons up what they have eaten, adding the cost of each item to the total as he goes along:

> *Four veals and hams is three [shillings], and four potatoes is three and*
> *four, and one summer cabbage is three and six, and three marrows is*
> *four and six, and six breads is five, and three Cheshires [portions of*
> *cheese] is five and three, and four half-pints of half and half is six and*
> *three, and four small rums is eight and three, and three Pollys*
> *[tip for the waitress] is eight and six.*

The treat costs each man two shillings and tenpence, though without the luxury of the rum each bill would be sixpence less. It is still extravagant for men earning a little above a pound a week, though Guppy gets £1 15s. The American visitor to early Victorian London, Henry Colman, reckoned he could dine for between 1s 6d and 2s without wine. A plate of meat was eightpence, potatoes a penny, celery twopence, greens twopence, bread a penny; apple pie was fourpence, a pint of ale a penny. With a penny for the waiter, the cost was 1s 8d, close to Jane Carlyle's bill at Verrey's.[22]

'Eat it and like it!'

The quality of the cooking and the service was another matter. Maria Manning would have learned, soon after she arrived from Switzerland, that in England it was not done to make a fuss. You ate what you were given and liked it. In any case, people who depended on credit in their local shop could not afford to complain. It was a long time before multiple grocers such as Lipton's and the famous Home and Colonial opened shops in London's local high streets, competing with the smaller shops on quality. One critic of about 1850 dared to complain, but only anonymously, about being served in London eating places with:

> *[. . .] parboiled ox-flesh with sodden dumplings floating in a saline,*
> *greasy mixture, surrounded by carrots looking red with disgust and*
> *turnips pale with dismay.*[23]

Few of these eating houses, dining rooms or chop houses were patronised by women, who did not eat out alone – perhaps Jane Carlyle's experience was exceptional – until much later in the century when the department stores began to open refreshment rooms, and even later when J. Lyons and Co. and the Aerated Bread Company opened teashops where the female office workers who handled the new typewriting machines and telephones could have something to eat at lunchtime, away from the overwhelmingly masculine atmosphere of the chop houses with their avuncular or gloomy waiters, their sawdust and spittoons and their stained cloths and heavy, coarse crockery and cutlery.

'Tis my delight on a Friday night . . .

If the Mannings were ever in funds, they might have rounded off a play in the West End with supper in the Haymarket, at the Café de l'Europe for instance, with partridge, fillet steak or truffles, or plain English chops, steak, kidneys, sausages or Welsh rarebit, washed down with stout, finished off for Frederick with a cigar and a glass of brandy and water. If they had no money left over for such luxuries, they could buy a tired ham sandwich or some poor quality pig's trotters from an old woman wearily carrying her tray in the street, or they could go to the Royal Albert at the junction of the Haymarket and Coventry Street and, for as little as a halfpenny, buy a baked potato.[24]

Fish was probably the best value for eating out. Shellfish were relatively cheap in London. At Greenwich Fair stallholders sold pennyworths of pickled salmon with fennel, oysters and whelks, unfamiliar to Charles Dickens, who wrote that he thought they were called *wilks*.[25] There was a shop in the Haymarket where oysters, lobsters, crabs, pickled salmon and sprats were on sale. You ate them standing at the wooden counter, with crusty bread and butter and a glass of stout. It must have been rather like one of today's 'gastropubs', one might think, or a Spanish-style *tapas* bar, until one reads that there were no napkins, not even of the paper variety, so you wiped your hands on a common roller towel!

Sprats were a favourite treat for supper. The tune of 'The Lincolnshire Poacher' was given the words:

Oh! 'Tis my delight on a Friday night,
When sprats they isn't dear,
To fry a couple of score or so
Upon a fire clear.[26]

Another treat on a bright summer's day was to take an excursion down-river to Lovegrove's East India Tavern at Blackwall, where you could have the speciality of the house, whitebait with a squeeze of lemon and cayenne pepper, or salmon, eels or stewed carp, accompanied by brown bread and butter and washed down with iced punch and followed by tart and custard.

Posh eating

This was quite different. The upper class dined starting with soup and fish, followed by the entrée and the roast, then the pudding, the savoury and a dessert. Dinner might be served *à la française*, where there were two courses, each with a wide selection of dishes, or *à la russe*, where each dish was presented in turn. Really wealthy folk employed French chefs, following the example of the Prince Regent who had paid a thousand pounds a year to his chef, somewhat contradictorily named Carême, which means 'Lent'.

Society festivities were catered for by Robert Gunter of Mayfair's elegant Berkeley Square, a renowned pastry-cook. He supplied lavish parties with trifles, ice cream, lobster salads, turkey in jelly, ham in broth and the like, and you always went to Gunter's for your daughter's wedding cake. Gunter's also supplied the china and the glass, as well as the requisite number of black-clad men with grave faces and butler-like mien. If not Gunter's, the wealthy patronised Fortnum and Mason of Piccadilly, which dated back to 1707 and is still pulling in well-heeled tourists and country cousins. Fortnum's specialised in sending out well-packed hampers for summer outings.[27]

On 24 August, 1867, *Punch* published a drawing depicting a fashionable outing on a hot afternoon. The ladies have had the carriage brought out to drive to Gunter's. Arriving there, they have sent the footman into the shop for an ice, and are consuming it in a leisurely manner as they recline in the carriage on the shady side of the Square. As the horse, the coachman on his high seat, and the footman wait, the ladies in the picture indulge themselves in Gunter's luxuries. But how striking is *Punch*'s social comment. Three barefoot, ragged little children, ranged in ascending height, the smallest first, the tallest at the back grasping his crossing-sweeper's broom, are standing silently gazing at the fine lady. Will there be anything for them when she finishes her ice? If they are lucky she will tell the footman to throw them a penny as the coachman whips up the horse and turns it sharply to trot out of Berkeley Square and make its way to Bond Street and Regent Street for some shopping.

Shopping in town

Usefully, considering its unreliable weather, London provided covered shopping in arcades and bazaars. The Adelaide Gallery in the Lowther Arcade near Trafalgar Square, 80 yards long, had shops lit by skylights, selling jewellery, millinery, cutlery, perfumes and fancy goods. Marks & Spencer in Oxford Street is on the site of what was called the Pantheon, a bazaar for accessories and fancy goods, toys, wax flowers and crochet work. It had beadles at the Oxford Street and Great Marlborough Street ends to prevent undesirables wandering in and annoying the customers. Remarkably, the Pantheon employed female assistants. A contemporary journalist wrote about the female assistants

> *The gentlemen, I am pleased, though mortified, to say, they treat with condescension mingled with a reserved dignity which awes the boldest spirit.*[28]

It would be interesting to know how the shop assistants were recruited. Obviously they would have to be quite well spoken and neatly dressed, but would middle-class families allow their daughters to serve in shops where, as the journalist suggested, bold gentlemen might make suggestions to them? Perhaps these shop assistants were the predecessors of the 'typewriters' and 'telephonists' of thirty years later. Along to the west the later famous department stores, mostly now gone, of Peter Robinson, Dickens and Jones, and Marshall and Snellgrove were flourishing as linen drapers, although not till after the Mannings were executed did Derry and Toms, John Lewis's and Liberty's open their doors. Henry Harrod, the tea merchant, had taken over a grocery shop in the Brompton Road, but Whiteley's would not open until 1863.

Regent Street was the prime shopping street for fancy and unnecessary luxuries. Henry Colman, the Bostonian visitor to London, admired the elegance of Regent Street's shop windows, with their plate glass, gaslight and gilding, stuccoed fronts, gold lettering, carpets and massive pillars:

> *Indeed, I think one of the most beautiful sights I have seen in London*
> *has been on a ride down Regent Street, on the box-seat of an omnibus,*
> *in the evening, when the streets are crowded with people elegantly*
> *dressed and the shops [. . .] with their illuminated windows of immense*
> *length [. . .] the whole of this magnificent street seems converted into*
> *the hall of an oriental palace.*[29]

Regent Street was 'a great trunk road to Vanity Fair', wrote the journalist George Augustus Sala in 1859. Between two and four in the afternoon was the fashionable shopping time. In Regent Street the assistants in the fashionable shops gave themselves airs as they showed silk stockings at four shillings a pair, lace cuffs at three shillings and shawls at two guineas, all with a languid air of indifference.

Indeed, the strange behaviour of London shop assistants and even proprietors – until almost the present day – was remarked on by a Parisian visitor in 1856:

> *The detached attitude of shopkeepers in London is amazing [. . .]*
> *they seem quite indifferent as to whether you make or do not make a*
> *purchase [. . .] the cashier took my money with the attitude of a*
> *man receiving a subscription for some charitable purpose [. . .]*[30]

In smart shops no bargaining was allowed, yet the price was not always indicated. Nor were you allowed to inspect goods at your leisure. Not until the drapers' shops became department stores with fixed and clearly signed prices, selling for cash and not credit, did things change.

Clothes make the woman

The wealthy had their clothes made personally for them. When they no longer wanted them they gave them away to their servants, who passed them on to the poor of the streets or sold them to the abundant market in second-hand clothes. Hippolyte Taine, the French observer, thought that the wearing of second-hand finery by the London poor was grotesque and debasing. The French peasant wore his own clothes. In England, he wrote, 'the poor resign themselves to being other people's doormats.'[31]

Maria Manning also wore clothes given to her by her employers. Lady Palk and Lady Blantyre would probably wear certain dresses, shoes and kid gloves only once or twice, so they were as good as new. Maria was able, however, to adapt the dresses in order to establish her image of respectable and stylish neatness. And she had a great quantity of clothes. When she fled to Edinburgh after the murder of O'Connor, she took so many trunks and boxes with her that the police later found an excess baggage receipt in her purse. She had already left so many clothes in the boxes that she had deposited at London Bridge Station that their inventory occupied four foolscap sheets of the police clerk's neat copperplate penmanship. Among them were 11 petticoats, 9 gowns, 28 pairs of stockings, 7 pairs of drawers, 19 pairs of kid gloves, as well as sheets, tablecloths, napkins, and 27 pillow cases.[32] This, however, was minor in comparison with the property she took with her to Edinburgh: morning wrappers, petticoats, nightgowns, handkerchiefs, shifts and chemises, stays, a mantilla, silk and cotton stockings, silk handkerchiefs, veils and aprons, gowns of sarsnet (a fine soft silk material), of merino wool and satin, a worsted shawl, lace flounces, lace veils, tippets, collars and gloves, thirty pieces of silk and satin, dress-lengths of material, skirts and bodices and much more.

Maria was skilled with the needle, but so were many women. The sewing market was saturated with women who needed work, which was why she could not bring any money into the household as a dressmaker. She sewed by hand. Sewing machines came into widespread use later, though ten patents for them were filed in 1849.[33] She had a wide choice of fashion magazines at her disposal, including *Le Petit Courrier des Dames* and *The Lady's Gazette of Fashion*. Later on, in the 1850s, the fashion magazines would compete for readers by including free paper dress patterns in each issue.

Maria dressed neatly, in good-quality clothes, in sober and elegant taste. She wore the wider skirts which came in after the simple lines of the Regency period began go out of style in the late 1830s, but she went to her death before the introduction of the exaggeratedly hooped skirt called the 'crinoline'. Nevertheless, the wider skirts of the 1840s required an ever-growing number of petticoats to support them and bulk them out. Maria wore as many as seven flannel or calico petticoats stiffened with horsehair or starched. These were required to produce the dome-like appearance of a skirt which was several feet in circumference. To create the essential small waist and generous pushed-up bosom of the time, Maria wore high-laced stays. They were essential. To leave them off was considered indecent and produced an unfamiliar female body outline. In very young and slim women, however, such as Marian Halcombe, whom Wilkie Collins introduces in Chapter V of *The Woman in White*, published in 1860, the waist was 'visibly and delightfully undeformed by stays'. Stays could be made to measure but also bought ready-made. They laced up behind, though there was a version called the new 'corset' which laced up in front. Maria Manning wore white cotton stockings, kept up with garters, which could be bought at Harvey Nichol's for 4s 11½d a pair, though a serviceable pair could be found in poor districts like Bermondsey for only 4½d. The police inventory of Maria's clothes also lists several pairs of drawers, a garment which came in before the crinoline, although it is often said that drawers were invented to avoid serious lapses of modesty when the wind got under the enormous hoops of the 1850s and blew women over and their skirts in the air. Wearing drawers was a marker of Maria's class, for working-class women adopted the garment much later.[34] On her head she wore black or white lace or muslin caps, and on all formal occasions a coal-scuttle bonnet, bought perhaps in Swan and Edgar on the corner of Regent Street and Piccadilly, trimmed with ribbon and with lace or muslin framing the face, which could be seen only straight on, so that the woman did not appear to be inviting attention. No real lady went out without a bonnet. The pictures of Maria, drawn in court by artists for the press, make it difficult to see how she wore her hair. In one, she appears to wear it in ringlets or curls cascading over her forehead and down the side of her face.[35] In the photograph of Madame Tussaud's waxwork figure, however, Maria wears her hair with a parting in the middle and drawn firmly down on either side. She wears a lace cap, tied under her chin, so the back of her head is not visible, but she probably had her hair firmly tied back over her ears and drawn together with a ribbon at the back.[36]

Maria appeared in court in elegant shawls in suitably matching colours. Certainly, had Taine, the critical French observer, seen her, he would not have said, as he did about Englishwomen in general, that her clothes were:

> [. . .] *badly-matched, striped, fussed, overdone, loud, with excessively numerous colours swearing at each other . . .*[37]

The American Henry Colman thought that upper-class Englishwomen were very neat, compared with the 'dirty pantalets bobbing about the ankles of our women'.[38] Englishwomen, he wrote, did not wear false curls or dye their hair as, presumably, American women did. By the end of 1843, however, his letters show that he was less sure of the taste of English ladies, and he writes that the 'dress and appearance of the middle classes, with many exceptions, are much inferior to ours'.[39] Colman, however, was prone to frequent changes of opinion.

Show me how you dress and . . .

As for men, a combination of evangelical seriousness and the dirty atmosphere of the city streets contributed to their clothes growing ever more sombre.[40] Gone were the padded shoulders and flamboyant waistcoats of the Regency. Policemen, stationmasters and men in authority wore top hats, as did some coachmen and even grocers, but they were not all made of silk. You could even get them in papier mâché.[41] Douglas Jerrold's fictional Mr Caudle once treated himself to a beaver hat costing a very dear 23 shillings, but after a night out with his friends he picked up somebody else's headgear that, as his wife sneered next morning, no second-hand dealer would give him fivepence for. When Dickens wrote *Nicholas Nickleby* in the late 1830s, in Chapter Two he dressed the eponymous hero's uncle Ralph Nickleby in decidedly old-fashioned mode, with a bottle-green coat called a spencer over a blue jacket, with a white waistcoat, grey mixture pantaloons and a frilled shirt. By 1849, however, men were wearing frock coats in brown, grey, dark blue or black, or black cutaway coats, as does Patrick O'Connor in the picture of him drawn for a contemporary magazine. Waistcoats could be white and gloves lavender. Trousers might be checked or in pepper and salt material, but usually the entire suit would be of the same drab colour. A black neckcloth usually hid the upper part of the white shirt, which by the end of the week was getting grimy, and if tied tightly enough, the neckcoth held the shirt collar high up against the ears. Except among the dandified swells and their vulgar imitators, the 'natty gents' with their flashy jewellery, greasy hair and false-fronted shirts, men's clothes, if they were to be 'decent' and 'respectable' – both terms suggested aspirations to something higher than one's class implied – had to be monotonous and unconspicuous.

Only a wedding was the occasion for wearing brighter clothes. At his marriage, Frederick Manning might have worn a blue coat with bright buttons and a white, watered-satin waistcoat, as did Mr Caudle in 1831.[42] In the 1840s, Dickens's Mr Dombey was also married in a blue coat, fawn-coloured pantaloons and a lilac waistcoat.[43]

Maria was given most of her clothes and altered them to suit her figure and style, but where did Frederick obtain his? One cannot imagine Maria consenting to his poking about in the second-hand clothes shops of Middlesex Street, still today called 'Petticoat Lane', or in the slums of Whitechapel and St Giles. Nor would he have bought the simple loose work clothes known as 'slop'. On the other hand, the Mannings could not afford tailor-made suits for Frederick. Did he patronise the most widely advertised outfitter of London, Elias Moses and Son, a firm with its head-quarters on the corner of Aldgate and the Minories, and with branches on the corner of Tottenham Court Road and the New Road, as well as in New Oxford Street? Beginning as a slopmaker, Moses sold jackets, trousers, waistcoats and ladies' riding habits. He offered bespoke suits, and others whose fit was assured by 'self-measuring', which probably meant that he could fit a range of sizes from his stock. Alterations were cheap enough. Unlike other shops, E. Moses and Sons neither embarrassed people by not stating its prices, nor expected them to bargain. Moses displayed his fixed prices on tickets, which was considered highly vulgar by those who had their clothes made for them by George Stulz of Bond Street, the tailor of fashionable London.

The firm of E. Moses and Son did not miss a trick in self-promotion. Its name appeared on the sides of omnibuses and on hoardings at the approaches to London's great railway termini, where boys thrust hand-bills into the hands of arriving travellers. Moses took advertising space in the newspapers and was on the front page of *The Times*, which at the time contained only advertisements and notices. He arranged for little advertising booklets to be inserted into the first four numbers of Dickens's serial *Martin Chuzzlewit* in 1843–1844, and he regularly bought the inside front or back wrapper of succeeding parts of Dickens's novels. Some of his advertising copy was flowery prose and some was doggerel verse, related to the season of the year or even to an episode in the particular part of the novel being serialised. One particular rhyme ran thus:

> *Attend to my ditty, attend, ev'ry one!*
> *For I owe my existence to MOSES and SON.*
> *I am viewed as the very perfection of dress,*
> *And wherever I go I am met with success.*
> *My fashion and elegance none will dispute,*
> *But all have pronounced me 'a beautiful suit' . . .*

These and the sixteen lines that followed were high poetry in comparison with the doggerel of:

> *Our waistcoats shall rival all others by far,*
> *And our trowsers shall prove that our House is the star.*[44]

The firm of Elias Moses and Son understood that if it was going to sell, as it claimed, 'ready-made suits that Beau Brummel would have been proud to wear, at prices that a mechanic could afford to pay' – an exaggeration at both ends of the phrase – the shops had to be different from the hushed pomposity of the traditional gentleman's tailor, as well as from the rough and ready crudeness of the second-hand clothes shop. The assistants at Moses' large shops were polite. They were trained not to be snooty but to sell by putting people at their ease. The premises were brilliantly lit with chandeliers with a reputed 700 gas burners. There were Corinthian columns, sculptured panels and soft carpets. Moses sold everything, as a contemporary journalist wrote, 'from a tin shaving pot to a Cashmere shawl',[45] as well as hosiery, hats, boots and shoes to everyone 'from prince to peasant'. By 1860, he was claiming that 80 per cent of the population were buying ready-made clothes. This was no wonder, if there was any truth in Thackeray's poem, published in *Punch* on 25 March 1848, which proclaimed that 'the poor are not done and the rich are not fleeced by E. Moses and Son'. No longer did ordinary people need to look like ludicrous caricatures of high life. That some of these puffs came from E. Moses and Son's own publications does not necessarily mean that they were not to a considerable extent true, as they would be decades later of E. Moses' cultural successors, Montague Burton and the Fifty Shilling Tailors. These were outfitters who could make a man look respectable in a new suit that fitted him, if to the trained eye it was not adapted to all the peculiarities of his body and was made in a standard style rather than to the individual's personal taste.

Frederick Manning could buy his cotton shirts at $4\frac{1}{2}$d each, but only because thousands of women were 'sweated', that is grossly underpaid by shops in harsh competition with each other. 'Sweating' was the root of much destitution, disease and prostitution among the 197,000 sewing outworkers in London, one quarter of all of those in England and Wales in 1861.[46] In 1843, *Punch* printed an anonymous poem (later the author was revealed as the poet Thomas Hood) called 'The Song of the Shirt':

> *With fingers weary and worn,*
> *With eyelids heavy and red,*
> *A woman sat, in unwomanly rags,*
> *Plying her needle and thread –*
> *Stitch! Stitch! Stitch!*
> *In poverty, hunger and dirt.*

When Elias Moses was accused of 'sweating', that is paying very low prices to the people who made his clothes, he defended himself fiercely, saying that he paid more than others, particularly more than the widely advertised Donald Nichol of Regent Street, who sold his patent 'paletot' or overcoat, and engineered the dismissal of Henry Mayhew from the *Morning Chronicle* after that investigative journalist accused Nichol of sweating.[47]

Beaver!

Pictures of O'Connor and Manning show both with clean-shaven faces. Military men affected moustaches, but facial hair was usually considered to be a sign of mental imbalance, eccentricity, immorality or being a revolutionary and very likely foreign into the bargain. Beards were so unfashionable that an enthusiast for them, W.H. Henshaw, published a pamphlet in 1847 entitled *Beard-Shaving, and the Common Use of the Razor, an Unnatural, Irrational, Unmanly, Ungodly, and Fatal Fashion among Christians*.[48] The clean-shaven fashion changed when conditions during the Crimean War of 1854–1856 obliged British troops to grow full facial hair, at which point hirsuteness became fashionable among Victorian men and would remain so until it became associated once more with assassins and bomb-throwers towards the end of the century.

One of the most widely advertised hair products for men was Rowland's Macassar Oil. While it was later discovered to be mostly olive oil,[49] it gave its name to the piece of white cloth which was laid over chairbacks until almost contemporary times, known as an 'antimacassar'. For their shoes, men used Warren's bootblacking, made in the factory close to the Old Hungerford Market, where the young Dickens worked and which he portrayed in *David Copperfield* as Murdstone and Grinby's. The paste, costing a sizeable one shilling per tin or bottle, was advertised with the picture of a cat surprised by its own reflection in a boot.

1849 was the year of an important discovery which would, in time, make a great difference to people's smartness. A Parisian tailor spilt turpentine over the tablecloth and noticed that it had removed some stains. This was the origin of *nettoyage à sec*, or dry-cleaning, which in time would make it less necessary, for men at least, to wear dark clothes now that stains could be got out of grey and brown.

The principles of style changed very slowly. Rumour, later proved untrue, had it that Maria Manning's choice of black satin in which to appear in court and for her execution had made that material unfashionable. On the contrary, despite the brighter fabrics that chemical dyes would in due course encourage, the dark suit and the black dress would always stay in fashion. But women would have to wait another sixty-five years until, with their entry into the mass labour market during the 1914–1918 war, they shortened their skirts and relaxed their stays, while men continued to wear stiff, even wing, collars, long-sleeved vests and long-legged underpants, heavy boots and wide-waisted trousers until American styles came in well after the Second World War. The butterfly collar, not to speak of the corset, survived into the age of terylene.

Notes

1 Burnett, J., *Plenty and Want: A Social History of Diet in England from 1815 to the Present Day*, first published 1966 (London: Scolar Press, 1979), pp. 78–9.

2   Reynolds, G.W.M., *The Mysteries of London*, ed. T. Thomas (Keele University Press, 1996), p. 234.

3   Sala, G.A., *Twice Round the Clock*, first published in 1859 (Leicester: Leicester University Press, 1971), p. 298. It had first appeared as essays in magazines in the 1840s.

4   Quoted in Ackroyd, P., *London: The Biography* (London: Vintage Press, 2001), p. 317.

5   Hoppen, K.T., *The Mid-Victorian Generation 1846–1886* (Oxford: Oxford University Press, 1998), p. 346.

6   Burnett, J., *A History of the Cost of Living* (Harmondsworth: Penguin, 1969), p. 209; Clapham, J.H., 'Work and Wages', in G.M. Young (ed.) *Early Victorian England 1830–1865*, 2 volumes (Oxford University Press, 1934), vol. 1, pp. 1–77.

7   Burnett, J., *A History of the Cost of Living* (Harmondsworth: Penguin, 1969), pp. 212–13.

8   Dodds, J.W., *The Age of Paradox: A Biography of England 1841–1851* (London: Gollancz, 1953), p. 430.

9   Burnett, J., *Plenty and Want: A Social History of Diet in England from 1815 to the Present Day*, first published 1966 (London: Scolar Press, 1979), p. 89.

10 Dodds, J.W., *The Age of Paradox: A Biography of England 1814–1851* (London: Gollancz, 1953), p. 299.

11 Briggs, A., *Victorian Things*, first published 1968 (Harmondsworth: Penguin, 1990), p. 216.

12 Peel, C.S., 'Homes and Habits', in G.M. Young (ed.) *Early Victorian England 1830–1865*, 2 volumes (Oxford University Press, 1934), vol. 1, pp. 79–151.

13 Sheppard, F., *London 1808–1870: The Infernal Wen* (Berkeley: University of California Press, 1971), p. 190.

14 Burnett, J., *A History of the Cost of Living* (Harmondsworth: Penguin, 1969), p. 216.

15 Holme, T., *The Carlyles at Home*, first published 1965 (London: Persephone Books, 2002), p. 6.

16 Dodds, J.W., *The Age of Paradox: A Biography of England 1814–1851* (London: Gollancz, 1953), pp. 121–3; Dickens, C., *David Copperfield*, Chapter XI. Dickens published *David Copperfield* in the late 1840s. His reference to seeing pineapples may be contemporary, though his novel is set ten years or so earlier.

17 Holme, T., *The Carlyles at Home*, first published 1965 (London: Persephone Books, 2002), p. 14.

18 Burnett, J., *Plenty and Want: A Social History of Diet in England from 1815 to the Present Day*, first published 1966 (London: Scolar Press, 1979), pp. 103–15.

19 House, H., *The Dickens World* (Oxford University Press, 1941), pp. 184–5.

20 Burnett, J., *Plenty and Want: A Social History of Diet in England from 1815 to the Present Day*, first published 1966 (London: Scolar Press, 1979), p. 119.

21 Holme, T., *The Carlyles at Home*, first published 1965 (London: Persephone Books, 2002), p. 85.

22 Colman, H., *European Life and Manners in Familiar Letters to Friends*, 2 volumes (Boston and London, 1850), vol. 1, p. 141.

23 Burnett, J., *Plenty and Want: A Social History of Diet in England from 1815 to the Present Day*, first published 1966 (London: Scolar Press, 1979), quoting from the anonymous *Memoirs of a Stomach*.

24 Sala, G.A., *Twice Round the Clock*, first published in 1859 (Leicester: Leicester University Press, 1971), pp. 322–4. It had first appeared as essays in magazines in the 1840s.

25 Dickens, C., *Sketches by Boz* (London: Chapman & Hall, 1913 edition), Chapter XII 'Greenwich Fair'.

26 Sala, G.A., *Twice Round the Clock*, first published in 1859 (Leicester: Leicester University Press, 1971), p. 22. It had first appeared as essays in magazines in the 1840s.

27 Altick, R., *The Presence of the Present: Topics of the Day in the Victorian Novel* (Columbus: Ohio State University Press, 1991), pp. 220–5.

28 Sala, G.A., *Twice Round the Clock*, quoted by Adburgham, A., *Shops and Shopping 1800–1914* (London: Allen & Unwin, 1964), p. 22.

29 Colman, H., *European Life and Manners in Familiar Letters to Friends*, 2 volumes (Boston and London, 1850), vol. 1, pp. 127–8.

30 Quoted by Adburgham, A., *Shops and Shopping 1800–1914* (London: Allen & Unwin, 1964), pp. 141–2.

31 Quoted by Laver, J., *Manners and Morals in the Age of Optimism 1848–1914* (London: Weidenfeld & Nicolson, 1966), p. 86.

32 The inventories are in the Public Record Office, Metropolitan Police (MEPO 3/54).

33 Hardyment, C., *From Mangle to Microwave: The Mechanization of Household Work* (Cambridge: Polity Press, 1988), p. 43.

34 Briggs, A., *Victorian Things*, first published 1968 (Harmondsworth: Penguin, 1990), p. 281.

35 Borowitz, E., *The Bermondsey Horror* (London: Robson Books, 1989), p. 15.

36 Ibid., p. 282.

37 Quoted by Seaman, L.B.C., *Life in Victorian London* (London: Batsford, 1973), p. 128.

38 Colman, H., *European Life and Manners in Familiar Letters to Friends*, 2 volumes (Boston and London, 1850), vol. 1, pp. 21–2.

39 Ibid., vol. 1, p. 166.

40 Laver, J., *Taste and Fashion from the French Revolution until Today* (London: Harrap, 1937), p. 57.

41 Briggs, A., *Victorian Things*, first published 1968 (Harmondsworth: Penguin, 1990), p. 267.

42 Jerrold, D., *Mrs. Caudle's Curtain Lectures* (P. Harvill, 1974), pp. 84–5.

43 Dickens, C., *Dombey and Son* (published in parts 1846–1848), Chapters 10 and 31.

44 From a New Year message by E. Moses and Son, quoted in Dodds, J.W., *The Age of Paradox: A Biography of England 1841–1851* (London: Gollancz, 1953), p. 279.

45 Sala, G.A., *Gaslight and Daylight* (London: Chapman & Hall, 1859), p. 260.

46 Sheppard, F., *London 1808–1870: The Infernal Wen* (Berkeley: University of California Press, 1971), p. 168.

47 Levitt, S., *Victorians Unbuttoned* (London: Allen & Unwin, 1986), p. 12.

48 Hoppen, K.T., *The Mid-Victorian Generation 1846–1886* (Oxford: Oxford University Press, 1998), p. 350.

49 According to an 1850 analysis cited in Dodds, J.W., *The Age of Paradox: A Biography of England 1841–1851* (London: Gollancz, 1953), p. 279.

CHAPTER 4

In sickness and in health

Physicians and surgeons

The prison doctors who examined the bodies of Maria and Frederick Manning after their execution may well have been the first medical men to see them. The doctor's page-boy, in his patent leather pot-shaped hat and his tight jacket decorated with several rows of silvered buttons, never delivered medicine to 3 Miniver Place. Maria and Frederick were young and in good health. Probably they had never needed to use anything but the common remedies of the day for minor illnesses. Apart from traditional home cures, such as goose fat rubbed on the chest for chills and poultices for boils, they could buy morphine, opium and even arsenic over the counter if they needed something to help them sleep and counter pain and fever. Constipation could be efficiently tackled by a dose of castor oil or liquorice powder. Laudanum, a tincture of opium in alcohol, was the common painkiller, pacifier and tranquilliser. They could take it as a cough suppressant or for binding the loose bowels which were so common in the unhygienic conditions of a London summer.

Medical practitioners sensibly recommended diet, exercise, rest, baths and massage, together with a battery of treatments of less efficiency, including purges and enemas, bleeding and sweating, which were intended to rid the body of whatever was causing its malaise. Doctors, who would send in their bills annually on New Year's Day, prescribed arsenic-based medicines for a number of illnesses, including fevers, epilepsy and even the deficiency disease of rickets. Thomas Carlyle, the author, dosed his rather vague ailments with castor oil and the 'blue pill', which consisted of five grains of mercury.[1] His wife's lack of appetite was treated by the doctor with quinine, as well as with a substance scraped from animals' stomachs called pepsin.

Medicines were still very much the stock in trade of patent-medicine vendors. Most were either palliatives of pain or simple laxatives. Forty thousand bottles of Atkinson's 'Infant Preservative', which was mostly tincture of opium, or laudanum, were sold annually in the 1840s[2] and 'Godfrey's Cordial' and 'Daffy's Elixir' served generations of mothers to silence their infants, sometimes permanently, while they went out to work or got on with the thankless tasks of the household. 'Holloway's Pills' were recommended for every illness from ague and asthma through constipation, dropsy and gout, to jaundice, lumbago and piles, ending the alphabet with ulcers and venereal disease and, in case the advertising copywriter suspected that those ailments he had missed would be suspected as incurable, he added 'and weakness from whatever cause'. When analysed, Holloway's Pills were found to contain aloes, rhubarb, saffron and Glauber's Salt (sodium sulphate). As a cure for constipation, which must have been endemic among those who ate so few vegetables and fruit, the best one could say about Holloway's Pills is that they would not have done much harm. In addition, the newspapers carried advertising for 'Parr's Life Pills', proclaimed contradictorily as good for both constipation and diarrhoea, and 'Morison's Vegetable Universal Pills', announced as recommended by the 'British College of Health'. This bogus institution happened to occupy the same address as the manufacturers of the pills, Morison and Moat in the New Road near King's Cross. The pills had a purgative effect and no more, which did not stop them selling 1 million boxes in 1834.[3] Another patent medicine, 'Barry's Revalenta Arabica', whose exotic name suggested mysterious cures from the Orient, turned out to be powdered lentils.[4]

Patrick O'Connor, the Mannings' victim, who was about twenty years older than them, was reported by an acquaintance to have once grown weak and faint, perhaps because of too much smoking. But heart disease related to smoking would not be recognised for another century. A doctor might have prescribed foxglove, known pharmaceutically as digitalis, a diuretic, to stimulate the heart if it was affected by rheumatic disease. But there was no medical treatment available for cancer, save extirpating a visible tumour, and none for arthritis, diabetes or asthma. Nor were there any techniques available to analyse or even identify blood. William Odling, the 20-year-old son of the police surgeon at the Mannings' trial, who had studied chemistry, could not positively state in court that stains on Maria's dress were of blood. Even if his tests could have ruled out iron oxide, or rust, he could not have proved whose blood it was, the murdered man's or, as her defence counsel delicately suggested, Maria's herself.

Using a stethoscope, a doctor might have recognised symptoms of advanced tuberculosis, though his main diagnostic tool would have been the patient's own medical history. Stool analysis and bacteriology were unknown tools. Liver and kidney disease, unless there was jaundice or a stone present, were often not recognised. Doctors were unfamiliar with resuscitation methods; there was no blood transfusion or intravenous fluid technique. If one suffered a multiple limb fracture with skin break or artery obstruction, and there was a risk of gangrene, amputation was the only solution.

Before the introduction of anaesthetics, surgeons, who were still seen as belonging to a profession which was somewhat inferior to physicians, employed a very limited range of procedures. They could set broken bones and lance boils, deal with external conditions or operate swiftly in places which they could reach with instruments. The leading practitioners amputated very skilfully and rapidly for compound fractures, cut for stone in the bladder, removed some cancerous tumours, repaired stran-gulated hernias, incised abscesses and carbuncles and couched the eyes to remove cataracts. All these procedures brought great apprehension to the patient, immeasurable pain – often thankfully brought to an end by unconsciousness – and frequently great loss of blood. The lack of asepsis in the operating theatre, added to infection in the recovery wards, meant that surgery was very chancy even if the patient did not perish from shock. Thus people would not submit themselves to the scalpel if they could possibly avoid it. In many matters, however, the Mannings lived on the edge of great advance. They were hanged before they reached an age where surgery might have been necessary, when they would have benefited from Joseph Lister's 1865 discovery of the antiseptic qualities of carbolic acid when used in surgical operations.

'In pain shalt thou bring forth children'

Sufferers from toothache usually had the tooth painfully pulled by a carpenter's pliers. However, soon after their marriage in 1847, the Mannings would have been able to have a dentist take a rotten tooth out painlessly. The power of nitrous oxide and sulphuric ether to render a person unconscious was known about earlier, but the first surgical operations under anaesthesia were being undertaken in the 1840s in the United States. In London in November 1846 ether was demonstrated at the Medical-Chirurgical Society on a Dr Duncan, whose arm was pricked with pins as he lay unconscious. Francis Booth administered ether before extracting a tooth on 19 December 1846, and two days later ether was administered at University College Hospital before the famous surgeon Robert Liston amputated a Belgravia butler's leg. By 1849 the use of ether, soon replaced by chloroform, was common in the United States and England, as well as in many European countries.

Despite some religious objection based on the Scriptural statement that Eve's sin required women to give birth in pain, other authorities quoted the earlier verse, 'And the Lord caused a deep sleep to fall upon Adam' before extracting Adam's rib, in order to demonstrate divine approval of anaesthesia. The argument became academic, or rather theological, when in April 1853 Queen Victoria availed herself of chloroform to ease the birth of Prince Leopold. Anaesthesia was now completely respectable.

Progress

Medicine, however, was on the brink of great advances. Between 1801 and 1850 8,000 university-educated men entered the medical profession in Great Britain. The number of practitioners was keeping pace with the increase in the population. Specialised medicine was practised in the many new hospitals founded between 1801 and 1860, including the London Fever Hospital, the Kensington Children's Hospital and the Free Cancer Hospital in Fulham. By 1850 there was hospital accommodation in London for more than twice the number of patients as in 1801. Many more drugs were available by mid-century than in 1800, including quinine, atropine, digitalin, codeine and iodine. Many diseases – emphysema, bronchitis, pneumonia – had been clearly described and differentiated from others. Just after 1849 Richard Bright observed that protein in the urine was associated with a big heart and shrunken kidneys (Bright's disease). Addison, Hodgkin and Parkinson gave their names to the diseases they described. But how capable were doctors of curing these diseases that they were beginning to know so much more about, and what were the chances of the Mannings and their victim reaching old age had the former not murdered the latter and paid the price?

Short and nasty lives

The annual death rate in England and Wales was about 22 per 1,000. The figure had fallen since the beginning of the century, particularly because of the spread of smallpox vaccination, but it remained at this figure until the 1870s when, with better public health, it began to decline, reaching 14.7 in 1906–1910.[5] Nevertheless, the annual rate of infant mortality was still 156 per 1,000 live births as late as 1871–1875,[6] that is ignoring stillborn babies. This figure conceals a wide variation: from a 10 per cent likelihood of infant death among prosperous families to 30 per cent among the poor. Thus, infant death was a common and accepted feature of Victorian family life. The absence of reliable contraception and the need to engender many children for a small number to survive to term and to resist the diseases of childhood – scarlet fever, diphtheria, measles, whooping cough and many others – meant that the national birthrate in the 1840s was as high as 32.5 per 1,000, compared with today's 17.5.

Death rates, however, were notably higher in London than in the rest of the country. The statistics given in the *Annual Register* for 1849 indicate a death rate of close to 33 per 1,000, magnified by high figures for children under fifteen. In 1841 the average expectation of life in England and Wales was 41 years but in London only 37.[7] Including infantile deaths, however, the average age of death in London was 27, among the working class it was 22, and half the burials in London in 1839 were for children under 10. Epidemics, added to the normal high incidence of death, only increased people's familiarity with the Grim Reaper. The black-plumed horse and the hearse were frequent sights in the narrow streets, and the passer-by would often hear the unmistakeable tapping of the undertaker's hammer hitting the brass-headed nails which fixed the black cloth to the coffin.

Dyspepsia and bad teeth, rheumatism, deficiency diseases such as rickets, infections such as ringworm, coughs and colds and 'the flux' (the common expression for diarrhoea), added to badly treated injuries, boils and sepsis, were part of most people's lives. If one survived childhood the main causes of death were infectious diseases. A quarter of London's population suffered typhoid fever in November and December 1847.[8] The death rate was also kept high by tuberculosis, known as consumption, and non-choleraic or English summer diarrhoea, which caused 3,899 deaths in 1849, together with the dread Asiatic cholera which was sweeping London during the hot summer of that year.

'The filthiest place that can be imagined'

Unaired rooms, persistent damp, people living hugger-mugger, and lack of drainage and washing facilities encouraged insanitary habits and made respiratory illnesses, bronchitis and intestinal infections prevalent. Diarrhoea, frequently stated as the cause of infant death, came from lack of food hygiene and the spread of infection. There were no facilities for washing one's hands after visiting the privy, and it is doubtful if people understood that they ought to do so before they touched other people's food or put their fingers into their own mouths. At the same time, the absence of adequate roughage in the diet and the sheer unpleasantness of going to the lavatory led to constipation.

The London sewers were inadequate. Edwin Chadwick, Secretary to the Poor Law Commission, produced a report in 1842 entitled *An Inquiry into the Sanitary Condition of the Labouring Population of Great Britain*, which provided a mass of detail about conditions in the poorer parts of London, now in a very grave state because of the rapid rise and concentration of the capital's population and because of the greatly increased number of connections of water closets to the sewers rather than cesspools, both of which were often choked with faecal material.

Asiatic cholera, which had killed several thousand in 1832, was approaching through Continental Europe once more in 1848. What was to be done? The commonest theory was that cholera was caused by the 'miasma' or the prevalent foul odours and emanations of the streets, by the stink from piles of rotting organic rubbish and from human beings who lived and slept in close proximity in ill-ventilated houses.

Certainly London was foul, not only, as everybody could see, because of the soot in the air, but also because it stood on a subsoil of decay. Broken down or insufficient sewers were blocked; they leaked into the wells and water supplies, or backed up into houses even in expensive parts of the West End. Prince Albert himself would die of typhoid arising from the bad state of the drains at Windsor Castle. The rookeries, where one foul privy might serve dozens of families, were regularly flooded by their own overflowing sewage, while Westminster Abbey itself lay over cesspools crammed with centuries of filth. In certain streets in Whitechapel there were no sewers at all, admitted the surveyor of the Tower Hamlets Commissioners to Chadwick's inquiry. In the surveyor's own words, the district was 'the filthiest place that can be imagined.'[9]

In 1847 an inspector reported that 'the filth [the propriety of the times meant that he could not bring himself to say 'excrement'] was lying scattered about [. . .] so thick and so deep that it was hardly possible to move for it'.[10] Excrement and urine ran down gutters in the middle of the street until stopped up in a court or an alley. Faeces oozed up through the shallow foundations of houses. The soil of London was sodden with filth. In mid-century London most of the poor simply threw their excrement into the streets where, hopefully, the rain would carry it into the main sewer and then the river. The same happened to dirty water of all sorts in the absence of sinks and house drainage.

In Bermondsey, where the Mannings lived:

> The whole borough was crossed and criss-crossed with filthy, stinking ditches which, receiving the contents of privies and the overflow from cesspools, sometimes also constituted the water supply for drinking and washing purposes.[11]

The entire area was ill-drained, especially in the marshy parts close to the river, which was not as yet embanked. Privies hung over ditches, and sewers backed up into houses, bringing foul smells. Excrement and other decaying matter was not cleared away. Weston Street, in one of whose continuations the Mannings lived, was not so bad because in September 1847 new sewers had been built, but Bermondsey also included the notorious Jacob's Island, marked today by Jacob's Street, an infamous rookery and the scene of Bill Sikes's death in *Oliver Twist*. This is how

Henry Mayhew described Jacob's Island in one of his perambulations among the London poor:

> [. . .] we were assured that this was the only water which the wretched inhabitants had to drink. As we gazed in horror at it, we saw drains and sewers emptying their filthy contents into it; we saw a whole tier of doorless privies in the open road, open to men and women, built over it; we heard bucket after bucket of filth splash into it . . .[12]

Dr Simon's report

The highly concentrated population and trades of the City of London, however, created very special problems. The City Sewers Act of 1848 required all new houses and all old ones of a certain size to be connected to sewers and to have storage facilities for water in the form of cisterns. In October 1848 the City appointed Dr John Simon as Medical Officer of Health. Highly energetic, Dr Simon sent out Inspectors of Nuisances to compel the cleansing of privies and the removal of waste. He forced the New River Company to supply water twice a day to standpipes. In November 1849, with strong support from The Times, Dr Simon published his first annual report, 'a classic document in the history of nineteenth century sanitary improvement'.[13] If the death rate in the City, where large numbers of the poorest still lived, was high at between 30 and 40 per 1,000, the causes could be put down to defective drains, an inadequate supply of water, the unhygienic personal habits of the people and, lastly, to offensive trades and intramural burials. Both animal slaughtering and burying people in overcrowded graveyards were causes of repellent odours and sights.

'That shameful place'

The huge numbers of cattle, sheep and pigs driven into London daily had to be slaughtered somewhere. There were no restrictions about where an abattoir could be opened, and some were to be found in the backyards or cellars of butchers' shops only yards from major and elegant streets. In Newport Market, for example, the smell, flies and terrified bellowing from the doomed cattle could be smelled, felt and heard by the visitors to

one of the tourist sights of London, James Wyld's Great Globe in neighbouring Leicester Square.

Hundreds of thousands of animals were driven to slaughterhouses
through the packed streets of the City, their dung adding to the filth.
Around Smithfield in particular, the great meat market, the streets were
littered with blood, gobbets of animal flesh, slimy entrails, hooves
and hides, all buzzing with flies. The scenes around Smithfield were
Dantesque. Dickens describes them in Chapter XVI of *Bleak House*:

> *The blinded oxen, over-goaded, over-driven, never guided, run into*
> *wrong places and are beaten out; and plunge, red-eyed and foaming,*
> *at stone walls; and often sorely hurt the innocent and often sorely*
> *hurt themselves.*

And again, in Chapter XX of *Great Expectations*, when Pip takes a stroll
to get out of the oppressive atmosphere of Mr Jaggers's office:

> *So, I came into Smithfield; and the shameful place, being asmear with*
> *filth and fat and blood, seemed to stick to me.*

Smithfield was the largest animal market in the world. Dr Simon, the
City's Medical Officer of Health, found it 'full of knackers' yards, tripe
dressers, cats' meat boilers, catgut-spinners, paunch-cookers, bladder-
blowers and all the stench and brutality of backyard butchery.'

One hot Friday evening, 7 September 1849, while the Mannings were
awaiting trial, a bullock being driven to be slaughtered at Smithfield
escaped, ran into the machine room of a newspaper and found itself
wedged between two gleaming new state-of-the-art steam presses.[14] The
technical brilliance of the age of steam and machinery had met the
mediaeval backwardness of the slaughterhouses of London. The situation
could not be allowed to go unreformed.

As so often, reform was obstructed by the interests of people who
lived far enough away from the trouble not to be bothered. The City's
Court of Common Council, a law unto itself, drew close on £10,000 a
year in the 1840s from its various taxes on Smithfield and the other City
markets, and of course resisted all attempts at reform.[15] In 1849, however,
a Royal Commission recommended that the great meat market be closed.
Despite the objections of the Court of Common Council, this 'reeking
central abomination', as *The Times* called it, had to go.[16] On 9 January

1849 the new Copenhagen Market was opened in Islington, still in the country north of the City. It could accommodate 8,000 cattle and 50,000 sheep, as well as large numbers of horses and pigs. Smithfield's last market would be held in 1855.

'A nauseating stench'

Every year in the 1840s tens of thousands of corpses were buried in London's churchyards and other burial grounds. Each layer of bodies took seven years to decompose, but new burials exceeded the rate of decay. Gravediggers beat and scattered the putrefying remains of the dead, raising a nauseating stench. The earth was a heaving, rotting mass of corpses at different stages of putrefaction. In George Reynolds's *The Mysteries of London*, Tidkins, the 'Resurrection Man' or supplier of recently dead bodies to the anatomists, observes as a matter of course that even in cold weather the clay does not freeze because the whole graveyard is greasy with human remains.[17] 'Horrible disclosures' were revealed by the rain, wrote the *Illustrated London News* on 15 September 1862, appalled by sights which were 'nauseous, disgusting and putrid' (22 September 1862). Adjoining Whitechapel Church:

> the ground is so densely crowded as to present one entire mass of
> human bones and putrefaction [. . .] They are exhumed by shovelfuls
> and disgustingly exposed [. . .] It appears almost impossible to dig a
> grave in this ground without coming into contact with some recent
> interment, and the grave digger's pick is often forced through the lid
> of a coffin when least expected, from which so dreadful an effluvium is
> emitted . . .[18]

Half-decomposed bodies, bones and bits of splintered coffins lay exposed. Graves were often not filled in until the piled-up coffins reached to within a foot or two of the surface. Thus the newest corpses were interred only eighteen inches below ground. Broken coffins, robbed of their brass fittings, were scattered all over the cemeteries.

'King' cholera

It was in these conditions of public squalor that cholera was anticipated to strike London in early 1849. On 22 September 1848, a case of cholera was diagnosed in Southwark, close to Bermondsey. This was followed by sporadic outbreaks all over the low-lying areas south of the Thames.

Cholera struck suddenly. Within hours it could kill half of those affected, sometimes within a day of the onset of the violent diarrhoea and vomiting which were its main and completely dehydrating symptoms. It struck with a high degree of randomness, sometimes missing entire towns, districts, streets and even sides of streets. By now it was accepted that cholera was not a contagious disease. You did not 'catch' it from other people in the way that you caught a cold. Since even the convict ship *Justitia*, moored in the river with no shore communication at all, was affected, it seemed obvious that the contagion theory was false and that the cholera was caused by some agent inherent to the place. But what could this be when some major institutions, such as Millbank Prison, standing on the south bank of the river where the Tate Britain art gallery is today, suffered while others, for instance Pentonville Prison and 'Bedlam', the Bethlehem lunatic asylum, now the Imperial War Museum in Lambeth, escaped? What was common to some but not to others?

There were theories which explained that cholera was caused by unhygienic living conditions, but in what particular way did these cause the disease? The most popular theory, however, which claimed that the solution was a major campaign against the insanitary condition of London, was the one which believed in miasmatic or atmospheric influences, that there was a poison in the air caused by lack of hygiene that permitted the emanations of animal and vegetable substances, largely human excrement and human and animal respiration, which were not sufficiently ventilated and removed from areas where people lived. In other words, excessive crowding together, animal and human effluvia, lack of air and dirty habits were the causes of cholera.

As for treatment for cholera, Holloway's Pills were touted as a remedy. If you took five or six a night, and the same quantity next morning for two weeks, you would be cured, said the puff on the pillbox. One of the methods of anaesthesia, nitrous oxide, or 'laughing gas', was recommended as a quack remedy for the dread disease which killed over 14,000 Londoners in 1849. The most popular remedy was opium, though this was effective only in the early stages of the disease. Other treatments used in London hospitals included electricity, brandy, turpentine, cayenne pepper, and the internal use of common salts enemas or the injection into the veins of saline solution, which suggests that there was some intimation that cholera had to be treated by urgent fluid replacement.

'The paradise at Tooting'

The worst single outbreak of cholera, and the one which changed the issue from a medical one to a question of wide-reaching social policy, occurred in Bartholomew Drouet's institution in Tooting, now a built-up area of South London but then a village in open fields. Drouet ran a home for pauper children, orphans with no means of support, whom some of the London workhouses farmed out to him until the children were old enough to be released into the world. In the first week of January 1849 there were 112 cases of cholera among the 1,300 children boarded out in Drouet's Infant Poor Establishment. The Surrey coroner, in whose juris-diction the asylum lay, did not think inquests were necessary. It was only because other children suffering from cholera were removed from Drouet's establishment and died in other coroners' areas that the scandal of the asylum came to public notice. On 19 January, an inquest con-ducted by a coroner, Dr Wakley, founder of *The Lancet* and an active social and medical reformer in contrast to other coroners who did not usually have medical qualifications, found that the children at the Tooting institution were badly fed, clothed and housed. The Poor Law Guardians of Holborn, who boarded their children at Drouet's, obtained a manslaughter verdict against him from another coroner's jury. Drouet was tried on 13 April 1849 but acquitted because it could not be proved that his negligence had caused the death from cholera of the particular child whose decease was being investigated.

Drouet did run his establishment inefficiently and cruelly. He underfed, overworked and beat the children. The final death toll from cholera in Drouet's establishment reached 180. As is so often the case, the scandal of the deaths of so many defenceless children sparked the public conscience in a way that the solid prose columns of medical and parlia-mentary reports on public health could not. Probably the most powerful broadside came from Charles Dickens, writing an article called 'The paradise at Tooting' in *The Examiner* of 20 January 1849. Dickens was already aware of the scandal of pauper baby-farms, which he described in *Oliver Twist*. Dr Grainger, a Board of Health inspector, had given evidence that the lack of ventilation, arising from Drouet's habit of nailing up doors and windows, 'exceeds in offensiveness anything yet witnessed [. . .] in hospitals or elsewhere, occupied by the sick.'[19] Drouet, despite warnings, had overcrowded his accommodation and had put four cholera patients in one bed. They lay, of course, covered with each other's diarrhoea, which the inspector described as 'every offensive, indecent and barbarous circumstance that can aggravate the horrors of their condition [. . .]'. The insufficient food and clothing, together with the cold, damp, dirty and rotten rooms, made it likely that infectious disease would break out.

Yet perhaps these circumstances, foul and intolerable as they were, were only the 'predisposing causes' of the cholera rather than its true origin. Was the disease caused by some other agent? The truth was that, contrary to what Dickens wrote and most medical opinion believed, cholera did not break out because Drouet's institution was, in Dickens's words, 'brutally conducted, vilely kept, preposterously inspected, dishonestly defended, a disgrace to a Christian community, and a stain upon a civilised land.' All these attacks were justified, but the conditions themselves were not the cause of cholera.

The epidemic raged throughout the summer, particularly in south London, Lambeth, Southwark and Rotherhithe: 250 died in June, 2,000 in July, and over 4,000 in August.[20] By early September 10,142 had died, two of them stockbrokers who were due to give evidence at the police court proceedings in the Manning case. Bermondsey stood second in the death rate; it had lost 591 people. The death knell tolled from morning to night, and mourners might return from the graveyard to find that yet another sick person in the house had succumbed.

Contaminated water – the true cause

Over 7,000 would fall victim to cholera in September. However, 3 Miniver Place was empty. Perhaps the Mannings would have been infected had they not fled from London after they had murdered O'Connor, or perhaps there was another reason. Their water supply may not have been contaminated by a broken sewer or cesspit, or maybe the Mannings drank only boiled water in the form of tea. Frederick Manning preferred to drink brandy in any case, but he also drank it specifically to ward off cholera.

Evidence was mounting that contaminated water might be the cause of the disease. The huge volume of new construction meant that cesspools and sewers overflowed or leaked, while the introduction of flushing water closets sent faecal material straight into the sewers, and from there it finally emerged in the Thames from which the water companies drew their supply and pumped it into London standpipes and dwellings for people to drink. Sewers, privies and open ditches were known to leak into water supply pipes and wells. Arthur Hassall's *Microscopic Examination of the Water supplied to the Inhabitants of London* of 1850 revealed that 'some of the inhabitants of the metropolis are made to consume, in some form or another, a portion of their own excrement [. . .].[21] Nevertheless, the cholera bacillus (*vibrio cholerae*) itself had not been isolated.

'A vast open cloaca'

The supply of water to London was a common scandal. On 29 September 1849, the *Illustrated London News* thundered:

> *The supply of water ought no more to be meted out to us as a matter of profits to individuals, than the atmosphere and the sunshine.*

London's water was supplied by eight companies, drawing their supplies from the Thames, from deep wells or from the River Lea. The Thames and the Lea were noisome with horse dung, dead and rotting fish, and, worst of all, with the discharge from the sewers. In the same year, 1849, as cholera scourged London, the novelist Charles Kingsley wrote:

> *I was yesterday [. . .] over the cholera districts of Bermondsey, and oh God, what I saw! People having no water to drink – hundreds of them – but the water of the common sewer [. . .] full of [. . .] dead fish, cats and dogs.*[22]

In Southwark, adjacent to Bermondsey, where the Mannings were to come to live, of 18,000 houses, only 4,000 had their own water supply. The inhabitants drew their water from standpipes in the road or the yard. These were turned on quite briefly. This slow and irregular supply of water was the occasion for quarrels among the dozens of mostly women waiting to fill their barrels and jars which could not be properly washed. The inhabitants kept water for as long as possible, using and reusing it, and drinking it when it was stagnant.

Having a relatively new house, Maria and Frederick probably did have a piped water supply to their basement kitchen or to a cistern in the area just outside. It cost a landlord £4 to install water and about six shillings a year rent for supplying a two-room flat and about twelve shillings annually for a four-roomed dwelling. Progress in the supply of constant piped water was very slow because landlords feared that the tenants would steal and sell the lead fittings. Water companies worried that the unmetered water would be wasted. Nor could landlords be sure of sufficient and regular rent to make up for the cost of installation. Besides, London plumbers who provided the internal arrangements were notoriously inefficient, while the cisterns were often allowed to become foul. In any case, the water was piped for only two hours daily, or on alternate days, and never on Sundays.

The way to prevent cholera was to keep the drinking water separate from the sewage. The cure for a person attacked by the violent stomach pains, vomiting and watery discharges of the cholera was to replace the lost fluid. The acute dehydration caused total collapse and a rapid drop in body temperature, ending with a disappearing pulse and a wizened and blue corpse. Yet neither the true cause nor the appropriate cure were known.

Dr Snow and the Broad Street Pump

It was Dr John Snow, the same who would administer chloroform to Queen Victoria during her labour in 1853, who implicated water as the carrier of cholera. Snow's first publication on the subject, *On the mode of communication of cholera*, came out in 1849, but attracted little attention given the predominance of the miasma theory. Dr Snow continued to study the subject and in 1855 published a full-size book with the same title as his 1849 essay. He demonstrated that the poor, who had little opportunity for washing, came into contact with the cholera bacillus and transferred it to their mouths. Doctors did not catch it because they washed their hands before eating and did not eat in their patients' houses in any case. However, cholera spread to better-off sections of the community because the bacillus got into the general water supply. Snow carefully crosschecked where people got their water with the incidence of cholera. The pump in Broad Street, now Broadwick Street, in Soho, provided water which was contaminated from a nearby cesspool whose brick revetment was cracked, thus allowing sewage containing the cholera bacillus to seep into the water supply. In the water Snow noticed the typical floccules or flakes sloughed from the intestines of cholera sufferers. People who drank water drawn from this pump got cholera while others who lived in the same street and had unpolluted wells did not. Final proof of this came when a widow, who had moved from Broad Street to Hampstead but continued to have the particularly sweet-tasting water of the Broad Street pump sent up to her, was the only person in Hampstead, which had its own wells, to contract and die from cholera. Snow persuaded the authorities to remove the pump handle and the cholera infections came to an end.

This, however, was a local outbreak. It was the discharge of sewers into the Thames above the part of the stream where some of the water suppliers, especially the Southwark and Vauxhall Water Company, drew their supplies, which caused the extent of the cholera outbreak of 1849.

On 16 November 1849, the entire British nation was summoned to thank the Almighty for the end of the cholera epidemic. Shops closed, although it was a weekday, and railways ran only a Sunday service. Church bells pealed. But *The Times* made the very valid point that 'It is not the part of a Christian or any rational man to implore the Almighty to remove evils nine-tenths of which we can remove ourselves.'[23]

Over 14,000 people had died of the cholera in London alone. The Mannings went to the scaffold three years before the Metropolitan Water Act of 1852 gave water companies until 1855 to stop taking their supplies from below Teddington and until 1857 to cover their reservoirs, filter their water and provide a constant supply. When the Lambeth Waterworks Company moved its intake above the tideway in 1853, as required by law, the death rate fell dramatically in the area which it served, compared with the area supplied by the Southwark and Vauxhall Water Company which still suffered 130 deaths per 10,000 inhabitants.

Between the two outbreaks of cholera in 1854 and 1856 a proper London-wide sewer authority, suggested long before by Edwin Chadwick, at last came into being when the Metropolitan Board of Works was established in 1855. It was not until Members of Parliament themselves were repelled by the stench from the Thames in the summers of 1857 and 1858, and Queen Victoria and Prince Albert had been forced to abandon a trip on the Thames by the nauseating smell stirred up by the paddles of the steamboat, that the Government gave the Metropolitan Board of Works the power to construct the drainage system it wanted. Its Chief Engineer, Joseph Bazalgette, built 82 miles of sewers. By 1865 these were working and collecting 420 million gallons daily of water and sewage and conducting them to outfalls outside the area of the river from which the water companies drew their supplies. Cholera was finally halted by the opening of the new sewers with their outfall far down the river. The problem of a regular, clean and affordable water supply was not, however, entirely solved until the Metropolitan Water Board bought out the water companies in 1902.

Notes

1 Holme, T., *The Carlyles at Home*, first published 1965 (London: Persephone Books, 2002), p. 43.

2 Dodds, J.W., *The Age of Paradox: A Biography of England 1841–1851* (London: Gollancz, 1953), p. 283.

3 Altick, R., *The Presence of the Present: Topics of the Day in the Victorian Novel* (Columbus: Ohio State University Press, 1991), p. 551.

4 Dodds, J.W., *The Age of Paradox: A Biography of England 1841–1851* (London: Gollancz, 1953), pp. 282–3.

5 Hoppen, K.T., *The Mid-Victorian Generation 1846–1886* (Oxford: Oxford University Press, 1998), p. 326.

6 Ibid.

7 Burnett, J., *A Social History of Housing 1815–1870* (London: Methuen, 1980), p. 101.

8 Ackroyd, P., *Dickens* (London: Sinclair-Stevenson, 1990), p. 384.

9 Quoted by Sheppard, F., *London 1808–1870: The Infernal Wen* (Berkeley: University of California Press, 1971), p. 256.

10 Quoted by Ackroyd, P., *Dickens* (London: Sinclair-Stevenson, 1990), p. 382.

11 Ibid.

12 Quoted in Wilson, A.N., *The Victorians* (London: Hutchinson, 2002), p. 155.

13 Sheppard, F., *London 1808–1870: The Infernal Wen* (Berkeley: University of California Press, 1971), p. 270.

14 *Illustrated London News*, 8 September, 1849, p. 163.

15 Sheppard, F., *London 1808–1870: The Infernal Wen* (Berkeley: University of California Press, 1971), p. 189.

16 *The Times*, 31 January 1851.

17 Reynolds, G.W.M., *The Mysteries of London*, ed. T. Thomas (Keele University Press, 1996), p. 163.

18 Walker, G.A., *Gatherings from Graveyards, particularly those of London* (London: Longman, 1839), p. 168.

19 Dickens, C., *Dickens's Journalism*, ed. M. Slater, 4 volumes (London: Dent, 1996), vol. 2 'The Amusements of the People and Other Papers 1834–1851', pp. 147–56 (specifically p. 150).

20 Longmate, N., *King Cholera, the Biography of a Disease* (London: Hamish Hamilton, 1966), p. 178.

21 Weinreb, B. and Hibbert, C., *The London Encyclopaedia* (London: Macmillan, 1983), pp. 930–1.

22 Ibid.

23 Quoted by Longmate, N., *King Cholera, the Biography of a Disease* (London: Hamish Hamilton, 1966), p. 180.

CHAPTER 5

Money, housing and class

Filthy lucre

Social status without money to live up to it was merely the genteel poverty in which so many of the middle class lived. Dickens's Nicholas Nickleby was paid very generously by the Cheerybyle brothers at £120 a year and a house. A more usual salary for a clerk was £80, so Frederick Manning's £2 a week plus commission as a commercial traveller seems quite fair. In Wilkie Collins's *The Woman in White*, serialised in 1860, the drawing master Walter Hartwright is offered four guineas a week 'on the footing of a gentleman' to teach drawing and to mount a collection of pictures. Well might he call these terms 'surprisingly liberal'.

There was no good reason why Frederick Manning should have been such a loser, given the capital he had inherited and his marriage to a strong and determined woman. His victim, Patrick O'Connor, demonstrated in a small way that money could certainly be made in London. It was helpful to have good connections and to know how to use them, and to discover a niche in offering people what they wanted, which in O'Connor's case were loans. According to the medical student who had lodged with the Mannings, William Massey, Maria had told him that Patrick O'Connor had amassed a fortune of about £20,000 and had made a will in her favour.

'There's gold in them thar hills'

Even larger fortunes could be made, however. By 1849, London had been thrown into excited tumult by the news of a gold strike in distant

California, where, it was said, the precious metal could be picked up from the ground. Enterprising steamship lines began to put on voyages direct from London to the west coast of America via Cape Horn.[1] The Californian gold rush became one of the topics of 1849 London. Tickets sold out for the farce at the Adelphi theatre in the Strand called 'Cockneys in California'. At Vauxhall and Cremorne Gardens people danced the 'Californian Polka' and the 'Golden Polka', and in London's famous supper and drinking rooms, the Cyder Cellars and the Coal Hole, cigar-smoking gentlemen sang 'The Race to California' and the still unforgotten:

In a cabin, in a canyon,
excavating for a mine,
lived a miner, forty-niner
and his daughter, Clementine.

During 1849 *Punch* joked continually about the gold rush. On 13 January the magazine published a cartoon showing a dustman with his three tiny children, his spade and his broom, announcing, 'Oh! I aint a-going to stop here, looking for teaspoons in cinders. I'm off to Kallifornier, vere there's heaps o'gold dust to be "ad for the sweepin".' Appropriately, the ship in which the dustman is going to sail is called the *Moonshine*. Another cartoon of the same date, called 'A few days at the diggings', illustrates the 'Californian prices' that journalists would complain about when they were heavily charged for vantage points to view the Mannings' executions later that year. *Punch*'s caricatured Yankee, 'Hiram K. Doughboy', was charging the huge sum of $30 (over £6) per day for board and lodging in the goldfields.

In more serious mood, however, *Punch* hoped that the abundance of gold would lead to lower interest rates. On 22 September 1849, as Maria and Frederick Manning lay in prison awaiting trial for murder, the *Illustrated London News* reported the arrival at the Bank of England, under huge police escort, of wagon loads of Californian gold and Mexican gold pesos worth over half a million pounds. The backing of the increased gold reserve allowed greater circulation of paper currency and, as *Punch* had forecast, an expansion of credit from 1850 onwards. Bank rate fell to 2 per cent in April 1851 and a boom was created by increased demand during the Crimean War of 1854–1856.

There was considerable confusion about how much of the gold and paper money, and the share certificates that were found in Maria's possession when she fled to Edinburgh after O'Connor's murder, belonged to the victim, to either of the Mannings (that is, in law, to Frederick) or to Maria personally as a result of the legacy she had received from her parents in Switzerland. When the Mannings' property was finally sold at auction by Debenham and Storrs of King Street, Covent Garden, it realised £56 16s, but the cash and shares raised the amount to £297 12s 5d.[2] Naturally, Maria had sought to find a good home for her savings. After the 1847 collapse in British railway shares there was a renewed flow of overseas investment in railways all over Europe, in public utilities and mines, all channelled through the City of London and often on the basis of loans floated by Rothschilds or Barings. Maria's investments were all in foreign funds, either in French railway certificates or in Spanish bonds, both of which were favourites among British investors, offering better rates of return than the classic 'Consols', which were originally the 3 per cent Consolidated Bank Annuities of 1751. Consols had paid 5.3 per cent interest since 1801, raising the national debt from £228 million in 1793 to £709 million by 1816, after the end of Britain's enormous effort against Napoleon. In 1841 interest on Consols had been slashed to 3.25 per cent. If one had £10,000, the interest would now be £325 rather than £530, a sizeable fall. The high rate of interest on Consols had been justified during the inflationary period of the Napoleonic Wars. Taking 1794–1795 as 100, by 1818 prices had doubled, but by 1849, they had fallen back to where they were before the surge caused by the war.[3] The tumbling interest rate on Consols was responsible for sending a flood of money into speculative shares and foreign bonds.

Patrick O'Connor, for his part, was a prudent investor, but investment was common by 1849 even among ordinary folk including, as a House of Commons report informed Parliament, country parsons, half-pay officers, servants, mail guards, butchers, cooks, coachmen and cotton spinners.[4] Many of them would be ruined by the collapse of the schemes in which they invested their life savings or even by dishonest manipulations of the Stock Exchange.

Plus ça change . . .

Charles Dickens's 'United Metropolitan Improved Hot Muffin and Crumpet Baking and Punctual Delivery Company' in *Nicholas Nickleby* was capitalised at the impertinently audacious and grotesquely exaggerated sum of £5 million in half a million £10 shares.[5] This, along with his Anglo-Bengalee Disinterested Loan and Life Assurance Company in *Martin Chuzzlewit*, are fictional examples of one of the notorious phenomena of the age: the share swindle. Innocent Nicholas Nickleby, father of the eponymous hero of Dickens's novel, speculates in shares and, as Dickens writes:

> . . . *a mania prevailed, a bubble burst, four stockbrokers took villa residences in Florence, four hundred nobodies were ruined . . .*[6]

David Copperfield's aunt Betsey Trotwood invested in a fanciful scheme for fishing up treasure, which Dickens may have based on a project which was suggested for recovering the lost treasures that the Israelites had supposedly jettisoned in their biblical escape from Egypt.[7] Until the Limited Liability Act of 1856, shareholders of a failed company would not lose just the value of their shares, but could also be required to surrender all their property to the creditors.

Another personage whose frequent appearance in fiction reflects his importance in real life was the usurer. Before the age of bank credit, a person in desperate need of capital had recourse to a moneylender. While in traditional fiction the wastrel son of a wealthy family goes for money to a Jewish moneylender because usury was forbidden to Christians, the reality was often otherwise. This was brought out by Charles Reade in his novel *It's Never too Late to Mend* (1856), which portrays Isaac Levi as a mysterious, noble and Oriental Jew, whom John Meadows, the Gentile usurer at 20 per cent interest, considers a competitor because his rates were lower and whom he tried criminally to put out of the way. Even 20 per cent interest, however, was little enough compared with Dickens's fictional Ralph Nickleby who, in his schooldays, lent at the simplest rate of 'two pence for every halfpenny', that is at 400 per cent.[8]

Bankruptcy

If one could not pay one's debts, bankruptcy or insolvency was the consequence. Did the Mannings have the humiliating experience, like Madame Mantalini in *Nicholas Nickleby*, of bailiffs pushing their way uncouthly into their beerhouse in Hackney and roughly making an inventory of the contents? Possibly, but not for sure, given that crockery inscribed with the name of the King's Head was found among Maria's possessions and inventoried by the police. Nor did the Mannings ever have to pawn anything, especially their jewellery, including a gold hunter watch, a gold chain, with seals and a key, which was found in Frederick's possession and was listed in the catalogue when the Mannings' property was auctioned after their execution.

Selling up the property of the insolvent was in the news in 1849. Count d'Orsay, lover and stepson-in-law of the Countess of Blessington, had had to flee to the Continent to escape his creditors. He must have had a great many, to judge by Jane Carlyle's description of his carriage, 'resplendent with skye-blue and silver' from which the 'Prince of Dandies' descended. 'Such a beautiful man', as the Carlyles' servant exclaimed, though Jane herself thought d'Orsay's beauty was 'of that rather disgusting sort'.[9] She meant he was slightly effeminate. Howell and James, silk mercers of Regent Street, tried to recover sums for the expensive furnishing of Gore House, Lady Blessington's residence, which stood on the site of the later Albert Hall in South Kensington. In May 1849, it was sold up. Lady Blessington, a novelist herself, had conducted a fashionable literary salon, attended by the novelist Thackeray, who was highly offended by the coarse handling of the items up for sale, although they were unpaid for and thus never his patroness's property.

Bankruptcy (at the time the term was reserved for trading failures rather than for insolvency caused by overspending or unwise investment) seems to have been a common fate, at least to judge by the list of failures in *The Times* for the first quarter of 1849. While this probably reflects the sequel of the bursting of the railway share bubble in 1847, bankruptcy seems to have been frequent in the rough and tumble of mid-nineteenth-century business. It certainly occurs often in Victorian novels. In a world of investment and share swindles, together with an enterprise culture in which a certain proportion, little protected by the law, was bound to fail, bankruptcies were part of the life of a pulsating city such as London. Wages and salaries were low, so a well-invested legacy, such as Nicholas Nickleby the elder received and unwisely invested, might make all the difference between a comfortable life and one in straightened circumstances. Such concerns must have been the daily conversation in the Manning household, after their two ventures into tavern-keeping had failed.

They seem, however, to have been free of personal, as opposed to trading, debts, probably through Maria's hard-headed attitude. Perhaps if they had owed money they would not have been able to pay cash or obtain credit to secure the pistol, the lime and the shovel, which were such important items in the prosecution's case.

Confinement in the debtors' prison was the frequent experience of the insolvent, as Charles Dickens knew from visiting his father in the Marshalsea debtors' prison. John Dickens owed the baker £40. He was taken first to a 'sponging house', from where he sent young Charles to try, unsuccessfully as it turns out, to collect enough money from friends and relations to pay something on account, before finally being imprisoned in the Marshalsea, an experience reproduced in *Little Dorrit*, whose eponymous heroine is called the 'Child of the Marshalsea', and earlier, when the novelist depicts kind, pompous Mr Micawber in the King's Bench Prison, just off the Borough High Street, not that far from where the Mannings lived.

Housing

There were a few large-scale builders in London, such as Thomas Cubitt who built the Calthorp Estate off Gray's Inn Road, Highbury Park, Woburn Place, Gordon Square, half of Belgravia, Eaton Square and most of Pimlico. But short terraces such as Miniver Place were built as speculations by small builders. Over 43,000 new houses were built in London between 1841 and 1851. A small builder would lay the foundations and build the walls, then finish the house by paying a subcontractor by mortgaging the property for a couple of hundred pounds to one of the new building societies. When the house was complete, the builder would pay off the loan by selling the house at a small profit to a landlord who wanted to invest a few hundred pounds.[10]

Maria might have noticed the house when she was living with O'Connor in Bermondsey a year or so earlier after running away from Frederick, but the usual method of renting was through an agent who had a baize-covered board in his window on which slips of paper were stuck with details of the property to be let. No. 3 Miniver Place was let to the Mannings by the builder himself, James Coleman. The amount of the rent was never mentioned at the trial. However, a similar property, number 16

Bayham Street in Camden Town in north London, was rented by Charles Dickens's parents at £22 a year plus rates, which the tenant had to pay if the house's rateable value was over £20.[11] A considerably better house, such as the one rented in Chelsea in 1834 by Jane and Thomas Carlyle, the writer, cost £35 a year, but in consideration of the improvements that the Carlyles continued to make, the landlord extended their lease, at the same rent, for thirty-one years.[12] Nobody expected inflation then. In addition, the water rate was £1 6s per year, the church rate £2 5s; there was a Lighting, Paving and Improvement Rate and a Poor Rate. The Carlyles also had to pay the Fire Insurance and a Sewer Rate.

Chelsea was considered a high-quality suburb with some excellent houses. The Carlyles' house had eight rooms, with a closet, large enough to be used as a dressing room, on each floor, and many cupboards. In the basement, just as in the Mannings's much poorer dwelling, there was a stone-paved back kitchen, off which were a larder and a coal cupboard, and a huge copper, as well as a fireplace with complicated arrangements of trivets and hobs. There was no bathroom; Thomas Carlyle rigged up a cold water shower in the kitchen. The servant slept in the front kitchen, which faced the street and, because it was below street level, was usually in semi-darkness.

It was usual for builders to number their new rows of houses from No. 1 or No. 2 onwards, depending on which side of the street they were. A street might have several little rows of houses like Miniver Place. Later, the Post Office would renumber the houses consecutively from the first one in the street. In time, 3 Miniver Place became 103 Weston Street. A photograph of it was taken in 1959, shortly before it fell victim to municipal demolition. Sadly dilapidated, in need of a coat of paint, it is hard to connect it with the white-painted terrace that was sketched in 1849 for Robert Huish's weekly penny parts of his sensational *The Progress of Crime; or Authentic Memoirs of Maria Manning.*

The house was built of brick, which was originally completely rendered with stucco, as the artist drew it for Huish's publication, though by 1959, when the photograph was taken, the upper floor had lost its rendering and was faced with bare brick.

The front door, with its decorated lintel and keyblock, opened on to a corridor and then a staircase leading to the two rooms on the upper floor. On the ground floor were the front and back parlours and there was a front and a back kitchen in the basement. Given that the average number of persons per house in England and Wales was 5.5 in 1851, the Mannings were spaciously housed, even if they had to take a lodger in one of the six rooms.[13]

No. 103 Weston Street was demolished in the 1960s, presumably because it could not be repaired to minimum standards. Throughout the 1840s, when the house was built, the battle for public health had been fought on the general issues of sanitation, overcrowding, alcoholism and social problems rather than on the housing question in particular. Several proposed building reforms were postponed because of property owners' objections. In 1844, when Miniver Place was built, the Metropolitan Building Act had legislated on minimum sizes for houses, on street widths and habitable cellars, but the law did not deal with drainage and sanitation until 1855. London was particularly behindhand in matters such as damp-proof courses and ventilation. In any case, the Act of 1844 applied only to the cities of London and Westminster and some adjacent parishes, not including Bermondsey. There were only 33 district surveyors at work in London at the time, so we cannot tell what minimum standards were applied in the Mannings' house.[14] On the other hand, London was spared the back-to-back houses of the northern industrial cities. No. 3 Miniver Place had a back garden, not very well cared for, according to the next door neighbour, but there were a few straggling scarlet runner beans.

The house in Miniver Place was of the lower class in the hierarchy of standard dwellings. Its only refinement was the railings which implied middle-class self-containment. The front parlour was wallpapered. About 8s 6d per week was the rent for this class of new six-roomed house.[15] One would need an income of about £5 per week to rent it, given that 8 per cent was considered appropriate to allow the rest of a middle-class income to be spent on a suitable standard of living.[16] The Mannings, however, had a particularly uncertain income. They did not think they could afford the house, which is why they were so angry with O'Connor because he promised to be their subtenant and then went back on his word when they had already signed the lease. William Massey, the medical student who took a room in the house, probably paid three or four shillings, inclusive of coal and candles.

Whatever its condition in 1959, Miniver Place was better than this description of a house in late nineteenth-century Bermondsey:

The house was one up, one down, with a small scullery and no backyard except a shut-in paved area three feet deep. Drying and washing was done in the front court, where at the other end there was a stand-pipe for twenty-five houses with the water on for two hours daily, though never on Sundays. There was no place to wash in, no other water to wash in . . . there was one w.c. for the twenty-five homes and a cesspool. Queues lined up outside that w.c., men and women and children.[17]

Maria Manning was well-equipped to make a home. Well-trained, probably when she was still at home in Switzerland, she had observed how an English aristocratic house was run. She was a competent needlewoman. She had no need of the books of advice which proliferated, such as *The English Wife, a Manual of Home Duties* of 1843, or Eliza Acton's *Modern Cookery for Private Families* of 1845, or even the hugely successful Alexis Soyer's *The Modern Housewife or Ménagère* of 1849. These books increased in number after 1850; Mrs Elizabeth Beeton's famous *Book of Household Management* appeared in 1861. But no guide to household economy was inventoried among Maria's possessions.

'My ball's in the airy'

It wasn't easy to run a house in 1849, at least not without a servant. Many Victorian kitchens were in the basement, dank and gloomy, though this house did have an 'area' at the front of the house, giving some light to the front kitchen. The area, known, perhaps because of its function, as the 'airy', rhymed with a common Irish name to create the children's song heard when children still played in London streets until not long ago:

One, two, three, O'Leary,
My ball's in the airy.

The only way Maria could heat water, save on the open fire, was in the copper, a metal cauldron under which she had to make a fire. The house almost certainly had piped water but it would have been only what was called 'low' service, not the 'high' version which reached the upper floor, and only into the sink in the basement kitchen where Maria invited the hapless O'Connor to wash that hot evening.

'A dandified folly'

Bathrooms were very rare, even in better-class houses. Sybarites could install cold shower-baths, as Carlyle did, though this required a piped water supply. In Chapter 29 of Thackeray's novel *Pendennis*, which was appearing in monthly parts in 1849, the younger barristers in the Temple have installed showers, but their elderly colleague Mr Grump declares that the practice is 'an absurd, newfangled, dandified folly'.

One of the improvements made by the great pressure for sanitary reform in the 1840s was the Public Baths and Wash-houses Act of 1846. This came a long time after the tax on soap had been reduced in 1833, to be removed altogether in 1853. The consumption of this necessary aid to hygiene doubled between 1841 and 1861.[18] A large public bathing institution was opened in Goulston Street, Whitechapel, in May 1849, with 94 separate warm and cold baths, as well as steam and sulphur baths. The demand was 30,000 baths per week as well as laundry facilities for 20,000 people.[19] During 1849, 96,726 baths were taken in the George Street Baths in Euston Square, that is 1,860 per week or about 300 daily. A cold bath cost a penny and a warm shower with a clean towel twopence.

As for the lavatory, the usual provision was a privy or 'necessary' at the end of the back garden. The excreta fell into a box and were covered with earth, either by a shovel or via a hopper. 'Night-soil men', who often worked as chimney sweeps during the day, came and emptied the box and sold the material for fertiliser. This was a very healthy way of ridding the area of offensive material. In the Manning garden, however, there was a closet connected to a cesspit, into which it was thought that the couple had thrown the gun and the crowbar which they had used to kill O'Connor and which were never found. The landlord protested that enough damage had already been done to his house without digging underneath the garden, though presumably the cesspit had to be emptied periodically by the night-soil men. They would first remove the top soil, and then get into the brick cesspit through a hole at the top covered with a stone slab. The process of getting into the pit, digging out the offensive material in it and carting it away must have contributed to the regular foul smells, which people were so accustomed to that they probably did not even notice.

The police report spoke of a 'water-closet' in the Manning house, but evidently it did not mean a lavatory with a cistern.[20] Even though the house was relatively new, the Mannings did not enjoy this state-of-the-art way of relieving themselves. At best, they may have tipped a bucket of water down the privy.

Even if there was piped water in the kitchen, the supply was irregular. Yet there was no way of storing any substantial quantity of water in the house. At the trial, the Attorney-General made the point that Maria had tried to clean the basket that held the quicklime, which the Mannings had poured over O'Connor's corpse, 'until she had exhausted all the water on the premises'. This suggests that she kept water in containers. No cistern is shown in the illustration of the kitchen, though one may have been installed in the area, as was commonly the case.

Home cooking

As for cooking, Maria Manning's kitchen had an open fire with enough space over it to hang a roasting spit (which is probably how she cooked the goose on the afternoon of the murder), but no range or 'kitchener' (a coal-burning stove with ovens and iron plates on the top for pans), which was just coming into use and was considerably more economical of coal and provided hot water as well. Expenditure on coal might be considerable; the Carlyles burnt 12 tons a year at 21s per ton, about the same cost as a servant. However, landlords would not install an expensive range – the average price was £7 15s plus cost of installation – unless they could charge more rent, and ranges were rare in poorer parts of London.[21] The range in the Carlyles' house in Chelsea did not work well. In 1852 Carlyle agreed to pay £7 3s for a new one, and the landlord promised to refund the money if Carlyle ever moved away.[22]

The fire would burn in the hearth of the Mannings' basement kitchen all through the year. As well as the roasting spit, there was a trivet over the open fire which could support one or more pots at a time, but the food was probably very smoky.

In the winter, what with London grime and fog, the cooking would have made the kitchen greasy and grimy. There was probably a lot of condensation and the floor would have been damp. Washing up was an unpleasant business. The butler sink was unglazed and perhaps there was a rough wooden draining board. The pots had to be scoured with wood ash. On the plus side, the Mannings not only had a larder for food storage, but also they lived in a large city where they could buy food in any quantities they needed whenever they wanted it.

Home comforts

Mr Bainbridge, the furniture dealer, was invited by the court to prepare an inventory of all the furniture in the house, which he had bought from Frederick, but the details were not mentioned during the hearing. Its second-hand value was £13 10s, though Frederick had asked for £16. It had cost £30, much more expensive than the price with which one could furnish a house at the end of the century when mass production had brought the cost down to £12 12s,[23] or just under ten weeks' wages for a man on 25 shillings a week.

The Mannings heated their house with coal, most of which still came in the 700 colliers which carried fuel from Tyneside to London. The coal was broken up and bagged by the coal-whippers on the Thames, brought ashore in barges and sold by the ton by merchants who brought it to the houses in carts drawn by huge shire-horses. The coal cupboard at 3 Miniver Place was off the back kitchen, so there probably wasn't a coal hole in the street outside the house, through which the coalman tipped the coal, creating as he did so immense clouds of coal dust and angering the local housewives whose laundry and white-scrubbed front steps became coated with black dust. The coalman carried the heavy sacks down into the area of 3 Miniver Place and emptied them into the coal cupboard. It would have been impossible to avoid creating a haze of black dust throughout the house.

Rooms were smoky in the winter because the downdraughts blew coal dust into the room. Chimneys were inefficient and carried a great deal of the incompletely combusted fuel out into the air in the form of soot, which created the black pall of smoke that struck all foreign visitors.[24] And sometimes, during high winds, chimney pots, which the builders had not properly fixed to the chimney stacks, would come crashing down with an explosion of shattered earthenware.

As for lighting, gas was rare even in middle-class homes until the 1850s, when its installation in the new House of Commons reassured many who suspected its safety. It was unlikely to have been laid on in Miniver Place. Gaslight was yellow and smoky until incandescent gas mantles were introduced in the 1880s. It was also quite expensive. Thomas Carlyle had gas put in, but he considered it a great extravagance. Gas for private houses was seen as garish and typical of the nouveaux-riches, making their houses resemble brilliantly lit gin palaces. It made the atmosphere even more hot and stuffy than it already was. Besides, the impurities in the supply created an unpleasant smell. Furthermore, gas was cruel to women's complexions, showing up every blemish.[25] Private kitchens were slow in adopting gas for cooking, though the famous chef Alexis Soyer used it in the Reform Club, where he produced legendary banquets from 1841 onwards.[26] The price of gas was falling, but too late for the Mannings, who used whale oil or colza, made from oil-seed rape, in their lamps, and in the bedroom probably smelly tallow or rendered animal fat candles. Lighting was expensive for the really poor, so they still used rushes dipped in hot bacon fat. They were called 'farthing dips', because a bundle could be bought for a quarter of one penny.[27] Candles cost tenpence per pound. The middle-class Carlyles burned 3 pounds in ten days, but this was because Thomas liked to stay up late.

As for laundry, Maria might have done the washing herself or she might have sent it out. Perhaps she had a washerwoman in once a week, maybe the wife of one of the Irish dockers who owed O'Connor money. The regular washing of Maria's voluminous petticoats, Fred's underwear, shirts and neckcloths, and the nightdresses, sheets and pillowcases of the household, required soaking in a tub, vigorous rubbing, boiling in the copper, rinsing, blueing and starching. As for the drying, fortunately the Mannings had the garden in the summer and the second kitchen in winter.

A steady £3 a week was considered the minimum income at which one could afford to employ a live-in servant of the least skilled sort, a 'maid of all work' or 'skivvy', who might earn between £6 and £12 a year with her keep. The Mannings' income didn't run to a servant, but Maria engaged a charwoman when she needed one, as she did when she brought in twelve-year-old Hannah Firman to clean up after she and Frederick had buried O'Connor's corpse. Hannah usually sold matches, bootlaces and laces for ladies' stays from a tray in the street. When she approached Maria, asking if she wanted the front step cleaned, Maria engaged her.

It took Hannah the whole day to clean up the mess of lime and earth produced by the disposal of O'Connor's corpse. Maria gave her sixpence. Hannah made up for the meanness of her reward by stealing stockings, a petticoat and an egg, as she unwillingly confessed when she gave evidence in court.

Home, sweet home

Maria Manning, who had never had to soil her hands when she was a lady's maid, was now obliged to shop, cook, clean and wash with little help. Whether or not her ideal had ever been cosy domesticity, a few months of this in Miniver Place with its minimum facilities, in smoky Bermondsey, where the air stank of the tanning workshops for which the district was famed, would have driven her to desperation. Even though she was no longer a servant, but a married woman running her own house, she must have felt that she had dropped in social class.

Class

> Oh! Let us love our occupations,
> bless the squire and his relations,
> live upon our daily rations,
> and always know our proper stations.

In Dickens's short novel *The Chimes*, this rhyme is set to music by the 'new system' – tonic sol-fa – for Lady Bowley, wife of Sir Joseph Bowley MP, who wants the men and boys of the village to sing it in the evening as they engage in pinking and eyelet-holing. But the rebel, Will Fern, politely refuses. Lady Bowley complains, 'Who can expect anything but insolence and ingratitude from that class of people?' She and her husband, who have spent money on the poor, agree that Fern should be punished as a vagrant.[28]

Middle-class people

Money and where one got it was indelibly associated with class in Victorian times. Frederick Manning came from a respectable family in trade in Taunton; Maria had been a very high class lady's maid. They belonged to the lower middle class of small manufacturers, shopkeepers, master tailors, innkeepers and commercial travellers, to which was now being added a growing array of clerks, schoolteachers and the lower ranks of the professions, together with railway and government officials. Such people were either 'in trade' or they provided a paid service, rather than living on their investments or rents. But they did not live by their own manual labour either, and this put them firmly among the middle classes, who opposed aristocratic idleness, preferring puritan values of 'seriousness', hard work and sobriety, unless they had a taste for sherry or port at 25 shillings for a dozen bottles. It was Frederick's inability to resist his vice of alcohol which would drag him down. On 7 July 1849, *Punch*, reflecting middle-class disapproval of high-spending Londoners' habits, quotes 'Mr Brown' who remarks cuttingly, 'Everybody lives as if he had three or four thousand a year.' 'Everybody' would include Charles Dickens's characters Hamilton and Anastasia Veneering in *Our Mutual Friend* (1864–1865), who live in 'a bran-new house in a bran-new quarter of London', and keep up with their friends by giving a dinner party which might have cost all of £50.

The lower middle class also feared atheists and disreputable agnostics. With little education and little artistic sensitivity, this class was 'respectable'. It disapproved of working-class and upper-class sexual misbehaviour, though Maria herself engaged in it. They held themselves up as examples to the feckless poor, preaching the doctrines of self-control especially in the area of having children. They had grown to maturity in the wake of the 1832 Reform Bill and the repeal of the Corn Laws. The increasing acceptance of middle-class values gave that class a sense of mission and identity. It also had a sense of responsibility. Charles Dickens's wealthy merchant Mr Dombey, for example, recommends Rob, nicknamed 'Biler', the son of Mr Toodle, the stoker and later engine driver, for a place at the Bluecoat School, fictionalised in *Dombey and Son* as the Grinders.

If the Mannings' income was insufficient for a middle-class standard of living, to allow them, for instance, to occupy their six-roomed terrace house without the help of a subtenant, they certainly had middle-class aspirations. When they ordered a crowbar, Mr Manning was quite annoyed that it was delivered unwrapped, though this was alleged to be because he did not want it seen as a potential murder weapon.

Despite their financial straits, the Mannings seem to have been able to dress well, they had money to buy things and to adopt the middle-class prestige symbol of inviting their friend to dine on poultry, even if the real purpose of the invitation was sinister. If Frederick Manning had been able to keep his salesman's job at Gover and Company, stationers in Holborn, at a salary of £2 per week and 5 per cent commission, he would have been well placed in the lower middle class at about the status of a higher clerk. As an employee he was probably lower in status than he had been as a publican, but a commercial traveller had the advantage of not having to deal with drunks. He was higher than the class that Dickens, in *Sketches by Boz*, the novelist's observations of London people, described as 'shabby-genteel'. At a fixed wage he was also in a better position than Mr Micawber in *David Copperfield*, who sold corn on commission only. This was a time when a builder's labourer in the season might be paid £1 a week (much more than he would have received as a Wiltshire or Essex farm hand), a postman received 22 shillings and a skilled worker in London would get thirty shillings, but only when he was in work of course. Frederick Manning had earned only 18s per week as a railway guard, the same as a policeman. Only printers, those aristocrats of the skilled working class, had a good wage of £4 4s a week, just a pound less than reporters for the newspapers they printed.

Charles Dickens, with his outstanding shorthand skills, was employed by the *Morning Chronicle* as a parliamentary reporter at 5 guineas (£5 5s) a week. With the development of his writing skills, there was always the chance that he could ascend one day to the heights of the deputy editor of the paper at over £500 a year, if not the editor, at the dizzy rate of over £1,000. An annual income of £500 would allow a man to rent a London villa, for £45 a year, with two drawing rooms, a breakfast room, kitchen and scullery and five bedrooms for his several children and perhaps two live-in servants.[29]

Just over two pounds ten a week

Most of the lower middle class earned between £100 and £200 per year, though clerks and teachers often got even less. Bob Cratchit, Ebenezer Scrooge's clerk in Dickens's *A Christmas Carol* of 1843, receives only 15s a week or £37 10s per year, though Scrooge recognises that this is particularly poor pay. The later novelist Anthony Trollope started as a clerk at the General Post Office in 1834 on £90 per year, but had risen after seven years to £140, which was considered the minimum at which to begin lower middle class married life. William Guppy, the solicitor's clerk, offers Esther Summerson marriage in Chapter IX of *Bleak House*. He sees himself as poor when he earns £1 15s a week (the wage of a well-paid working man), but now, having had his salary raised to £2 and with the promise of another 5s a week in a year's time, he spends money on his clothes and wears a flashy ring. He lives in Penton Place, Islington, considered a good, healthy address.

Patrick O'Connor, however, for his sinecure in the docks, received £300 a year. Fees for lecturers at the Mechanics' Institutes were between three and twelve guineas a session, but of course they had no fixed annual salary. A popular lecturer could earn between £500 and £1,000 a year.

As for hours, the seven or eight hundred clerks in the Bank of England, whose employment practices provided a model for City firms, worked from 9 a.m. to 3.30 p.m., or 5 p.m. if they took an hour and a half for dinner (perhaps to go home, unless they lived in distant Islington or Camberwell), but the work had to be finished and the daily balance struck before they left in the evening. Most offices closed at six. Below the Bank of England clerks came those who worked in insurance or the Stock Exchange. They worked six days a week and had no annual holidays save Christmas Day and Good Friday. In fact the early nineteenth century clerk worked harder than his predecessor in the eighteenth, when there had been a much larger number of statutory 'holy days'.

When in 1842 Sir Robert Peel reintroduced income tax, abolished after the Napoleonic wars, on incomes of over £150 per year, Patrick O'Connor, who had a salary of £300, would pay 7d in the pound tax on £150, that is £4 7s 6d. Even on a comfortable £500 a year, tax on £350 would be only £10 4s 2d. But class was determined by the house you could afford to rent and the number and type of servants you could employ. That £10 4s 2d tax would pay the wages, though admittedly not the food, board and clothes, of a teenage servant-girl, so in one sense, the income tax of the 1840s, even though it seems a bagatelle to us today, could be judged a burden. The Carlyles had been paying £17 12s 8d in taxes (including local rates) but in 1855, with the inflation caused by the

Crimean War, Jane Carlyle, who paid all the accounts, expostulated to her husband that she needed a larger allowance because she was having to pay out £7 16s 8d more.[30] This was principally because income tax was doubled to 1s 2d in the pound in 1855 before being cut back to 7d in 1857.

Jane Carlyle went to beard the Commissioners of Income Tax in protest at their high assessment of her husband's tax debts. The Commissioners asked Jane whether they were expected to believe that the Carlyles lived on the £150 a year that Mr Carlyle had quoted as his average annual income from writing. No, of course not, retorted Jane, adding coldly that Thomas had no obligation to give the Commissioners any account of his other income, which came from land and was not subject to tax. The Commissioners conceded the point and knocked £50 off their assessment of Mr Carlyle's earnings.

While 111,000 families in 1850 had over £150 a year and thus came into the tax bracket, only 39,000 had as much as £200, fewer still £200–£300 and even fewer had between £300 and £400. A total of 194,300 families, perhaps a million people in all, enjoyed what might be called lower and 'middle' middle class incomes.[31]

Four-figure men

A 'gentleman' needed £1,000 a year at least to maintain his standard, keep horses and employ several male and female servants. Maria Manning had worked for ladies whose husbands had incomes of at least £10,000 a year, the least they needed to be able to spend the season in London and maintain a country house and large estate. The major dukes of the kingdom, however, Bedford, Bridgewater, Devonshire and Northumberland, had £50,000 a year or more.[32]

At the bottom of the heap

Below the lowest of the middle class, the Bob Cratchits trying to keep 'respectable' on fifteen shillings a week, were London's mass of working men. One class knew little enough about the other, as Benjamin Disraeli's oft-quoted lines from his novel *Sybil* (1845) reflect:

Two nations, between whom there is no intercourse and no sympathy,
who are as ignorant of each other's habits, thoughts and feelings, as if
they were dwellers in different zones, or inhabitants of different planets;
who are formed by a different breeding, are fed by a different food, are
ordered by different manners and are not governed by the same laws . . .
THE RICH AND THE POOR.[33]

The 1844 Factory Act had cut children's hours of work to six and a half per day and women's to twelve. In 1847 the Ten Hours Act had further limited women's working hours. Yet the law was often ignored and not applied, particularly in smaller workshops. As for men, in the London building trade they worked about 54 hours a week in the summer and slightly fewer when there was less light in the winter. But if they wanted the work, or were on piecework, working people themselves conspired to frustrate the factory inspector. For those who worked in factory and workshop, the exhausting tedium and monotony, together with the noise, dust and poor light, especially in the winter months, made labour an experience of suffering only relieved by the hard drinking of the weekend.

The 1851 census revealed that in England and Wales there were 24,000 male servants and 39,000 female housekeepers, cooks and maids, as well as 121,000 general domestic servants, mostly under the age of thirty. Their wages, at about £10 a year besides their board, clothes, lodging and medical attendance, contrasted favourably with the £26 per annum that an average working woman could earn at the time. A woman had little alternative work, particularly in London which did not have the factories employing armies of females that were to be found in the north of England. The needle trades were notorious for sweating and slack time.

The workhouse

Very few people enjoyed pensionable employment. If one had not been able to save sufficiently for one's old age, the workhouse was the grim answer. On Sunday 5 May 1850, Charles Dickens visited the Marylebone workhouse, and wrote his visit up in a piece in *Household Words* on 25 May.[34] The institution had 1,715 inmates, as well as a further 345 in the infirmary, including 79 lunatics and those in the 'itch' ward. Most of the young inmates were fatherless children, the sort who might have been farmed out to cruel moneymakers such as Bartholomew Drouet of the Tooting Baby Pauper Farm ravaged by cholera the previous year. Others were widows without support. In his article Dickens wrote:

> *Aged people were there, in every variety. Mumbling, blear-eyed, spectacled, stupid, deaf, lame: vacantly winking in the gleams of sun that now and then crept in through the open doors, from the paved yard . . . There were weird old women, all skeleton within, all bonnet and cloak without, continually wiping their eyes with dirty dusters of pocket-handkerchiefs, and there were ugly old crones, both male and female, with a ghastly kind of contentment upon them which was not at all comforting to see.*

Servants in particular, if they lived long enough and worked for employers who did not think it their responsibility or were not able to support them in old age, took refuge in the workhouse. Dickens saw a young woman, pretty and well-mannered, who had been brought to the workhouse because she was subject to epileptic fits and had no friends who could take her in. It is difficult to know what the elderly middle class did if they could no longer pay the rent, but Dickens underlines that the young woman in question 'was by no means of the same stuff, or the same breeding, or the same experience as those by whom she was surrounded', so it would seem that the workhouse was very much restricted to the poor, ignorant and rough.

The workhouse that Dickens visited, in contrast to the one under the rule of Mr Bumble in *Oliver Twist*, was well run and clean. The paupers were kindly treated, but there was no stimulus for the mind. Was it any substantially different in this respect from some old people's homes today, except that Dickens says nothing about the separation of husbands from wives in different wards which was what elderly and poverty-stricken couples most dreaded? He visited the workhouse on a fine May day. The windows and doors were probably open, which may be why Dickens says nothing about the smell.

The permanent smokiness of London, together with the filthy state of the streets and the repellent drains, created the smell, the miasma, which worried doctors so much. But people smelled badly also. The Baths and

Wash-houses Act of 1847 allowed some improvement in the body odour of manual workers who, unwashed, reeking of sour sweat, stale tobacco and beer, their jackets, trousers and shirts rarely changed, carried with them the odours of their work: paint, turpentine, coal and glue. On 11 December 1849, the opening of the public baths at Marylebone gave occasion for the socially concerned middle-class inhabitants of the parish to congratulate themselves on facilitating the cleanliness of the common people. They did so at what the press described as 'an elegant déjeuner', laid out for the occasion.

The working class not only smelled differently; in London they also spoke a different language. If written records are trustworthy, one of Henry Mayhew's contacts among the London common people revealed, perhaps for the first time, the characteristics of cockney rhyming slang:

> *Suppose I want to ask a pal to come and have a glass of rum and smoke a pipe of tobacco and have a game of cards with some blokes at home with me. I should say, if there were any flats present, 'Splodger, will you have a Jack surpass of finger-and-thumb and blow your yard of tripe of nosey-me-knacker, and have a touch of the broads with me and the other heap of coke at my drum?*

Most of the rhyming is obvious, but 'flats' were flatfoots or police. 'Nosey-me-knacker was 'tobacco', pronounced 'terbacker', while 'broads' were cards, pronounced 'cords'.[35]

Notes

1 Dodds, J.W., *The Age of Paradox: A Biography of England 1841–1851* (London: Gollancz, 1953), p. 360.

2 Public Record Office, MEPO 3/54.

3 Burnett, J., *A History of the Cost of Living* (Harmondsworth: Penguin, 1969), pp. 200–1.

4 Sheppard, F., *London 1808–1870: The Infernal Wen* (Berkeley: University of California Press, 1971), p. 71.

5 This was the same capitalisation as Nathan Rothschild's Alliance Fire and Life Assurance Society of 1824: see Altick, R., *The Presence of the Present: Topics of the Day in the Victorian Novel* (Columbus: Ohio State University Press, 1991), p. 643.

6 Dickens, C., *Nicholas Nickleby* Penguin English Library edition, ed. M. Slater, 1978, p. 63.

7 Dickens, C., *David Copperfield*, Chapter 35.

8 Ibid., p. 61.

9 Holme, T., *The Carlyles at Home*, first published 1965 (London: Persephone Books, 2002), p. 28.

10 For these details see Burnett, J., *A Social History of Housing 1815–1870* (London: Methuen, 1980), p. 20. See also Sheppard, F., *London 1808–1870: The Infernal Wen* (Berkeley: University of California Press, 1971), pp. 101–3.

11 Johnson, E., *Charles Dickens, his Tragedy and Triumph* (Harmondsworth: Penguin, revised edition, 1986), p. 28.

12 Holme, T., *The Carlyles at Home*, first published 1965 (London: Persephone Books, 2002), p. 76.

13 Hoppen, K.T., *The Mid-Victorian Generation 1846–1886* (Oxford: Oxford University Press, 1998), p. 339.

14 Sheppard, F., *London 1808–1870: The Infernal Wen* (Berkeley: University of California Press, 1971), p. 95.

15 Burnett, J., *A Social History of Housing 1815–1870* (London: Methuen, 1980), p. 78.

16 Ibid., p. 145.

17 Quoted in Hardyment, C., *From Mangle to Microwave: The Mechanization of Household Work* (Cambridge: Polity Press, 1988), pp. 17–18.

18 Perkin, J., *Women and Marriage in Nineteenth Century England* (London: Routledge, 1989), p. 142.

19 See *Gentleman's Magazine* for July 1849.

20 Public Record Office, MEPO 3/54.

21 Burnett, J., *A Social History of Housing 1815–1870* (London: Methuen, 1980), p. 211.

22 Holme, T., *The Carlyles at Home*, first published 1965 (London: Persephone Books, 2002), p. 10.

23 Burnett, J., *A Social History of Housing 1815–1870* (London: Methuen, 1980), p. 171.

24 On this, as on many other details, see Cruickshank, D. and Burton, N., *Life in the Georgian City* (London: Viking, 1990), p. 78.

25 Altick, R., *The Presence of the Present: Topics of the Day in the Victorian Novel* (Columbus: Ohio State University Press, 1991), pp. 343–4.

26 Ibid., p. 122.

27 Cruickshank, D. and Burton, N., *Life in the Georgian City* (London: Viking, 1990), p. 74.

28 Dickens, C., *The Chimes* (1844) 2nd quarter.

29 Burnett, J., *A History of the Cost of Living* (Harmondsworth: Penguin, 1969), p. 242.

30 Holme, T., *The Carlyles at Home*, first published 1965 (London: Persephone Books, 2002), p. 147.

31 Altick, R., *The English Common Reader: a Social History of the Mass Reading Public 1800–1900* (Chicago: University of Chicago Press, 1957), p. 277.

32 Burnett, J., *A History of the Cost of Living* (Harmondsworth: Penguin, 1969), p. 221.

33 Quoted in Altick, R., *Victorian People and Ideas*, first published 1973 (London: Dent, 1974), p. 11.

34 Dickens, C., *Dickens's Journalism*, ed. M. Slater, 4 volumes (London: Dent, 1996), vol. 2 'The Amusements of the People and Other Papers 1834–1851', pp. 234–41.

35 Pearsall, R., *The Worm in the Bud: The World of Victorian Sexuality*, first published 1969 (Harmondsworth: Penguin, 1971), p. 79.

CHAPTER 6

Learning, literature and liturgy

'Widely diffused ignorance'

The Victorian passion for elaborate and precise statistics allowed the novelist and journalist Charles Dickens to conclude, from the Metropolitan Police figures, that out of 20,500 London women convicted of offences in 1847, 9,000 were totally illiterate and 11,000 could read and write only imperfectly. Only 14 of these women could read and write well. These probably belonged to the middle class or were perhaps superior servants like Maria Manning. As for the men, only 150 out of 41,000 could read and write well.[1] The rest, where they could read, could do no more than, in Dickens's pathos-inducing words, 'blunder over a book like a little child'. In any case, the standard of literacy was often very basic, perhaps no more than being able to stumble through an elementary reading book. Dickens linked women's illiteracy with their incapacity to do simple household tasks or basic sewing, and he allied these deficiencies to the general immorality of such women's lives. He took the view – and he may be assumed to represent a great deal of progressive opinion at the time – that education had to have a practical and moral end, to be 'immediately applicable to the duties and business of life, directly conducive to order, cleanliness, punctuality and economy'. The Gospels were not supposed to be used merely as a reading primer (in Dickens's words, 'a dog-eared spelling book'); they had a moral purpose as well.[2]

In the next issue of *The Examiner*, Dickens used his fluent and compelling pen to launch an attack on the schools of the National Society for the Education of the Poor in the Principles of the Church of England in England and Wales, known for short as the National Schools. A London servant girl, Susan Grant, had recently been tricked out of her savings by a fortune-teller who claimed, for money, to be able to change the influence of the planets on Susan's future life. When the fortune-teller was had up in court, the magistrate expressed surprise that Susan had been so credulous. Dickens used her example to lambast the teaching of the National Schools. Susan Grant could probably parrot her catechism without the slightest idea of what it meant, but her so-called education had not taught her that, for a pious person, the planets were controlled by the Divine will, and thus could hardly be affected by crossing somebody's palm with silver.

There were also non-sectarian schools run by the British and Foreign School Society. However, in Dickens's view, their severe utilitarianism would have crushed the sense of wonder of any child who mused 'Twinkle, twinkle, little star, how I wonder what you are'. Eight years later Dickens wrote about the same jingle in his novel *Hard Times*, where he attacks the harshness of a utilitarian education limited to pure facts. 'No little Gradgrind,' he wrote, 'had ever known wonder on the subject [of the stars], each little Gradgrind having at five years old dissected the Great Bear [. . .].'

While Susan Grant seems to have been simple, whatever the deficiencies of her education, the fact was that in 1834, of 130,000 couples who married, one-third of the bridegrooms and half of the brides could not even manage to sign their own names in the register.[3] Later, the 1851 Census showed similar figures: 30.7 per cent of the males and 45.2 per cent of the females could not sign the marriage register.[4] These figures hid an even greater proportion of the population who were illiterate for all practical purposes, even if they could manage to scrawl their names. The newly-wed Mr and Mrs Manning, however, signed the register with practised hands.

Yet Frederick, who was probably educated up to the age of twelve or so in a National School in Taunton, had left school before the State's concern with education began. In 1839, Parliament established a committee of the Privy Council to administer the annual education grants voted by the Commons. In 1840 the Treasury Grant for elementary education was £50,000. Although there were substantial increases, it remained below a very inadequate £200,000 throughout the next decade. Tens of thousands of London children never went to school at all, or attended for only a short time and irregularly. Elementary education taught religion, together with reading, writing and arithmetic ('the three Rs'). It was based on the monitorial system, by which the teacher taught pupils who in turn taught sections of huge classes of up to one hundred children.

SQUEERS: That's our system, Nickleby.
What do you think of it?
NICHOLAS: It's a very useful one, at any rate.
(*Nicholas Nickleby*, Chapter 8)

Middle-class children were educated in private schools. There were 30,000 of these in England and Wales, teaching 700,000 children. They varied greatly. Some were 'dame' schools, costing fourpence or sixpence per week, beyond a working-class pocket and some middle-class ones also if several children had to be educated. Even the grammar schools, with their humane traditions, which catered for children of the higher classes who did not go to the great 'public schools' such as Eton, Harrow and Rugby, interpreted their foundation statutes in a way which had hardly changed their practices from when they had been founded, often centuries earlier. And for not too great a sum, guardians who wished to get rid of inconvenient children could board them out permanently for twenty guineas (£21) a year in places like Wackford Squeers's Dotheboys Hall, which Dickens based on a true instance. Squeers's educational system is truly utilitarian. In Chapter 8 of *Nicholas Nickleby*, after learning that 'window' was a 'noun substantive', a boy is made to clean the casement in question. Unfortunately, the practicality of the education is marred because Mr Squeers thinks that 'window' is spelled 'winder' and that 'botany' is written 'bottiney'.

Self-help

After leaving a private, British or National school, or no school at all, a person was not completely abandoned to brutish ignorance, but immense efforts had to be made to use one's scant leisure profitably. Henry Brougham, a distinguished polymath and statesman who became Lord Chancellor in 1830, was one of the founders in 1828 of University College, precursor of London University. It was known as 'the Godless Institution of Gower Street' because, unlike Oxford and Cambridge, it did not impose religious tests for entry. Brougham also founded the Society for the Diffusion of Useful Knowledge, which set up Mechanics' Institutes, places where the working man who wanted to get on, improving his mind or his skills, could attend lectures and borrow books. Liberal utilitarians such as Brougham saw the Mechanics' Institutes as valuable not only in themselves, but also as firebreaks against revolutions. They encouraged respectability, keeping men out of gin palaces and pubs, while giving them peaceful rather than violent amusements. By 1850 there were 610 Mechanics' Institutes in England alone with 102,000 members, including the London Mechanics' Institute, now Birkbeck College, today a part of London University where classes are held at night. This institution offered a wide range of lectures on subjects including literature, elocution, the topography of the British Isles and history.

To be a railway guard required a certain level of education. Frederick Manning had to be able to read instructions and to write brief reports. The travelling salesman's job that he obtained shortly before he was charged with murder also required literacy and some ability at figures, particularly since his earnings depended to some extent on commission. But, while Maria Manning had ambition, Frederick seems to have been a weak drifter. Devoted to the brandy bottle, he does not give the impression of being interested in the key phrase of the Victorian age – self-help – which expressed itself in the form of mutual improvement societies with subscribing members, lending libraries and regular discussions.

'Pulling oneself up by one's own bootstraps' was an article of faith for progressive utilitarians in the early nineteenth century. Weekday utilitarians were often Sunday evangelicals, Christians of the most 'serious' persuasion. Both believed in the value of serious literature which conveyed the immutable truths of religion and economics. Both evangelicals and utilitarians were profoundly convinced of the value of self-improvement. For both, reading had a purpose, and it was not the frivolous one of amusement.

Classes in self-help groups and Mechanics' Institutes were inevitably utilitarian. How to read and write a business letter, how to estimate builders' quantities, together with some factual information about geography and history, were in most cases their limits.

'Always got his nose stuck in a book'

In 1849, Karl Marx, the political refugee and author of *The Communist Manifesto*, came to London to join the leisured and the studious and to read some of the hundreds of thousands of books in the Reading Room of the British Museum. Before Panizzi's great circular reading room was constructed, readers sat in the King's Library, which was infested by monomaniacs and eccentrics. No lights were allowed for fear of fire. The rolling London autumn and winter fogs often sent readers home early. Most literature, however, whether in the form of books, pamphlets, religious tracts or newspapers, was being read by a growing number of people who had acquired the habit from publications which were written for their pleasure as much as for their improvement.

The Mannings owned few books.[5] They were all Maria's. She must have brought most of them with her when she came to England. She owned a book called *Souvenirs Historiques* (*Historical Memories* – of what?), the Psalms in French and a volume of sacred poetry, also in French. She possessed a French–English dictionary and a useful guide called *Cook's Letter Writer*.

While their trial provided no further information about what the Mannings read, an undoubted expansion was taking place in newspaper, magazine and book publishing. Both Mannings were to some extent products of their time. Did both or either form part of the increasing mass reading public? Two popular weeklies, the *London Journal* and the *Family Herald*, enjoyed combined sales of over 750,000 in the mid-nineteenth century. Each had 16 pages closely printed with adventure stories, general fiction, answers to readers' questions, serious essays and household hints.[6] The Stamp Act of 1818 had not taxed papers which published serials, so Charles Dickens remembered as a boy having bought a penny magazine called the *Terrific Register*: 'There was an illustration to every number in which there was always a pool of blood and at least one body,' he recalled.[7] People read sensational thrillers, ballads and broadsides sold in the streets, published in London mostly by James Catnach in the slummy Seven Dials district. The Catnach Press would sell two and a half million broadsides on the Manning murder. Probably the Mannings could be numbered among the millions who read such material, but occasionally they might have been among the thousands who took advantage of the limited but growing availability of better literature.

From 1827 onwards, Brougham's Society for the Diffusion of Useful Knowledge issued a series of volumes called, appropriately, the *Library of Useful Knowledge*. The books were published in parts every two weeks, each costing sixpence, which bought 32 closely printed pages. The *Library of Useful Knowledge* was probably not to be found in Bermondsey, but when Frederick went to his new job at the stationer's in Holborn, probably on foot, he could have looked in a bookseller's window and seen the volumes in question, as well as the Society's next series, called the *Library of Entertaining Knowledge*. 'Useful Knowledge' explained, among other topics, differential calculus and the art of brewing (which should have been interesting for Manning, who had been the landlord of two pubs). The *Library of Entertaining Knowledge* discussed subjects such as the Elgin Marbles, on show in the recently completed British Museum building. Rather more intriguing, perhaps, was the issue describing 'Secret Societies of the Middle Ages'. Even cheaper enlightening literature was available. The Society for the Diffusion of Useful Knowledge also published the *Penny Magazine* and the *Penny Cyclopaedia*, while Cassell's *Popular Educator* came in 1852, too late for the Mannings. Its appealing style was more attractive to the man or woman who had remained untouched by the turgid offerings previously available. By 1862, Cassells was selling 25 to 30 million annually of its penny publications. The Mannings were unlikely to have read Wordsworth or the next Poet Laureate, Alfred, Lord Tennyson, but they might well have come across Martin F. Tupper's banal moralisations in his *Proverbial Philosophy* of 1838, which by 1849 had reached its 9th edition and finally sold half a million copies in Britain and a million in the United States. Would Maria have agreed with Tupper's sententious proclamation, 'Yea, there is no cosmetic like unto a holy conscience'?[8]

In the twenty years or so of the Mannings' literate lives, say between 1829 and 1849, books fell in price because of cheap reprints and the expansion of publication in periodical parts. Perhaps what marked the change was the phenomenal success of the parts of Dickens's

Pickwick Papers. The publishers, Chapman & Hall, printed 400 copies for the first number in April 1836. By the last number, in November 1837, they were selling about 40,000. An early biographer of Dickens wrote that he visited a locksmith and 'I found him reading *Pickwick* [. . .] to an audience of twenty persons, literally, men, women and children. They had clubbed together to borrow it for twopence from a circulating library because the shilling that the number cost was beyond them.'[9]

The written equivalent of the 'Penny Gaff' theatre was the 'Penny Dreadful', and the most famous of these was George William McArthur Reynolds's *Mysteries of London* (1847) and his *Mysteries of the Court of London*, which were published in penny numbers from 1849 till 1856. Thirty or forty thousand of these eight-page booklets with their 7,500 words of tight double-columned prose, enlivened with occasional woodcuts, were sold every week. Reynolds also edited a family magazine called *Reynolds' Miscellany of Romance, General Literature, Science and Art*, and he wrote novels prolifically. In March 1848, Reynolds, a man of progressive ideas, chaired the great revolutionary Chartist assemblies in Trafalgar Square and on Kennington Common. He also edited a newspaper called *Reynolds' Weekly* which played an important part in forming radical thought and which survived, under different names, until January 1967. Reynolds's lurid episodes in the *Mysteries* contained populist politics, moving social comment, together with dramatic and even voyeuristic illustrations of depravity in high and low places. They were not, of course, meant to be 'improving' and, to this extent, Charles Dickens's *Household Words*, another well-selling family magazine of the time, was a rival to the *Mysteries*. Even today's reader finds Reynolds's text vigorous, though parts of it would be hard going. Perhaps language such as in the following extract was expected and appreciated, even by the illiterate to whom the *Mysteries of the Court of London* had to be read aloud:

> *'Indiscreet, my sweet girl!' cried her lover.*
> *'Oh! How can you suppose that I would entertain a harsh feeling with regard to that goodness on your part which doubtless instigated you to afford me the happiness of this meeting?'*[10]

Marie de Roux herself, after seeing Lady Palk or Lady Blantyre to bed, may have read this aloud in her elegant French accent to the kitchen maids and the cook.

Melodramatic serials like Reynolds's *Mysteries* had their sensational news equivalent in the threepenny weekly newspapers such as the *News of the World* and *The Weekly Times*, which exposed corruption and upper-class immorality. These newspapers also reported crimes and disasters with a wealth of detail. A diligent search through these and through the four and a half million words of Reynolds's *Mysteries* might even turn up an example of a murder where the victim is buried under a scullery flagstone and covered with quicklime, just as Patrick O'Connor was.

Henry Mayhew's influential articles, which became the famous *London Labour and the London Poor*, were announced in the *Morning Post* on 18 October 1849, as the Mannings awaited trial at the Old Bailey. In a piece on 'The literature of costermongers', one of his favourite subjects, Mayhew reported that Reynolds was their favourite reading material. A literate coster read it to groups who could not do so for themselves, and the reading was interrupted by queries and comments. Reynolds's *Mysteries* and similar works, despite being sneered at by the higher classes, some of whom must have been tempted by the racy style and the occasional bit of titillation, had, perhaps without realising it, a true educational function in increasing vocabulary and expression among their readers. Abel Heywood, a Manchester bookseller, reported in 1851 that Reynolds's *Mysteries of the Court of London* was selling 1,500 copies a week even away from the capital. Penny fiction was, he said, read by 'a *spreeing* sort of young man, the type who visits taverns and puts cigars into their mouths in a flourishing way (sic)', as well as by many women.[11]

So, despite the low level of literacy, many factors, especially in a great city like London, stimulated the urge to read, not least of which were the cheapening of printed matter and the rise of popular journalism. As in so many things, here also the Mannings lived on the brink of a new age. Stamp Duty on newspapers was reduced to one penny in 1836. The penny post, introduced in 1839, already allowed Maria and Frederick to correspond cheaply with their friends and relatives. Tax would be removed from advertisements in 1853, from newspapers in 1855 and from paper in 1861, allowing *The Daily Telegraph* to halve its price from twopence to a penny. But there had also been a technical revolution, especially in newspaper production. By 1848, state-of-the-art machines could print both sides of 4,000 sheets in an hour. By 1854, the circulation of *The Times* had reached 55,000.

High-quality and expensive magazine journalism of a surprisingly modern kind, but beyond the Mannings' purse, appeared in the *Illustrated London News* and *Punch*, both of which date from the 1840s. Just after Frederick and Maria went to the gallows, Charles Dickens began to publish *Household Words*. Competent and professional, it did not patronise its readers, and its cover price was modest. It was well designed to appeal to a large public, but it came too late for the Mannings. They, however, might have read Dickens's articles in *The Examiner*, founded in 1808, which had been converted from 1830 onwards by Albany Fontblanque, known as the wittiest journalist of his day, into a serious but easily read journal, one that a modern critic has called 'a mixture of the *New Statesman*, *The Times*, and the *News of the World*'.[12]

Maria Manning could have added to her small collection of books by buying reprints costing between one and six shillings. John Murray was producing his *Home and Colonial Library*, for example, including George Borrow's *The Bible in Spain*, arguably one of the best travel books ever written, while novels by Fenimore Cooper and Captain Marryat came out in Bentley's series of *Standard Novels*.

'Has Mudie's box come?'

The Mannings died too soon to make use of the free public library. That spring and summer of 1849, a House of Commons committee was meeting to discuss free libraries. It heard evidence from Continental librarians, perhaps including some from the 107 French public libraries with their 4 million books. A Bill was proposed allowing one halfpenny in the pound of local rates to be spent on public libraries. Despite opposition, the Bill became law on 14 August 1850. Few London parishes, however, adopted the Act. Prosperous people borrowed their books from private circulating libraries, such as Mudie's.

Maria might have heard her employers, Lady Palk and Lady Blantyre, ask whether the box from Mudie's had arrived. Mudie's Circulating Library was not wound up until 1937, when Harrod's Library bought up its stock.

Charles Edward Mudie was a hymn writer and lay preacher who set up his circulating library in Southampton Row in London in 1842, moving to New Oxford Street ten years later. It cost a guinea a year to belong.

The firm had branches in London, and sent down boxes of books by train to country subscribers. Mudie's library was big business. In the years between 1853 and 1862 it bought 960,000 volumes. Mudie provided his subscribers with a range of new books in history, biography, travel and religion, as well as novels and poetry. He took large quantities of each book, negotiating substantial price discounts. He took 2,400 copies of volumes 3 and 4 of Macaulay's *History of England* and 2,000 of George Eliot's *The Mill on the Floss*. A novel, usually published in three volumes, cost £1 11s 6d, a substantial sum for even a three or four hundred pounds a year man. The high prices of books kept up the number of Mudie's subscribers, who could borrow freely for the price of their annual one guinea subscription.

In the bookselling world, W.H. Smith was up and coming. His slogan was 'first on the road'; he made his fortune by distributing newspapers faster than his rivals, using the railway network. In 1848 he took leases of the bookstalls on the London and North Western Railway and later secured the monopoly. Perhaps Maria bought something to read from one of Smith's bookstalls to while away the hours of her journey to Scotland after the murder of O'Connor. It certainly would have been nothing even mildly salacious. Smith came from a strict Methodist background and acquired the name of the 'North-Western Missionary'.[13]

At Paddington Station there was a lending library with a thousand volumes, mostly of fiction, which passengers could browse through while they waited for their trains. A slightly higher charge allowed them to take the book with them on their journey to Oxford, Hereford, Cornwall or Wales, and give it in at the station bookstall when they arrived. It wasn't long before special literature for railway journeys was appearing. George Routledge launched his *Railway Library* and John Murray his *Literature for the Rail*.[14] But serious, particularly religious, literature was much in demand at railway stations. Some readers feared to meet their Maker if a fatal railway accident caught them with a frivolous work of fiction in their greatcoat pocket or lady's reticule.

Apart from the Penny Dreadfuls and the under-the-counter erotica sold in Holywell Street, popular literature was decorous. Even the highly successful *Pickwick Papers* was thought by the *Eclectic Review* to be somewhat near the knuckle, while Anne Brontë's *The Tenant of Wildfell Hall*, her sister Charlotte's *Jane Eyre*, *Villette* and *Shirley*, and Emily

Brontë's *Wuthering Heights*, were all criticised for coarseness and indelicacy.[15]

The late 1840s were halcyon years for the English novel. In 1846–1848, Dickens published *Dombey and Son* in monthly parts. From May to November 1849, he was issuing *David Copperfield*. At the same time, Thackeray was bringing out *Pendennis*. The Mannings lived before the age of the ubiquitous cheap reprint, but they may perhaps have bought the odd monthly number of these novels which would become so famous. Nothing, however, would equal the triumph of *Uncle Tom's Cabin* when it appeared in 1852. In its first six months Harriet Beecher Stowe's novel about slavery in the southern States of the USA sold 150,000 copies; by the end of its first year it had sold 1.5 million. Other great publishing hits of the mid-century included the first two volumes of Macaulay's *History of England from the Accession of James II*. They sold like a novel. From their publication in November 1848, the bookshops ran through five printings in six months; 22,000 copies were sold within a year at the high price of 32 shillings. The next two volumes produced £20,000 in royalties for the author within eleven months of publication. Had authors been protected against American pirate publishers, Macaulay would have done even better.

For large sections of the reading population, however, novels were out of the question on principle. Many people considered novels a waste of time during the utilitarian week, and sinful on the evangelical Sunday, when only improving religious literature was thought appropriate.

Do you believe in . . . ?

Fiction, drama, poetry and science all together scarcely equalled the amount of religious literature among the 45,260 titles appearing during the years 1816–1851, at a rate of about 1,300 new works annually. The artisan, shop assistant or the servant could not afford or find time to read a daily newspaper. The pious alternatives to the sensational serial or paper which came out on Saturday, and would be read in the leisure hours of Sunday, were the tracts which the Religious Tract Society, founded in 1799, distributed in their millions in the streets of London. Arthur Clennan, in the third chapter of Dickens's *Little Dorrit*, sits in a

Plate 1: Maria Manning

Plate 2: Frederick Manning

'*The murderers*'
Huish, R: *The Progress of Crime* (1849). Bodleian Library,
University of Oxford Pettingell 216

Plate 3: Patrick O Connor. '*The victim*'.
Huish, R: *The Progress of Crime* (1849). Bodleian Library, University of Oxford Pettingell 216

Plate 4: '*The foul crime discovered*'.
Huish, R: *The Progress of Crime* (1849). Bodleian Library, University of Oxford Pettingell 216

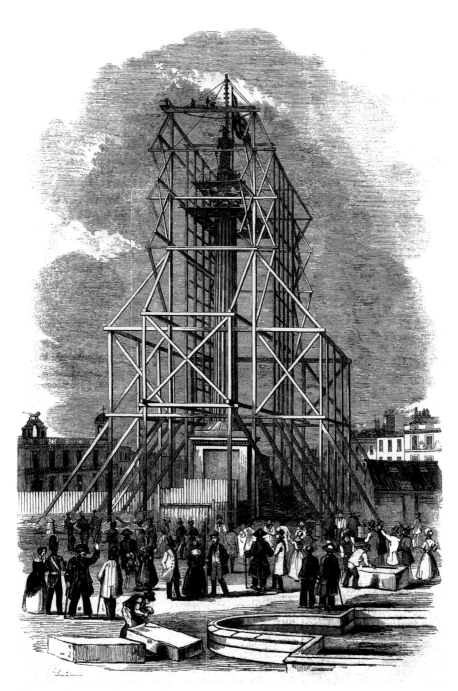

Plate 5: Nelson's Column. '*Nelson, our national hero*'.
Illustrated London News, 18 Nov 1843, Bodleian Library, University of Oxford, 2288 b.6

Plate 6: Ludgate Hill. '*Spoils the view*'.
Doré, Gustave and Blanchard, Jerrold: *London, a pilgrimage* (1872)

Plate 7: The docks. '*The riches of the world*'.
Doré, Gustave and Blanchard, Jerrold: *London, a pilgrimage* (1872)

1847. Marriage solemnized at *the Church* in the *Parish* of *St James Westminster* in the County of *Middlesex*

No.	When Married.	Name and Surname.	Age.	Condition.	Rank or Profession.	Residence at the Time of Marriage.	Father's Name and Surname.	Rank or Profession of Father.
295	May 27th	Frederick George Manning / Maria Roux	full / full	Bachelor / Spinster	Clerk or Servant on Taunton Railway	Stevens. / Stevens.	Joseph Manning / John Roux	Gentleman / Restaurateur or Traiteur &c

Married in the *Church* according to the Rites and Ceremonies of the Established Church, by *Licence* by me,

This Marriage was solemnized between us, *Fred. G. Manning / Maria Roux* in the Presence of us, *Jean Simon Beaurieu / Louisa Antrobus*

1847. Marriage solemnized at *the Church* in the *Parish* of *Lower Wedmore* in the County of *Middlesex*

No.	When Married.	Name and Surname.	Age.	Condition.	Rank or Profession.	Residence at the Time of Marriage.	Father's Name and Surname.	Rank or Profession of Father.
296	May 30	Alfred Erby / Mary Nicholson	full / full	Bachelor / Spinster	Butcher, Master	Oxford St. / Oxford St.	George Erby / John Nicholson	Carpenter / Master / Farmer

Married in the *Church* according to the Rites and Ceremonies of the Established Church, *after Banns* by me,

This Marriage was solemnized between us, *Alfred Erby / Mary Nicholson* in the Presence of us, *Frederick Evans / London Court*

Plate 8: Marriage entry of the Mannings. 'If only they had never wed'.
Westminster Local Archives, photographer Geremy Butler

Plate 9: Burlington Arcade. '*High quality whoredom*'.
Mary Evans Picture Library

Plate 10: Regent Arcade. *'Demolished because of the tarts'.*
Mary Evans Picture Library

Plate 11: A fashionable haberdasher. '*I really can't make up my mind*'. Punch, 18 August 1849. Bodleian Library, University of Oxford, 2706 d.10

Plate 12: Regent Street at 4pm. '*There doesn't seem to be a rule of the road here*'. Punch, 25 August 1849. Bodleian Library, University of Oxford, 2706 d.10

Plate 13: Ice being eaten in Berkeley Square. '*Will the lady give them a penny?*' Punch, 24 Aug 1867. Bodleian Library, University of Oxford, 2706 d.10

Plate 14: The clerks in the slap-bang. '*Pushing the boat out*'.
Dickens, Charles: *Bleak House* ChXX

Plate 15: Blackwall, the public dining on whitebait. '*Not a woman to be seen*'.
Punch, 8 September 1849. Bodleian Library, University of Oxford, 2706 d.10

Plate 16: 'Water, water everywhere'.
Punch 1849. Bodleian Library, University of Oxford, 2706 d.10

Plate 17: St Giles Rookery. '*Where policemen walked in pairs*'.
Thornbury, W G (Walford, E): *Old and new London: a narrative of its history, its people and its places* (1897). Drawings by William M'Connell

A REGULAR GOLD DUSTMAN.

" Hollo! Where are you off to now?"

"Oh! I aint a going to stop here, looking for Teaspoons in Cinders. I'm off to Kallifornier, vere there's heaps o' Gold Dust to be had for the Sweepin'!"

Plate 19
Punch, 13 Jan 1849. Bodleian Library, University of Oxford, 2706 d.10

Plate 18: 'Cholera, the silent highwayman'. Punch, 10 July 1858

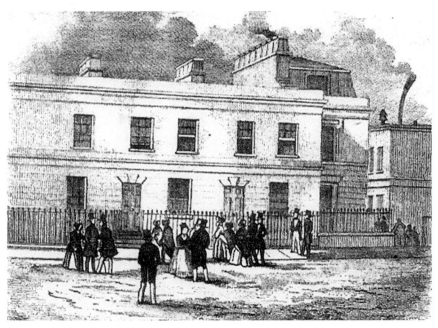

Plate 20: Miniver Place (when new). '*A nice young couple moved in*'.
Huish, R: *The Progress of Crime* (1849). Bodleian Library, University of Oxford Pettingell
216

Plate 21: Miniver Place in 1959. The murder house was second from the right.
Southwark Local Studies Library

Left and Right-hand Views of the Back-Kitchen where the Body was found.

A. Wall at the bottom of the kitchen-stairs, on which spots of blood were discovered, and near which it is supposed the pistol was discharged.
C. Iron-barred window, through which the shadow of the Mannings was reflected on the garden-wall, late on the night of the murder.
D. Entrance to the kitchen where the body was found.

F. Fire-place where a goose was roasted, on the day after the murder, by Mrs. Manning.
G. Stone, under which the body was found.
E. The Sink in which O'Connor was in the habit of washing his hands.
H. Copper.

Plate 22: The kitchen at Miniver Place. '*Where the deed was done*'.
The New Wonderful Magazine (1849)

Plate 23: Panorama of London. '*The vast metropolis*'.
Thornbury, W G (Walford, E): *Old and new London: a narrative of its history, its people and its places* (1897)

Plate 24: Tom Thumb with Queen Victoria. '*Much amused*'.
Mary Evans Picture Library

Plate 25: A poster advertising Vauxhall Gardens. 'Once glamorous, it had grown vulgar'. Bodleian Library, University of Oxford. J Johnson Collection (London Play Places (6) 11)

Plate 26: Astley's amphitheatre. 'A place to take the children at Christmas'. Bodleian Library, University of Oxford. J Johnson Collection (67-73 Entertainment II)

Plate 27: Pepper's ghost. '*One of the best shows at the Polytechnic, Regent Street*'. Illustrated London News, 2 May 1863. Bodleian Library, University of Oxford, 2288 b.6

Plate 28: Madame Tussaud and her waxworks – the chamber of horrors. '*The Mannings would be on show one day*'. Punch, 17 September 1849. Bodleian Library, University of Oxford, 2706 d.10

Plate 29: Victoria Theatre and the New Cut. '*Blood and thunder for threepence*'.

Plate 30: The public – its excitement on the appearance of Miss Jenny Lind, the Swedish nightingale. Punch, 12 May 1849. Bodleian Library, University of Oxford, 2706 d.10

THE THIN END OF THE WEDGE.

DARING ATTEMPT TO BREAK INTO A CHURCH.

Plate 31
Punch, 16 Nov 1850. Bodleian Library, University of Oxford, 2706 d.10

USEFUL SUNDAY LITERATURE FOR THE MASSES;

OR, MURDER MADE FAMILIAR.

Father of a Family (reads). "The wretched Murderer is supposed to have cut the throats of his three eldest Children, and then to have killed the Baby by beating it repeatedly with a Poker. * * * * * In person he is of a rather bloated appearance, with a bull neck, small eyes, broad large nose, and coarse vulgar mouth. His dress was a light blue coat, with brass buttons, elegant yellow summer vest, and pepper-and-salt trowsers. When at the Station House he expressed himself as being rather 'peckish,' and said he should like a Black Pudding, which, with a Cup of Coffee, was immediately procured for him."

Plate 32
Punch, 22 Sept 1849. Bodleian Library, University of Oxford, 2706 d.10

Plate 33: Ragged school. '*Small-group teaching, Utilitarian style*'.
Mary Evans Picture Library

Plate 34: Exeter Hall. '*No Popery here!*' Punch, 19 May 1849. Bodleian Library,
University of Oxford, 2706 d.10

A PARCEL OF OLD ——— FRIGHTENED AT A NASTY!
GREAT! UGLY! JEW BILL.

Plate 35
Punch, 14 July 1849. Bodleian Library, University of Oxford, 2706 d.10

Plate 36: Policemen at Bonner's Fields ready for the Chartists. *'Just in case. Was there going to be a revolution?'* Illustrated London News, 17 June 1848. Bodleian Library, University of Oxford, 2288 b.6

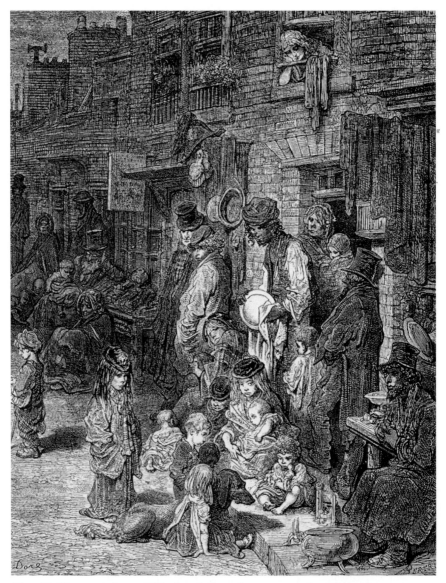

Plate 37: Wentworth Street, Whitechapel. '*I can fit you out nicely, sir, if you're not too particular*'. Doré, Gustave and Blanchard, Jerrold: *London, a pilgrimage* (1872)

Plate 38: Exterior of entrance to Euston station. '*Gateway to the North*'. Thornbury, W G
(Walford, E): *Old and new London: a narrative of its history, its people and its places*
(1897)

Plate 39: Entrance hall at Euston Station. '*Maria Manning walked through this hall to take
the train to Edinburgh*'. Illustrated London News, 2 June 1849. Bodleian Library,
University of Oxford, 2288 b.6

Plate 40: The steam excursion. '*Down to Margate for the holiday*'. Sala: *Twice round the clock or The Hours of the day and night in London* (1859). Drawings by William M'Connell

Plate 41: Omnibus at Bank. '*How long are you going to wait here?*' Sala: *Twice round the clock or The Hours of the day and night in London* (1859). Drawings by William M'Connell

Plate 42: Shillibeer's omnibus. *'Persuading the lady to get on the bus'.*
London Transport Museum

Plate 43: Ticket for the London to Greenwich railway. These arches are still standing.
London Transport Museum

FATAL FACILITY; OR, POISONS FOR THE ASKING.

Child. "PLEASE, MISTER, WILL YOU BE SO GOOD AS TO FILL THIS BOTTLE AGAIN WITH LODNUM, AND LET MOTHER HAVE ANOTHER POUND AND A HALF OF ARSENIC FOR THE RATS (!)"

Duly Qualified Chemist. "CERTAINLY, MA'AM. IS THERE ANY OTHER ARTICLE?"

Plate 44
Punch, 8 Sept 1849. Bodleian Library, University of Oxford, 2706 d.10

THE EXECUTION OF
FRED. GEO. MANNING,
AND
MARIA, HIS WIFE.

At Horsemonger Lane, November 13th, 1849,

For the MURDER and Robbery of PATRICK O'CONNOR.

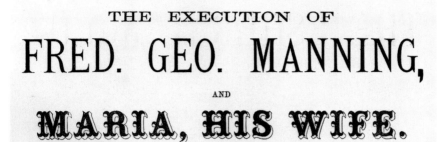

This morning the last act in the tragedy of the Mannings' was performed on the roof of Horsemonger Lane Gaol, in the presence of an immense assemblage.

The gardens in front of the houses opposite the prison, and from which the best view could be obtained, commanded high prices, and were occupied by persons of apparent respectability, and amongst them were many well-dressed females.

A few minutes before the clock struck nine, the bell of the prison chapel was heard to give forth the fatal toll, and those who had collected in the vicinity of the scaffold were observed to uncover, which was taken up by the populace below as a signal to do the same, and to call for silence. Immediately the roar of voices which had previously prevailed became hushed and still, and the mournful cavalcade ascended the steps of the scaffold, —Calcraft first, then the Chaplain, followed by the wretched man Manning, who ascended the stairs with a firm step, but appeared pale and emaciated. He was dressed in deep black, with a long frock-coat. The rope having been adjusted and the cap drawn over his face, Mrs. Manning, the female partner in his crime was brought up. She was dressed in black satin, tightly bound round the waist, with a long white collar fastened round her neck. On advancing up on the drop, and observing her husband at her side, as if acting upon the sudden impulse of the moment, she seized his right hand and shook it for several minutes. The hangman then hurriedly completed his deadly preparations, the next minute the slam of the drop was heard, and the dread sentence of the law had been accomplished. Manning gave a few convulsive jerks, and all was over, but his wife had a long struggle with death, and it was some moments before the immortal spirit had quitted her body for ever.

THE BERMONDSEY TRAGEDY.
BY J. CLARKE.

Come all you good people of every degree,
I pray you give attention and listen to me,
'Twas in the county of Somersetshire where I was bred and born,
And my wife she is a foreigner,—with her must die in scorn.

For the murder of O'Connor we are condemned to die ;
My wife she said I'm innocent of that sad tragedy,
But 'twas she who shot O'Connor and swore she would shoot me,
Unless I would assist her to bury his body.

Four months before his murder his doom was ready sealed,
His grave made ready under ground his body to receive,
He little thought his death so near when to the house he came,
But his death was plann'd all by our hands his money to obtain.

For murder and plunder they both were fully bent,
They shot him with a pistol, and to his lodgings went,
They got his cash and jewels and quickly did repair,   [pair
To hide the guilt for the blood they'd spilt—oh! what a wretched

At the Old Bailey, London, the trial it came on,
They were arraigned before the judge and English jurymen,
The counsel for the prisoners they nobly did defend,
And tried to prove their innocence, this point they did contend.

After the trial, Mrs Manning said,
I do protest I'm innocent and been unfairly tried,
Though you've pronounced me guilty, and doom'd me to be hung,
More like a dog than Christian, to a being thus undone.

With rage and desperation the keepers by them stood,
And to their gloomy prison they quickly were removed,
The coolness and courage which they before displayed,
Had now forsook them for a time, and they look'd quite dismay'd.

This wicked woman taken was unto Horsemonger Gaol,
Her husband followed after, and very soon did feel
Contrition for his guilty deeds, and to his wife he wrote,
Begging of her to think how soon she was to meet her fate.

The end of poor O'Connor will long in memory reign,
And shew the vice and folly which followed in its train.
Oh! may it thus a warning prove to shun bad company,
Never like the Mannings commit such a tragedy.

Now in their gloomy prisons bound down in irons strong,
Awaiting for the fatal morn when they will meet their doom,
For the murder of O'Connor—oh! what a horrid crime,
Now they are both cut off in the height of their prime.

Stewart, Printer, Botchergate, Carlisle.

197

Plate 45: Broadside sold at the execution of the Mannings. '*The wages of sin*'.
Hindley, Charles: *Curiosities of Street-literature: comprising 'cocks' or 'catchpennies, street drolleries etc* (1871). Bodleian Library, University of Oxford, 270 h.36

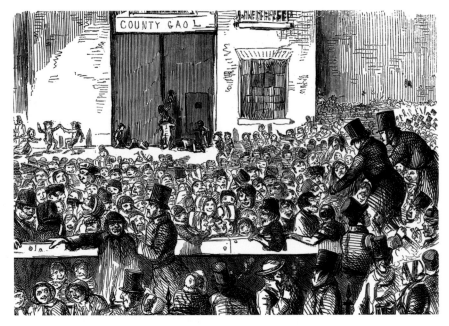

Plate 46: The great moral lesson at Horsemonger Lane Gaol. '*We went for a bit of a laugh, didn't we?*' Punch, 16 Nov 1849. Bodleian Library, University of Oxford, 2706 d.10

Plate 47: The crowd await the executions. '*They paid the price*'. Huish, R: *The Progress of Crime* (1849). Bodleian Library, University of Oxford, Pettingell 216

London coffee house on a gloomy Sunday evening listening to the church bells. They remind him of:

> [. . .] *the dreary Sunday of his childhood, when he sat with his hands*
> *before him, scared out of his senses by a horrible tract which commenced*
> *business with the poor child by asking him in its title, why he was going*
> *to Perdition? [. . .] and which, for the further attraction of his infant*
> *mind, had a parenthesis in every other line with some such hiccupping*
> *reference as 2.Ep. Thess. c.iii. v.6 and 7.*

The Mannings were probably bothered by what we would now describe as the 'cold calling' of the British and Foreign Bible Society and other such hawkers of religious literature, as they tried to place the books, pamphlets and tracts that were printed in their millions. One indefatigable young man was reported to have made 18,727 calls in a year, selling 3,795 pious items!

Religion was almost an obsession among the middle class. Some questioning of religious belief was already evident, however, among intellectuals. Sir Charles Lyell's *Principles of Geology*, whose three parts were published in the 1830s, offered a different view of the age of the Earth from that of the biblical account. Robert Chambers's *Vestiges of the Natural History of Creation* of 1844 was a popularisation of recent thought about evolution, defending the theory that nature, not a force outside it, was responsible for change, while in 1846 Mary Ann Evans, who would later write novels under the pseudonym of George Eliot, translated David Strauss's historical account of the life of Jesus, *Das Leben Jesu*. Nevertheless, until Darwin published his *Origin of Species* in 1859 and Bishop Colenso began to issue his *The Pentateuch . . . Critically Examined* in 1862, there was little to be read on the question of the absolute truth and authorship of the biblical narrative. Today, when indifference is widespread, it is hard to imagine the emotions aroused in Victorian times by the theological and doctrinal aspects of religious faith, as well as by its public manifestations. The House of Commons no longer argues about whether or not there should be candles on the altars of Anglican churches, or whether Church of England priests should wear vestments and hear confessions. Today's *The Times* does not often express a view on the restoration of the images of saints to Anglican churches. But in 1849 most educated people would have been well aware of the importance of such questions as they discussed the progress of Christian life in England.

Hi, Mass! 'Lo, Church!

The majority of English people belonged to the Church of England; some to the 'High' version, which meant tending towards the ceremonies – the 'bells and smells' as they were called by their enemies – of the Catholic Church, and others to the 'Low' Church, meaning that they leaned towards the starkness of the Dissenting or Nonconformist Churches. The American visitor Henry Colman noted that the Church of England, as integral a part of the Establishment as the House of Commons, was very formal in contrast with the 'naked simplicity' of the churches of his native Boston.[16]

New England churches, the successors of the Pilgrim Fathers, were by definition Dissenting. Some of their English equivalents were old, going back to the seventeenth century, such as the Congregationalists, the Baptists and the Quakers, but new Dissent was growing. Its history can be seen in the little Bethels, Mount Zions or Ebenezer chapels made of corrugated iron, located in dim alleys, where many in the grim industrial towns and in London found comfort in their toilsome lives.

Ventura de la Vega, the Spanish dramatist who visited London at mid-century, was impressed by the devoutness of the worshippers in Westminster Abbey. He noticed that they did not indulge in the habit of looking up to see who was there, as was common in Spain where church attendance was a social as much as a religious act.

Never on Sunday

The Spaniard was struck also by the closed shops and the sepulchral silence of the London Sunday, enlivened only by church bells, so different from the animated Sundays of Spain.[17] The Society for Promoting the External Observance of the Lord's Day was founded in 1831 in order to keep Sunday free of most recreation, shopping and travelling. This restriction bore heaviest on the poor, who only had Sunday in which to enjoy themselves. Public entertainment on the Sabbath was seen by many as devilish, with the exception perhaps of the essential wholesomeness of the 'Swedish Nightingale', Jenny Lind. While the sacred oratorio in which she performed might just about be tolerated on the Sabbath, even though many people had to work to allow it to be staged, the public house was of course out of the question for a Sabbatarian, so the reading of improving literature flourished during the endless Sunday hours spent at home.

Benjamin Disraeli, the future Conservative Prime Minister, who though of Jewish parentage had been baptised in his youth, took a train one Sunday in 1849 from his country home to London. On receiving an admonition from his local vicar to set a better example, Disraeli replied that only public urgency had compelled him to take the train. In any case, more pointedly, he retorted that when he attended Divine Service, he did so to worship his Maker, not so that others should emulate him.[18] Although it was in vain that the Bishop of London, having failed to stop trains running on Sundays, hoped for accidents on Mondays as a sign of divine wrath, he was nevertheless successful in banning the opening of museums, picture galleries and the zoo, as well as in silencing military bands in parks.[19] People of course were free to frequent the gin palace, but the Sabbatarians forced the Great Exhibition of 1851 to close on Sundays, thus preventing large numbers of people from seeing it on their only free day. At a demonstration in London's Hyde Park, on Sunday 30 September 1855, against a proposal to limit Sunday trading in London, a measure which would bear heaviest on the poor, the demonstrators hissed the splendid equipages of the swaggering aristocrats in Rotten Row, shouting, 'Go to church!' In 1856, Sabbatarian opposition defeated proposals to open the British Museum and the National Gallery on Sunday afternoons. Band concerts, however, were later permitted to provide civilised and orderly entertainment on Sundays in London parks. On 30 May 1850, the powerful Sabbatarian lobby persuaded the House of Commons to end Sunday collections and deliveries of letters. Charles Dickens, a noted enemy of the Sabbatarians, thundered against them in the leading article in *Household Words* on 22 June 1850, quoting the words: 'The Sabbath was made for Man and not Man for the Sabbath.' More pointedly, Dickens asked whether Lord Ashley, the proposer of the Parliamentary motion to stop Sunday postal services, did not require his servants to work on Sundays. And what about the police? Were citizens not to have their protection or did criminals observe the Sabbath?

Finally, Sunday working in the Post Office was allowed to continue. But London Sundays remained gloomy, as Dickens described in Chapter 13 of *Little Dorrit*:

> *It was a Sunday evening in London, gloomy, close and stale. Maddening church bells of all degrees of dissonance, sharp and flat, cracked and clear, fast and slow, made the brick-and-mortar echoes hideous. Melancholy streets in a penitential garb of soot, steeped the souls of the people who were condemned to look at them out of windows in dire despondency. In every thoroughfare, up almost every alley, and down almost every turning, some doleful bell was throbbing, jerking, tolling, as if the Plague were in the city and the dead-carts were going round. Everything was bolted and barred that could by possibility furnish relief to an overworked people. No pictures, no unfamiliar animals, nor rare plants or flowers, nor natural or artificial wonders of the ancient world – all* taboo *with that enlightened strictness, that the ugly South Sea gods in the British Museum might have supposed themselves at home again. Nothing to see but streets, streets, streets. Nothing to breathe but streets, streets, streets. Nothing to change the brooding mind or to raise it up. Nothing for the spent toiler to do, but to compare the monotony of his seventh day with the monotony of his six days, think what a weary life he led, and make the best of it [. . .].*

George Augustus Sala offered a very balanced view when he pointed out that people like himself might claim that the 'serious' (that is, pious) world was 'an amalgam of bigotry, hypocrisy and selfishness', but at the same time there were millions of sober and solid citizens who, he wrote, 'are honestly persuaded of the sinfulness of many things which we consider harmless recreations'.[20]

Hanging concentrates the mind wonderfully

In the final days before his execution for murder, Frederick Manning's mind was fixated on religion. In Taunton he had probably been brought up piously. On the Sunday after the murder of Patrick O'Connor, Maria Manning told O'Connor's colleagues that her husband had gone to church.[21] A few days before he was to be hanged, Frederick wrote a note to the prison chaplain, asking him to arrange an interview with Maria:

[. . .] as it is truly awful to contemplate the wickedness of any one
who shall enter the presence, the awful presence, of God without being
at peace with all men.[22]

Yet Maria, though she would weep bitterly when called on to repent in
the prison chapel on the last Sunday of her life, refused to see her husband
unless he affirmed her innocence. On the eve of her execution she again
insisted to the chaplain that she had had no part in the murder, blaming
it on 'the young man from Jersey'. But she could not explain how she had
obtained possession of the victim's keys.

In the hours before his death, Frederick read and reread the Psalms.
On Maria's last morning on Earth, Tuesday 13 November 1849, as she
knelt in the chapel, she still refused to confess her part in the murder of
Patrick O'Connor.

There was some confusion about what happened next. Did the Rev.
Rowe, the prison chaplain, administer the Sacrament to the Mannings
even though Maria had not expressed repentance? This question was
asked in a letter to *The Times*, signed 'Northumberland Rector'. The Rev.
Rowe admitted that he had administered the Sacrament, but only after
gravely exhorting the couple to receive it in a true spirit of remorse.

Religion and repentance do not seem to have meant very much to
Maria. True enough, among her few books were the Psalms, but this
was probably a childhood memento, given to her by a doting relative.
Frederick told the chaplain that she was an atheist, a view which the Rev.
Rowe, who seems to have wanted to give her the benefit of the doubt,
did not subscribe to, given that Maria had always been, in his words,
'anxious to receive spiritual instruction'.

Not for the likes of us

Marie de Roux and Frederick Manning had been married in St James's,
Piccadilly. Victorian London combined the greatest incidence of
Anglican marriages with the lowest level of church attendance.[23] In 1851,
a 'religious census' was taken of attendance at places of worship on
Easter Sunday, 30 March. The result shocked many people out of their
complacency. Large numbers did not go to any place of worship at all.
Only half of all attendances were at Anglican churches. About one

quarter of the population worshipped with the Church of England on that day; a quarter went to churches of other denominations, but half went nowhere at all.[24]

It was easy to see that the urban working class had turned their backs on the Church, and this was despite the fact that most of them had, at some time or other in their childhood, attended Church day or Sunday schools. Commentators claimed that charges for pews, the general boredom and the upper-class accents and views of Anglican clergymen led working people to feel that the Church was not for them. One study in 1849 wrote that 'the poor man is made to feel that he is a poor man; the rich reminded that he is very rich.'[25] Henry Mayhew repeated the words of a mid-century London costermonger who had 'heerd a little about our Saviour'. 'They seem to say,' added Mayhew, ' "he were a goodish sort of man; but if he says as how a cove's to forgive a feller as hits you, I should say he'd know nothing about it".' Charles Kingsley, the novel-writing Anglican vicar, wrote boldly in 1848: 'It is our fault. We have used the Bible as if it were a mere special constable's handbook – an opium-dose for keeping beasts of burden patient while they are being overloaded.'[26]

Middle-class Christians were not, however, content to allow the situation to remain as it was. Two major movements, Evangelism and Tractarianism, strove to rechristianise society.

Meet the Lord in Exeter Hall

Evangelism was concerned with disciplining sinful people's lives with the aim of fitting them to receive Divine Grace and thus to merit Eternal Salvation. The evangelical side of Anglicanism linked up with the more introspective, conscience-watching, Methodist spirit. Evangelism had a wide meaning and appealed to a spectrum of Christian opinion, from Low Church of England to Dissenters. It could be combined with the harsh spirit of utilitarianism, provided that the latter's frequently secular attitude was ignored. Evangelism chimed well with the Victorian social ethic of 'God helps those who help themselves' and with the spirit of self-help.

Evangelism spread like a brush-fire, led by Victoria and Albert's Court, which was a model of respectability compared with the Court of

William IV. From the Court, 'seriousness' spread to the aristocracy, which began to behave as properly as the new rising middle class demanded. 'We must go with the times, my Lord. A virtuous middle class shrinks with horror from French actresses; and the Wesleyans – the Wesleyans, must be considered,' the young Benjamin Disraeli put into one of his characters' mouths.[27] Things had certainly changed since Lord Melbourne, Prime Minister when Victoria came to the throne in 1837, had complained that 'things have come to a pretty pass when religion is allowed to invade the sphere of private life'.[28]

For all its emphasis on the private conscience, Evangelism went in for major religious events. It had a purpose-built London location in which to do so. Exeter Hall had been opened in the Strand in 1831 as an evangelical convention centre. It had a massive organ, 4,000 seats and 500 choir places. Mass evangelical rallies were held there as well as the annual meetings of several religious, missionary and philanthropic organisations. For the Low Church and Dissenting population, these meetings were what the contemporary Royal Academy Exhibition, held at the National Gallery in Trafalgar Square just along the Strand, was for the fashionable set. Exeter Hall had been financed by a company of rich evangelicals, including prominent members of the 'Clapham Sect' (known also as 'the Saints'), who lived in that healthy semi-rural suburb of the capital, and counted among their number the historian Macaulay and the humanitarian William Wilberforce, who led the campaign to free slaves in the British Empire.

In novels of the time, however, Exeter Hall symbolised sanctimoniousness. Godfrey Ablewhite in Wilkie Collins's *The Moonstone* of 1868 orates in Exeter Hall in defence of good morals and on behalf of many philanthropic causes, but he turns out to be a hypocrite and a swindler. Dickens's Luke Honeythunder in *Edwin Drood* (1870) presides at Exeter Hall over the meetings of the 'Convened Chief Composite Committee of Central and District Philanthropists', a target of the novelist's dislike of a particular class of do-gooders.[29] Philanthropy and social concern were, nevertheless, essential if England was to avoid the threat to the very foundations of society implicit in the three great revolutions that had taken place in France within human memory: 1789–1792, 1831 and 1848.

Can I interest you in a tract?

The decline of the religious spirit, which the 'religious census' of 1851 demonstrated so alarmingly, was energetically tackled. If Evangelism's target was social improvement by making the better-off classes more responsive to their consciences, the Tractarians, in contrast, urged a more devout attitude towards the liturgy, to ceremonial, to the observance of the holy days and to the role of the Church in general.

In one sense, both movements, Evangelism and Tractarianism, began as protests. Tractarianism, also known as the Oxford Movement, rebelled against the feared subjection of the Church to the State. Close ties with the State had been appropriate when the House of Commons had been an Anglican institution. But now, the reformed House included Roman Catholics and Dissenters. Tractarians saw it as controlled by secularists and Utilitarian Liberals, who were notoriously hostile to the Church of England, which they saw as the Tory party at prayer. Why should the Church of England be a department of the State? Why should its bishops be nominated as a political or other favour by the Prime Minister, who might be a non-believer? The Government was proposing, outrageously in the Tractarian view, to abolish 10 out of the 22 Irish Church of England Dioceses on the grounds that 6.4 million Irish Catholics paid tithes to an Anglican Church with only 850,000 members. By the Act of 1837 Dissenters had been granted the scandalous, in Tractarian eyes, right to celebrate legal marriages and baptisms in their own churches. The Government was reforming, by unjustified interference, the scandals of the Anglican Church: nepotism, pluralism, absentee vicars and sinecures such as the one the Reverend Mr Harding enjoyed in Trollope's novel *The Warden* (1855). To retain its independence, thought the Tractarians, the Church needed to break away from the State.

Tractarianism – so-called because its doctrines were expressed in a series called 'Tracts for the Times' – was launched when the Professor of Poetry at Oxford, John Keble, who, like all Oxbridge dons, was an ordained Anglican clergyman, preached a sermon in July 1833 on 'National Apostasy'. He advocated returning religious authority to the bishops and augmenting discipline by reducing the Protestant tendency towards emphasis on the individual's personal understanding of Scripture. John Henry Newman, the author of the famous hymn 'Lead, Kindly Light'

('And look where it led him,' sneered his detractors), vicar of St Mary's, Oxford, was at the time insisting that the Anglican Church was still the Catholic Church.

Tractarianism's main effect on ordinary people, however, was that it excited traditional English anti-Catholicism. Tractarians were accused of 'Popery' and 'Ritualism'. Ritual – candles, gorgeous vestments and the rich odours of incense – was probably the Tractarian movement's most visible outward sign. The Mannings might have attended a marriage or baptism in St George's, Southwark, built in Pugin's Gothic style and reflecting the Tractarian mood. Riots broke out in 1850 and 1851 in the London suburb of Pimlico following the opening of St Barnabas, with its ornate liturgical practices, its candles and its clouds of incense.[30] One of its enthusiastic young curates paid choirboys to throw rotten eggs at a sandwich-board man who had been employed to walk around with anti-ritualistic slogans on his back[31].

Both Tractarians and Evangelists were enthusiasts: personal ecstasy on one side; on the other a sense of awe and mystery. But farm-labourer or factory-hand Methodists could hardly meet ecstatic Oxford University gentlemen on equal terms. Nevertheless, the Evangelist and the Tractarian movements between them saw off the old three-bottle, hunting parson who performed his duties only cursorily, and they shook the Church of England out of its sloth.

However, though the Oxford Movement aimed at keeping Popery away by returning the Church of England to its earlier glory, its leader, John Henry Newman, went over to Rome. As *Punch* jeered, to the tune of a famous song:

> *Though crosses and candles we play with at home, To go the whole gander, there's no place like Rome.*

And fear of Rome was profound in the English psyche.

Notes

1 'Ignorance and Crime', published in *The Examiner*, 22 April 1848: see Dickens, C., *Dickens's Journalism*, ed. M. Slater, 4 volumes (London: Dent, 1996), vol. 2 'The Amusements of the People and Other Papers 1834–1851', pp. 91–5.

2 Ibid., p. 94.

3 Cruickshank, D. and Burton, N., *Life in the Georgian City* (London: Viking, 1990), p. 88.

4 In this discussion of reading, most of the factual statements have been taken from Altick, R., *The English Common Reader: a Social History of the Mass Reading Public 1800–1900* (Chicago: University of Chicago Press, 1957), p. 170.

5 Maria's library is listed in Borowitz, E., *The Bermondsey Horror* (London: Robson Books, 1989), p. 301.

6 Hoppen, K.T., *The Mid-Victorian Generation 1846–1886* (Oxford: Oxford University Press, 1998), p. 388.

7 Forster, J., *Life of Dickens*, cited in Altick, R., *The English Common Reader: a Social History of the Mass Reading Public 1800–1900* (Chicago: University of Chicago Press, 1957), p. 321.

8 Quoted in Dodds, J.W., *The Age of Paradox: A Biography of England 1841–1851* (London: Gollancz, 1953), pp. 371–2.

9 Ackroyd, P., *Dickens* (London: Sinclair-Stevenson, 1990), pp. 195–7.

10 Reynolds, G.W.M., *The Mysteries of London*, ed. T. Thomas (Newcastle-under-Lyme: Keele University Press, 1996), p. 169.

11 Ibid., Introduction, p. XV.

12 Dickens, C., *Dickens's Journalism*, ed. M. Slater, 4 volumes (London: Dent, 1996), vol. 2 'The Amusements of the People and Other Papers 1834–1851', p. XV.

13 Weindling, D. and Colloms, M., *Kilburn and West Hampstead Past* (London: Historical Publications, 1999), pp. 23–4. W. H. Smith lived in Kilburn.

14 Dodds, J.W., *The Age of Paradox: A Biography of England 1841–1851* (London: Gollancz, 1953), p. 374.

15 Trudgill, E., *Madonnas and Magdalens* (London: Heinemann, 1976), pp. 220–1.

16 Colman, H., *European Life and Manners in Familiar Letters to Friends*, 2 volumes (Boston and London, 1850), vol. 1, p. 5.

17 Vega, V. de la, *Cartas familiars inéditas* (Madrid, 1873), p. 9.

18 Cruickshank, D. and Burton, N., *Life in the Georgian City* (London: Viking, 1990), p. 192.

19 Ibid., p. 193.

20 Sala, G.A., *Twice Round the Clock*, first published in 1859 (Leicester: Leicester University Press, 1971), p. 294. It had first appeared as essays in magazines in the 1840s.

21 Borowitz, E., *The Bermondsey Horror* (London: Robson Books, 1989), p. 40.

22 Ibid., p. 244.

23 Hoppen, K.T., *The Mid-Victorian Generation 1846–1886* (Oxford: Oxford University Press, 1998), p. 465.

24 Ibid., p. 431.

25 Ibid., p. 453.

26 Ibid., p. 453.

27 Disraeli, B., *Sybil* (1845), vol. 2, p. 289, quoted in Trudgill, E., *Madonnas and Magdalens* (London: Heinemann, 1976), p. 176.

28 Cruickshank, D. and Burton, N., *Life in the Georgian City* (London: Viking, 1990), p. 173.

29 Altick, R., *The Presence of the Present: Topics of the Day in the Victorian Novel* (Columbus: Ohio State University Press, 1991), pp. 423–5.

30 Hoppen, K.T., *The Mid-Victorian Generation 1846–1886* (Oxford: Oxford University Press, 1998), p. 463.

31 Altick, R., *The Presence of the Present: Topics of the Day in the Victorian Novel* (Columbus: Ohio State University Press, 1991), p. 102.

CHAPTER 7

* * * * * * * * * * * * * *

'A burst of applause that made the building ring'

Patrick O'Connor, the Mannings' murder victim, with his well-paid job and his income from smuggling and moneylending, might have done many other things than walk over to Bermondsey on that hot afternoon in August 1849 to dine with the Mannings. Perhaps, as he plodded over London Bridge, he glanced down at the steamboat pier and thought that he might go to Margate on the Sunday. The day excursion left at eight on a fast steamer, the *Herne* or the *City of Canterbury*. Or he might take the Saturday off and spend a couple of days at Gravesend. This town was then a pleasure resort, with its promenade, its yacht club, its gardens at Rosherville and its villas on Windmill Hill where a pleasant day could be spent, followed by dancing and fireworks in the evening. Gravesend was nearer to London and a very convenient holiday place for men who could not stay too far away from business. But Margate, further down the river, and Ramsgate were places of a better class, or so Mrs Caudle nagged her husband in Douglas Jerrold's immensely successful *Mrs Caudle's Curtain Lectures*, a set of half-hour tirades, first published in *Punch* in 1845 and often reprinted, which Mr Caudle endures from his wife as he tries to get to sleep night after night. In the end, Mr Caudle gives in and the family goes to Herne Bay. One day they venture across the Channel to Boulogne. Despite Mrs Caudle's insistence on going, she doesn't like France, beginning with her outraged objections to being searched by a woman in the French customs shed, even though she herself is not above smuggling lace, velvet and silk stockings when they return to England.

Continental travelling was beginning to take off. Thomas Cook organised visits to Paris from 1855 onwards. Mrs Caudle, however, is shocked at the bare legs of the Boulogne fisher-girls and perhaps would have preferred to take a 'really genteel' cottage at Brixton, Balham, Clapham, Hornsey or Muswell Hill, suburbs of London today but still semi-rural in 1849.

Drink

Mrs Caudle is always scathing about Mr Caudle's visits to the public house and his 'drinking friends'. Maria Manning, with her Swiss Protestant background and her middle-class aspirations, would have looked down her nose as she passed a rowdy pub. Not for her the words of a prostitute recounted by an officer of the Salvation Army: 'The drink drowns all feelings of sorrow and shame, deadens the conscience, and hundreds could not live the life they do were it not for the excitement of alcohol.'[1] A working man, earning his paltry fifteen shillings to a pound a week in 1841, drank a mere pint of beer a day, but this cost one shilling and twopence per week. Some families spent over 20 per cent of their income on drink.[2]

That was at home, but the pub was warm and cheerful when home was cold and probably dark and the family comprised a worn-out slattern and a crowd of screaming children. For London's 2.3 million inhabitants, there were about 7,000 retailers of alcohol, one for every 330 people, and an outlet could be found, on average, every hundred yards.[3] Annual beer consumption in England and Wales was 19.4 gallons per head in 1849, or about three pints a week for every man, woman and child. Of course most of them drank much more, given the substantial number of teetotallers in the Evangelical and Methodist movements.

Unlike Frederick Manning, his victim, Patrick O'Connor, was not a drinking man. The gin palaces with their brilliant gas lighting reflected in abundant mirrors, and their roaring crowds held no attraction for him. But he had lots of alternative ways of amusing himself.

Neither the Mannings nor O'Connor had any means of entertainment at home. No piano was reported among their possessions. Maria and Frederick don't seem to have made a practice of receiving visitors except O'Connor himself. However, in this enormous and incomparable city, the

Mannings and O'Connor had at their disposal a wide range of public entertainment, depending on their inclinations, purses and the company with which they preferred to mix.

Much entertainment was as traditional as it had always been. The stage offered a wide variety, from the West End theatre to a sixpenny melodrama. One could eat out in pubs, in the street, where you could buy oysters or hot potatoes from ambulant vendors, or in West End supper-rooms where obsequious waiters took your order.

The stage had always been there, but other entertainment was new: promenade concerts or musical shows and circus-type spectacles, such as the trained horses at Astley's Amphitheatre. Shopping was becoming a diversion as well as a need. Maria, who liked clothes and was an expert seamstress, could saunter up the quite new Regent Street and have the assistants display endless trays of buttons and lace.

Panoramas, dioramas, cosmoramas

The growth of scientific knowledge and its application to mechanical devices overflowed into the world of entertainment. If the Mannings or O'Connor had any interest in going out at all, they would have visited a panorama, which was all the rage in 1849. The Burford Brothers were running one on the east side of Leicester Square. You could see immense circular pictures of the Alps, the Himalayas, Naples by moonlight or Cairo, as well as Arctic expeditions and the search for the lost explorer Sir John Franklin. But this panorama did not move, unlike what was probably the best known one of all.

This was the New Yorker John Banvard's Moving Panorama with its 36 scenes taking the spectator on a thrilling 3,000 mile trip from Yellowstone Bluffs down the Missouri and Mississippi rivers to New Orleans. Banvard invited Charles Dickens to a private showing. The novelist, who had done the trip in real life and describes James Steerforth taking David Copperfield to a panorama, guaranteed the accuracy of the experience that Banvard offered to the spectators.[4]

Banvard's panorama opened at the Egyptian Hall, an exhibition hall fronted by sphinxes and built in 1811–1812 on the site of the present Nos. 170–173 Piccadilly, a building opposite Burlington Arcade, now called Egyptian House in memory of the previous occupant of the site.

The panorama created an instant sensation. Banvard's canvas unrolled for two hours before the spectators' open-mouthed gaze. If you wanted to take part in dinner table conversations you really had to go and see the bluffs, the lonely cabins, the prairies with their vast herds of bison, the swamps and the alligators, the riverboats and levees of the South with slaves picking cotton and cutting sugar cane, the Red Indian wigwams and the waggon trains of emigrants. Banvard accompanied his show with witty remarks, which some found to be the height of Yankee vulgarity but which amused others. His panorama was a runaway success and Banvard was even invited to Windsor Palace.

As in the case of silent films half a century later, it helped to have music as an accompaniment. Banvard himself used the piano and a sort of harmonium called a seraphine. Spin-offs, as we would say, were profitable. Banvard sold sheet music, probably including the popular 'Oh, Susanna!' that the mob, replacing 'Susanna' with 'Mrs Manning', sang as they waited all night to see the Mannings hanged.

To see one of the greatest shows, an omnibus ride along the New Road or up Regent Street and Portland Place would bring you to within a few minutes' walk of the Royal Colosseum, built in 1825 on a site where the Royal College of Physicians now stands beside Regent's Park. It was a many-sided structure behind a classical portico. As you went in you entered a rotunda hung with silk and lined with classical and modern statuary, while behind the Colosseum was a garden with reproductions of ruins such as the Arch of Titus, the Temple of Vesta and the Parthenon, and in the centre was the Saloon of the Arts, with paintings, sculptures and casts of famous works of art. The main entertainment consisted of moving panoramas, called dioramas or cycloramas, including 'Paris by Night' as seen from a balloon hovering over the Tuileries. On one side of the Colosseum there was a luxurious little auditorium which recreated for spectators, as if they were floating down the Tagus, the great Lisbon earthquake of 1775 with spectacular lighting effects. Sound was provided by an enormous organ called the Grand Apollonicon, which thundered out the descent-into-hell music from Mozart's *Don Giovanni*.

The main exhibit of the Colosseum was a great panorama with 46,000 square feet of canvas, depicting twenty miles around London, as seen from the dome of St Paul's Cathedral, but without its usual covering of smoke, cloud and fog. To see it you had to go high into the building, hoisted by the first hydraulic passenger lift in London, called an 'ascending room'.

On the north side of the Colosseum was a 'Swiss Cottage', through the windows of which one could see Mont Blanc and a waterfall. It was occupied by an employee who, far from being Swiss, was Irish or a London cockney (reports vary) and had the catering concession.

Slightly to the south of the Colosseum, at Nos. 9 and 10 Park Square East, in one of Nash's new fashionable terraces, stood a building which housed Daguerre's Diorama. The age was one whose inventiveness with gaslight, mirrors and sound allowed the creation of illusion on a major scale for people who had not seen any sort of moving picture and to whom the photograph was new and unfamiliar. Here there was an ingenious system of lighting which could at once change a gentle landscape into a stormy sea, or give the illusion of depth to a flat picture. The circular viewing area held two hundred people. You entered through a dim corridor, groping your way or led by an usher (an experience which would be reproduced years later in the cinema). The auditorium moved through an arc of 73 degrees, but the spectator had the illusion that the scene itself was moving. By an intricate system of lights and prisms, shutters and pulleys, the pictures dissolved into each other with such variation that the viewer saw them with an almost kinematic effect. The diorama was very effective at producing the effects of light and clouds, sunshine and shadow. Thus, instead of dining with the Mannings that evening, O'Connor could have seen a thrilling depiction of an eruption of Mount Etna:

> [. . .] first beheld at evening in moonlight, then in sun, then night.
> Flashes of light from the mountain; clouds over the summit, changing
> colours from burning lava, streams of liquid fire rush down . . .[5]

Dioramas and panoramas offered what newspapers, magazines and finally the cinema would do later when pictures could be better reproduced and made to move. They offered fidelity to fact. You could see what you had read about in the newspapers. Like the later screen newsreel, the panorama was 'first with the news'. Only a week after the Houses of Parliament burned down on 16 October 1834, a panorama of their destruction was on show.

These shows reflected and to some extent satisfied British curiosity about foreign parts. In one sense, they were the middle class's alternative to the aristocracy's Grand Tour. In two hours, for a shilling or at the most two, a sum large enough to keep the rowdies out, you could see glamorous places such as Lake Maggiore, the Rhine, the Alhambra at Granada, St Petersburg, Cairo, Venice or Niagara Falls. Perhaps Frederick Manning, whose overseas journeys had been limited to a trip to the Channel Islands, fancied going to a panorama or a diorama. Maria, on the other hand, who came from Switzerland (which was often depicted in the panoramas) and who, as a lady's maid, had travelled more than most, would probably have been snooty about armchair tourism.

The fashion for still and moving panoramas stimulated the production of large canvases with a multiplicity of scenes. They contributed to for the popularity of Frith's famous mid-century paintings of Paddington Station and Ramsgate Sands. Maria, of course, was accustomed to seeing paintings hanging in her aristocratic employer's mansion and in the houses they visited. Her arrogance would have led her to sneer at Frederick's ignorance. He is unlikely to have seen much in the way of painting. Still, had he not had to keep his appointment with the hangman, perhaps he would have taken an interest in the National Gallery, which was free to the public. The number of its visitors doubled in the 1840s. In 1847 the Gallery acquired the Vernon collection of modern British art, though throughout 1849 *Punch* was complaining about its poor lighting.

'Nothing half so good'

Mechanical and scientific curiosity could be satisfied at the Royal Polytechnic Institution at the top of Regent Street:

> *We have given a very long account of the visits we paid to the Polytechnic Institution, because we saw nothing in London – nothing in England – half so good!*[6]

So wrote two Indian students of naval architecture who spent two and a half years in London. The Polytechnic, founded in 1838 in newly-built Regent Street and today the main building of the University of Westminster, was a place to visit which was indeed unlike anywhere else. It popularised science and technology. It gave free space to inventions and offered a programme of lectures and demonstrations for lay people. For a shilling you could visit the Polytechnic for several hours during the day or in the evening. A band played as visitors toured the thirty rooms and particularly the Great Hall, which was over a hundred feet long and had miniature canals dotted with models of locks and dockyards, printing presses and other highly specialised machines. A great attraction was the Polytechnic's 3-ton diving bell, in which the public could descend, and a diver who walked around the bottom of a tank and collected coins thrown by the spectators. Along the gallery were models of all sorts of inventions, which fascinated the two Bombay students. Experts lectured on coal gas, the adulteration of food, electricity, hydrostatics and chemistry, or demonstrated microscopes, particularly one which revealed the rich animal life of the Thames water which Londoners drank. On the roof stood one of the earliest photographic studios in the world. Under the hall could be found an Aladdin's cave, 'an infinite variety of ingenious models', wrote Dickens in his magazine *Household Words*.[7]

In 1847 John Pepper was appointed Lecturer in Chemistry at the Polytechnic. In 1852 he became the Polytechnic's Honorary Director and Professor of Chemistry. Pepper established regular classes in Drawing, French, German, Maths, Chemistry and Physics, and he used his skill with mirrors to produce the illusion known as 'Pepper's Ghost'. This was first displayed at a performance of Charles Dickens's *The Haunted Man* at the Polytechnic on Christmas Eve 1862. A quarter of a million people came to see it in the first fifteen months and a royal performance was given at Windsor.

There was something similar to the Polytechnic, but perhaps a little less earnest, called the National Gallery of Practical Science, at the Adelaide Gallery at the north end of the Lower Arcade, a passage that ran from the Strand to Adelaide Street, just east of Trafalgar Square, a site later occupied by Coutt's Bank. The Adelaide was a long, narrow room on two levels. The lower level had a miniature canal containing 6,000 gallons of water and some model steamboats. The new photograph, the Daguerrotype, had been exhibited there since 1839, developing views taken from the roof. Laughing gas, whose anaesthetic properties were only now being put into use, was demonstrated on Tuesday and Saturday evenings, more for curiosity than anything else. The most striking exhibit was a steam-powered machine-gun, which gave noisy demonstrations of firing a thousand shots per minute into an iron plate. But, compared with the Polytechnic (which was successful until challenged by the South Kensington museums, opened in the 1850s and 1860s, which then became the famous educational institution known as the Regent Street Polytechnic) the Adelaide Gallery was already going downmarket. By 1846 the scientific exhibits had been dispersed and the Adelaide soon became a dance hall.[8]

'Benighted heathens'

In east London, nearer to where the Mannings' victim O'Connor lived, the papers were full that summer of articles and pictures of the brilliantly painted three-masted Chinese junk, built of teak, which had been moored since May 1848 in the East India Docks, near the Blackwall pier where the river steamboats tied up. The junk had a Chinese crew who sang Chinese songs, and there were models of a mandarin of the first class and his lady with her bound feet. At Hyde Park Corner stood a Chinese pagoda, a conspicuous landmark for years, with two storeys and green roofs supported on vermilion columns. It contained an exhibition hall full of items of chinoiserie.

China apart, there was much interest in the exotic. From 1810 the enormously buttocked 'Hottentot Venus', a native woman brought from South Africa, had been on public view until she died of smallpox in 1814. George Catlin exhibited Red Indians for five years in the Egyptian Hall. These savage and exotic exhibits both provoked and satisfied the spectators' curiosity and encouraged their sense of racial superiority. While Catlin's Red Indians were still in the mould of the 'noble savage' of earlier times, by the 1840s theorists of race had stereotyped other peoples as inferior. In 1847 Bushmen were exhibited, posed on a stage against an African background. *The Times* saw them as 'benighted heathens', little superior to monkeys. Yet the interest in such unfamiliar peoples would soon change into a climate of intense if sentimental sympathy, reflected in the enormous success in 1851 of Harriet Beecher Stowe's antislavery novel, *Uncle Tom's Cabin*, which sold one and a half million copies in a year.

The Egyptian Hall, one of the great London exhibition venues, had opened its premises in Piccadilly in 1812, catering to the vogue stimulated by Napoleon's expedition to Egypt. The Hall contained models of sphinxes and stones inscribed with hieroglyphics, together with innumerable curiosities from many other exotic places. There were models of giraffes, rhinoceroses and elephants set among African and Indian plants and curios, while Laplanders, Egyptian mummies and Bedouin competed for space. The Egyptian Hall also hired out a room where one could hold one's own exhibition of freaks, such as a multi-limbed male child, or prodigies such as a six-year-old pianist, a group of Indian dancing girls and the strongman advertised as the 'Modern Samson, the Wonderful Fistic Stone-Breaker', who could lift 500 pounds with his teeth. Museums in the modern sense were not yet on the British scene, so the Egyptian Hall exhibited at one time or another in the late 1840s both clairvoyants and the Burmese State Coach, together with John Sainsbury's massive collection of Napoleonic relics. The famous 'General Tom Thumb', a midget, was exhibited by P.T. Barnum, the legendary showman, together with sundry other dwarfs, giants and the inevitable bearded lady. Tom Thumb's *pièce de résistance* was to stand on a chair and take off Napoleon. This brought the house down at the Egyptian Hall in 1844 and led to an invitation to perform at Windsor Castle, where Queen Victoria was reported to have been much amused.

Freaks were there, of course, to be shown off for money. Political correctness had only just reached the stage of making people ashamed of going to see the lunatics at Bedlam 'for a laugh'. But how else could the freaks live? It would have been considered absurd to say that they were exploited if their exhibitor took responsibility for their welfare and treated them well. What would have happened to the two-headed female baby, for instance, had she not been exhibited for a penny at Smithfield Fair in 1842?

Chamber of Horrors

Londoners who could afford it could also visit the waxworks that Madame Tussaud was exhibiting at her premises in Portman Square, including the room known since 1843, and still today, as the 'Chamber of Horrors' where in 1849 she was showing newly made models of James Rush, who had committed the ferocious Norfolk murders in the previous November. Rush was a farmer who had shot and killed his landlord and creditor, Isaac Jermy, together with Jermy's son, and had wounded Jermy's wife and her maid. The multiple shootings with their irrational ferocity horrified the sensation-hungry public. At his trial, Rush acted as his own counsel, subjecting his mistress Emily Sandford to rigorous cross-questioning to try to prove that he was with her and not at the scene of the murders. Although the killings were sparked off by hatred arising from prosaic matters such as mortgages, loans and leases, the press suggested that Rush had been inspired by revolutionary agitators, which increased the anxious interest of the public. The Mannings once gave themselves a treat and went and stared at Rush's replica in the Chamber of Horrors. Frederick asked William Massey, the medical student who lodged with them, whether he thought that a murderer could go to Heaven. Did he ever dream that he and Maria would soon be exhibits there themselves?

Queen Victoria's coronation in 1837 was on permanent show at the waxworks, as was Napoleon's carriage, captured at Waterloo and presented to the Prince Regent, who gave it to the Egyptian Hall, from which Madame Tussaud had bought it. She was constantly up to date with her tableaux and she probably gave people the best view, in the absence of photographs or film, of the politicians of the time such as Sir Robert Peel, Lord John Russell and Viscount Palmerston, as well as of stars of the stage such as the actor William Macready and Jenny Lind, the 'Swedish Nightingale', who was singing to packed houses at Covent Garden.

Unlike some other London waxworks, Madame Tussaud maintained very high-class premises with brilliant gas lighting, mirrors, sofas and an orchestra. But some of Napoleon's personal relics that she exhibited were activated by internal mechanisms, and in this she indulged the passion for clever tricks with which the showmen of London sought to attract the capital's growing audience for the spectacular and the curious. In one case, at the so-called Anatomical Waxworks in the Strand, one could see a female body being dissected. According to the blurb of the exhibition, the body was of the Venus de Milo. Of course, the show could not dare to advertise its real purpose – to titillate the sexually curious – but merely to display 'the order and beauty created by God'. Private showings could be arranged for modest ladies, claimed the publicity disingenuously.[9]

'No, they don't move'

A rather more suggestive spectacle was available for gentlemen. On the principle that anything French was daringly sexy, a certain Mrs Wharton and a 'Professor' Keller (this title was often affected and should not be taken to suggest a connection with a university) put on *Tableaux Vivants* with *Poses Plastiques*, that is nude scenes from history, mythology or scripture. As at the Windmill Theatre a century later, the participants in these scenes did not move. In 1849 their nudity could be no more than suggested by the use of skintight pink 'fleshings'. The journalist George Augustus Sala saw such a performance at Saville House in Leicester Square, the centre of London's more tawdry entertainment world. The man representing Adam in the Garden of Eden scene was suddenly arrested as an army deserter and marched off with a greatcoat over his fleshings.[10]

Spangles and sawdust

Lightly clad ladies might also be seen in the more respectable context of Astley's Amphitheatre in Westminster Bridge Road. This was one of the great permanent shows of London. Dickens captured the anticipation of a visit there in his *The Old Curiosity Shop*:

> [. . .] what a place it looked, that Astley's; with all the paint, gilding and looking glass; the vague smell of horses suggestive of coming wonders; the curtain that held such gorgeous mysteries; the clear white sawdust in the circus; the company coming in and taking their places; the fiddlers looking carelessly up at them while they tuned their instruments. What feverish excitement when the little bell rang and the music began in good earnest [. . .]

There were clowns who engaged in badinage with the ringmaster: 'I say, sir!' 'Do you know, sir?' There were acrobats and conjurors, but the real spectacle was horsemanship. Horses were trained to feign dropping dead, to rise from stage traps and descend into them, and to sit and eat a meal. In 1849 the famous exhibition rider Andrew Ducrow was playing the horseback hero. His great act was 'Mazeppa's Ride', in which he was bound flat on the horse's back. The most popular performance was 'The Battle of Waterloo', but 'The Burning of Moscow', 'The Crusaders of

Jerusalem' and 'The Conquest of Mexico' were among Ducrow's other dramatic compositions. In the summer of 1849, Ducrow put on his 'New Grand Equestrian Military Spectacle', subtitled 'Mooltan and Goojerat, or the Conquest of the Sikhs', which allowed the audience to share vicariously in that recent victory of British arms. If the depiction was not as accurate as it would have been in the panorama or the diorama, the bugle calls and cannon fire at Astley's Amphitheatre made up for it and gave the children, especially, a thrilling treat.

'An increasingly notorious haunt'

In the summer, Vauxhall and Cremorne Gardens were the places to go. Just behind today's Albert Embankment, Vauxhall's groves, bosky paths, statuary and coloured lanterns, its fireworks on summer nights, its cascades and its balloon ascents were widely mentioned in Victorian fiction. When Thackeray's *Vanity Fair* first appeared in monthly parts in 1847, older readers could indulge in nostalgia as they enjoyed the description of an evening spent there over thirty years earlier by a group of characters in the novel. Its refreshment booths served slices of ham whose thinness was one of the oldest jokes in town.[11] In earlier days, Vauxhall had fitted the poet Wordsworth's picture in *The Prelude* of 'green groves, and wilderness of lamps [. . .], gorgeous ladies, fairy cataracts, and pageant fireworks'. In the 1830s, Dickens evoked Vauxhall's magic by night:

> *The temples and saloons and cosmoramas and fountains glittered and sparkled before our eyes; the beauty of the lady singers and the elegant deportment of the gentlemen captivated our hearts; a few hundred thousand additional lamps dazzled our senses; a bowl or two of punch addled our brains; and we were happy.*[12]

Vauxhall had a theatre where one could hear the renowned Madame Vestris and the famous tenor John Braham sing 'Cherry Ripe'; as well as a supper room, an ice house and a remarkable construction called, unpronounceably, a 'Heptaplasiesoptron', which reflected the passion of the age for optical illusions, for it consisted of glass plates reflecting revolving pillars, palm trees, serpents and a fountain.

On Thursday 9 August, the day the Mannings murdered O'Connor, Vauxhall was offering Hernandez the Equestrian, a military band and another one with fifty instrumentalists and singers, American-style bowling, fireworks and the 'magic faerie land' of 60,000 lamps. Yet, by now, Vauxhall Gardens were beginning to be seen as tacky. In his *Pendennis*, which followed closely on *Vanity Fair*, Thackeray gave a more harshly realistic portrait of Vauxhall Gardens: '[. . .] how dingy the pleasure garden has grown, how tattered the gardens look,' he wrote.[13] Women might be accosted, while there were 'goings-on' in the bushes. Vauxhall had to halve its entry charge and was going downmarket by 1849 despite its flashy attractions. It had become a magnet for the yob clientele and for young men on the prowl for girls who were happy to be whirled around shrieking in the disreputable polka. Vauxhall was now described as 'the increasingly notorious haunt of London lowlife'.[14] Complaints multiplied about its vulgarity, the rowdiness of the customers, the high cab fare to get there and the toll to cross the bridge, not to speak of the infamously poor refreshments on sale. Closed in 1849, Vauxhall Gardens are recalled today only by Jonathan and Tyers Streets, which bear the names of an eighteenth-century manager.

Vauxhall's rival, Cremorne Gardens, just west of Battersea Bridge on the north bank of the Thames, opened in the 1840s. Hundreds came by riverboat on summer days and paid the one shilling entrance fee. Cremorne had a theatre, a bowling saloon and an orchestra. There were wooded paths, delightful bowers and a dancing platform, as well as the ubiquitous pagodas, kiosks, temples and Swiss chalets.

At Cremorne, a more original show, with which the management competed with Vauxhall for customers, was the Aquatic Tournament on the lake. This was described by one of the rare Spanish visitors to London, the playwright Ventura de la Vega. He visited Cremorne one summer evening in 1853. The lake was surrounded by false mountains; there was a harbour and ships. Suddenly the orchestra stopped playing, ships emerged from between the mountains and fired rockets and shells. Finally the ships exploded in a multicoloured and patterned conflagration.[15]

At dusk you could buy a half-crown supper in the long banqueting hall and eat it as you admired the firework displays. During the day there were balloon ascents by Charles Green, billed as the 'aeronautist', whom the Mannings might well have seen from their back garden in Bermondsey, sailing over their heads in a brightly coloured balloon, perhaps even with an acrobat twirling and swinging from a trapeze suspended beneath the gondola. A certain Herr von Joel yodelled peripatetically in the gardens, until his gurgling got on people's nerves.

In 1849 Cremorne was still new. Never having enjoyed the high-class reputation of Vauxhall, it had less to lose. It put on concerts and a ballet, whose title *L'Amour et la Folie* suggested that it was a little risqué. There was a tournament using fifty horses hired from Astley's Royal Amphitheatre, and the band of the Life Guards. It was admittedly rather flashy, but not until twenty years later did it begin to go downhill because of the behaviour of the customers. It became known, in the words of a local minister, as 'the nursery of every kind of vice'. In 1877 Cremorne closed; Lots Road power station was built on the site.

In the street

The Mannings would probably have made most of their journeys in London on foot. Cabs were expensive and horse-drawn omnibuses were slow. Traffic jams were monumental. In their perambulations they would have avoided what *The Times* of 20 February 1849 called 'disgraceful exhibitions' of brutish games and obscene peep-shows. Cock-fighting and prize-fighting had by now been prohibited, but the Mannings would have seen street shows everywhere. Men made their livings from the pennies which they hoped to collect from spectators as they showed their menageries of cats, mice and birds living amicably in the same cage, a show known as 'Happy Families'. There were five different Happy Families shows in London at the time, the largest with 54 birds and animals in one cage, exhibited at a spot near the south end of Waterloo Bridge.

There were acrobats, jugglers, the musician who could play several instruments at once, the Italian barrel organists, other Italians with dancing dolls which they dexterously moved with a string attached to their knees while they played the pipe and drum, and the Italian boys who played the concertina and exhibited white mice in the street. There was the Punch and Judy show, the strongmen, conjurors and fireaters, and the ubiquitous seller of street poetry about current events, such as, for example, the vast number of verses about Mrs Manning herself which were hawked in the streets while she awaited justice that summer and autumn of 1849.

'All the fun of the fair'

Patrick O'Connor may have been too careful with his money to frequent the Greenwich Fair, one of the best known of the more popular London places where one could have a good time in 1849. With its showgirls in spangly dresses, its clowns and fat ladies, its dancing at night, including the intriguingly-titled 'chin and shoulder French dance', its rows of stalls selling food and cheap toys, the 'raree shows' with their strange exhibits, tin trumpets blasting the ears, and Richardson's Show, which gave the impatient audience a tragedy, a comic song and a pantomime all in thirty minutes, you could have fun if you liked that sort of thing. For the nineteenth-century middle class, Greenwich was where one's servants went, as later they would have a day out at the fair on Hampstead Heath; Charles Dickens recounts that David Copperfield had to dismiss the maid who went off to Greenwich Fair wearing Mrs Copperfield's bonnet. But then, as so often now, public entertainment in London led to the stench of cheap liquor and cigars, of onions frying in overused fat, and drunks, cheating gamblers and the ever-menacing, swearing and violent rough. None of this would have suited the proud Maria Manning, nor probably Frederick, who was more used to the gentler public manners of his native West Country.

'Oh, Susanna!'

Perhaps Maria would have been more entertained by an amusement which in today's age seems distant and distasteful. Yet 'Nigger Minstrels' survived well into the epoch of television as the Black and White Minstrels. The first to appear in London were Dan Emmett's Virginia Minstrels, who played to packed houses at the Adelphi Theatre in the Strand in 1843. They were followed by the Ethiopian Serenaders in 1846 with their songs, dances and jokes and the Banjo and Mr Bones characters. In the streets, the buskers imitated them, singing 'Old Mr Coon', 'Buffalo Gals' and 'Oh, Susanna!' which became 'Oh, Mrs Manning!' when roared out by the crowd on that last night of Maria's life.

'Hallelujah'

Not all London entertainment was either spectacular or vulgar, however.
A mania for singing from sheet music swept over the country in the 1840s,
started by Joseph Mainzer, who came from Germany in 1841 and devised
a catchphrase which sounds as if it belongs to the twentieth rather than
the nineteenth century: 'Singing for the millions'. One of the biggest
halls for mass singing was the Exeter Hall in the Strand. On the site of the
present Strand Palace Hotel, this was a building hired out for political
and religious meetings, and those of the antislavery and the temperance
societies.

Public singing was intended to wean the lower classes from drink and
to encourage them to be patriotic and industrious. Like the Mechanics'
Institutes at which working men could make up for some of the education they had not enjoyed in their childhood, it was allied to the contemporary movement for the improvement of the 'industrious classes'. Still,
it doesn't seem likely that the gin and beer drinker would be attracted
to public singing any more than he would to the Exeter Hall to hear
oratorios or revivalist preachers. The Mannings' trial revealed some few
vestiges of religious feeling in Maria and Frederick, which could have
taken them to the Exeter Hall to be among the audience of 3,000 which
heard Handel's *Messiah* there at Christmas 1848, or Mendelssohn's *Elijah*
the year before, performed by the Sacred Harmonic Society before the
Queen and Prince Albert with a chorus and orchestra of 500. The 1840s
saw a flood of oratorio performances. Handel and Mendelssohn were the
most popular. Oratorio was respectable, 'the opera of the serious-minded
middle classes', wrote George Augustus Sala in 1858.[16] At an oratorio
people of the 'serious' tendency, as the pious were known, could share
their pleasure with the easy-going agnostic.

Concerts with immense orchestras were very popular at mid-century.
By 1849, the moustachioed and white-waistcoated Monsieur Louis-
Antoine Jullien, one of the best-known names on the London music scene,
was conducting orchestras of between 300 and 400 instrumentalists at
the Surrey Gardens, a venue which could hold 12,000 people. The
concerts were held on summer evenings, ending at dusk, when fireworks
were let off. Yet one wonders whether even the most spectacular firework
display could match Jullien's 400-piece orchestra, his three military

bands, his three choirs and his Roman march led by twenty trumpeters blowing into instruments 3 yards long.[17] In the winter, Jullien held his concerts at the Drury Lane Theatre. The crowd stood or, if there was room, walked about in the pit, whence the name promenade concerts.

'The management reserves the right . . .'

The more sophisticated audiences went to the Italian Opera House at Her Majesty's Theatre, on the corner of the Haymarket and Pall Mall. On 4 May 1847 Jenny Lind, known as 'the Swedish Nightingale' because of her vocal mastery, made her English debut in Meyerbeer's *Robert le Diable* and was received with acclaim. Her private life was blameless and her voice matchlessly beautiful. Long queues formed to pay the high prices demanded to hear her. Stars like Jenny Lind could earn vast sums. But Nowrojee and Merwangee, the Bombay Parsees who wrote an account of their stay in London, thought the English absurd to pay the ballerina Madame Taglioni 150 guineas a night for 'jumping about'.[18]

Covent Garden's interior was redesigned in 1847 as the Royal Italian Opera House, opening with Rossini's *Semiramide*. The theatre was managed by the singer Madame Vestris. But the bar was reputed to be full of whores. The Theatre Royal, Drury Lane, was also notorious for the prostitutes who haunted its Grand Saloon until the actor William Macready put a stop to their activities when he became manager in 1841. Both Covent Garden and Drury Lane were very large. They lacked intimacy. Refreshments were on sale during the performance at Drury Lane, which itself caused disorder. It had no lounge stalls; the pit had hard benches which you had to rush for after you paid the 8s 6d just to get in. Women roamed the theatre selling apples, oranges, nuts and ginger beer from large baskets, just like Nell Gwynn 200 years earlier.

In 1849 theatres and their audiences were changing. In some, behaviour was unrestrained; the audience let off steam by shouting at the actors. Charles Dickens had found the audience 'ruffianly', swearing, blaspheming and fighting, when he visited Sadler's Wells in 1841. Later, however, the Wells came under the very firm hand of the manager Samuel Phelps, who strove to make people sit to hear Shakespeare as if they were in church. The Wells was at the height of its Shakespearean fame in the latter half of the 1840s, *Hamlet* alone being performed

400 times as well as 34 other plays by the Bard. William Macready was playing the lead in *King Lear* during the Manning trial in autumn 1849. 'At the close of the tragedy,' wrote Dickens in *The Examiner* on 27 October, '[the audience] rose in a mass to greet him with a burst of applause that made the building ring.'[19]

Until 1843 Covent Garden and Drury Lane had enjoyed a monopoly of theatre plays. Other halls might 'give musical performances of a dramatic nature'. There were more than twenty other theatres in London by 1843 when Parliament ended the monopoly. The theatres had been limited to operettas and burlettas – musical plays, usually in rhyme – where the speeches grew longer and the musical pieces shorter, but as long as there was some music they did not trespass on the two big theatres' monopoly. But after 1843 plays could be put on anywhere.

Managements responded with superb new halls, and disciplined their audiences into a more subdued mood. A Victorian husband could take his wife to see Douglas Jerrold's *Black-Eyed Susan*, a popular melodrama about a sailor's last-minute reprieve from execution after he strikes his officer in defence of his wife's honour. This was put on at the Royal Marylebone Theatre in Church Street, Paddington, by now a well-conducted house. 'The audience laughed and wept with all their hearts,' wrote Charles Dickens in *The Examiner* on 12 May 1849, and continued, 'It is a pleasant duty to point out the deserts of this theatre as it is now conducted, and to recommend it.'[20]

'Unhand me, Sir!'

Drury Lane, Covent Garden and the West End theatres were expensive, but plenty of places would give you a play for sixpence or even less. It wasn't a long walk for the Mannings to go to have an evening out at the Royal Victoria in the New Cut in Lambeth. In 1850, Charles Dickens visited this theatre, long known as the Old Vic and now restored to its original glory. He saw a melodrama called *May Morning, or the Mystery of 1715, and the Murder*. 'May Morning' turned out to be the name of the main character. The heroines swooned, the heroes were noble and the villains dastardly. The pit cost 6d and the gallery 3d. The house was full. Some of the audience were none too clean, but Dickens observed some good-humoured young working men with their wives. They had brought their babies too, as well as cold fried fish and stone bottles of drink. You didn't expect solemn behaviour from them. People whistled, booed and shouted their way through the evening. They refused to put up with delays and loudly instructed the scene shifters in their duties.[21]

At a somewhat lower level, Dickens also visited the Britannia Saloon in Hoxton, called thus because the only way in was through the saloon bar of a tavern. Whole families were enjoying a night out to see the melo-drama. As Dickens noted, the common people were in the pit, and the play was directed to them. They were not shut away in the gallery as in the more expensive theatres. Everybody was attentive, despite the ham sandwiches and other comestibles being hawked around the closely packed and not very sweet-smelling audience.[22]

'Ladies and Gentlemen, at eno-o-o-rmous expense . . . !'

If you couldn't afford even as little as 3d and wanted some entertainment, you went to the 'Penny Gaff' as it was called. This was a room, often an empty shop front, where bawdy songs and pantomimes were put on every evening. Usually the Penny Gaffs suited the crowds of adolescents who thronged the streets rather than go back to the one or two squalid rooms where their parents quarrelled and a horde of younger children squalled. There were three Penny Gaffs in the New Cut alone, putting on shows from 6 p.m. until 11 p.m. James Grant, who published his book *Sketches in London* in 1838, calculated that 24,000 people attended Penny Gaffs every night. Just like the early cinema, people blamed these theatres for juvenile crime. With bare brick walls and wooden joists, a candle-lit stage close into the audience, a crudely painted backcloth, a couple of fiddlers and actors who couldn't get any better work and to whom the owner paid a pittance, they put on melodramas with titles such as 'The Red-Nosed Monster and the Tyrant of the Mountains', 'Sweeney Todd the Demon Barber' and 'Maria Marten and the Red Barn', but also cut-down versions of Shakespeare. *Hamlet*, for example, would be done in 20 minutes, followed by a singsong. *Othello* and *Macbeth* were also favourites. It was the blood and gore that mattered. Like the early Music Halls, of which the Penny Gaffs were a predecessor, the actors and the audience exchanged witticisms, obscene insults and the occasional bottle.

The first Music Halls were opening at the end of the 1840s. The nearest one to the Mannings' house was the Surrey in Southwark Bridge Road. Later, after the Manning case was over, the Canterbury Music Hall opened at 143 Westminster Bridge Road, with luxurious fittings and a chairman who controlled the audience and announced the turns. The Canterbury heralded a new age with its Nigger Minstrels, 'Hieland Laddies' and ribald, well-upholstered female singers. It was a pity that Frederick Manning did not have the personality to emulate the manager of the Canterbury, Charles Morton, who like him had run a pub in Hackney, but had taken over the Canterbury Arms and introduced his Musical Saturday Nights. The entertainment was free but people spent so much money on food and drink that Morton soon enlarged the hall to accommodate 1,500 spectators, who paid 6d to sit at the tables or 9d in the gallery. It was Morton who later engaged Geoffrey Leybourne to sing his immortal ballad 'Champagne Charlie is my name'.

'The Ratcatcher's daughter'

Like many other husbands, tired of crying children and complaining wives, Frederick Manning might have had enough of Maria's sneering at his incompetence and gone out on his own and spent an extravagant two shillings on the show and supper at the famous Cyder Cellars near Covent Garden. This was one of the song and supper rooms – the Coal Hole was another and the slightly up-market Evans's a third – open from 10 p.m. until 2 a.m. Only men went. You could eat – poached eggs and roast potatoes were a favourite dish – drink, sing songs and smoke. Percival Leigh's Mr Pips, a nineteenth-century fictional comic version of Samuel Pepys, went to the Cyder Cellars on 10 March 1849. He consumed kidneys and stout, followed by brandy and a cigar. He listened to the lugubrious song of 'The Ratcatcher's Daughter' who, like the Mannings, lived 't'other side of the water', as Londoners still refer to the south side of the Thames. Sadly for her, she fell into the river and was drowned, leading her fiancé, who sold 'lily-white sand' for caged birds' trays, to cut his throat with a pane of glass. Mr Pips also heard G.W. Ross perform the famous macabre tale of Sam Hall the Chimney Sweep, with a soot-blackened face, wearing a battered hat, smoking a short clay pipe and leaning over a chair as if over the side of the tumbril, cursing them all ('I'll see yer all in 'ell/ And I 'opes yer frizzle well, Damn yer eyes!') as he was being taken to Tyburn to be hanged for theft[23].

Improving one's mind

If Frederick had been a different sort of man, the upwardly-aspiring Maria and he would have made a point of improving their minds by taking advantage of the views of the Liberal administrations of the time, which wanted to make public monuments such as St Paul's, Westminster Abbey and the British Museum more accessible to ordinary people. The crowd's behaviour at public events had much improved of late, according to *Punch* and the press. The evangelical or 'serious' mechanic out for the afternoon would avoid the tawdry delights of Greenwich Fair, preferring to admire the contents of the glass cabinets of the British Museum, where several new galleries opened in 1847. As a result, the following year visitors totalled 897,985 compared with 81,228 who had visited the exhibits twenty years earlier.[24]

Two years previously, Victoria Park had opened in Hackney, lungs for the serried houses of the East End, and the zoo in Regent's Park had been open to the public since 1828. The manager, David Mitchell, reduced the entrance charge to 6d on Mondays, and had added to the popularity of the zoo by acquiring numerous and fearsome reptiles.

The information which has come down to us reflects the Victorian Age's interest in observing society. Charles Dickens and George Augustus Sala, with their interest in local colour, together with Henry Mayhew's investigative journalism and the anonymous collectors who gave their ephemera to museums, tell us a great deal about the Penny Gaff and the threepenny melodrama. The Manning trial record itself says nothing about how Maria and Frederick amused themselves but, living in London, they had ample possibilities of enjoying a wide range of entertainment. However, unlike the cinema or a lot of television today, entertainment in mid-nineteenth-century London was sharply differentiated in its appeal to different classes of society. Entertainments were well contrasted in price and attracted very different types of people. A Penny Gaff cost one penny, while a panorama or a visit to the Royal Polytechnical Institution cost a shilling, or twelve times as much, and the West End theatre pit cost very much more.

Notes

1 Cited in Barret-Ducrocq, F., *Love in the Time of Victoria* (London: Verso, 1991), p. 13.

2 Burnett, J., *A History of the Cost of Living* (Harmondsworth: Penguin, 1969), p. 263.

3 Hoppen, K.T., *The Mid-Victorian Generation 1846–1886* (Oxford: Oxford University Press, 1998), p. 353.

4 Dickens, C., *Dickens's Journalism*, ed. M. Slater, 4 volumes (London: Dent, 1996), vol. 2 'The Amusements of the People and Other Papers 1834–1851', pp. 134–7.

5 Altick, R., *The Shows of London* (Cambridge, Mass: Harvard University Press, 1976), p. 171.

6 Nowrojee, J. and Merwangee, H., *Journal of a Residence of Two Years and a half in Great Britain* (London: W.H. Allen, 1841), pp. 138–9.

7 Dickens, C., *Dickens's Journalism*, ed. M. Slater, 4 volumes (London: Dent, 1996), vol. 2 'The Amusements of the People and Other Papers 1834–1851', p. 180.

8 Altick, R., *The Shows of London* (Cambridge, Mass: Harvard University Press, 1976), p. 514 ff.

9 Ibid., pp. 514 ff.

10 Sala, G.A., *Gaslight and Daylight* (London: Chapman & Hall, 1859), p. 177. Though the collection was published ten years after the Manning case, it consists of much earlier journalism.

11 Altick, R., *The Presence of the Present: Topics of the Day in the Victorian Novel* (Columbus: Ohio State University Press, 1991), p. 432 note.

12 Dickens, C., *Sketches by Boz* (London: Chapman & Hall, 1913 edition), p. 98.

13 Quoted in Altick, R., *The Presence of the Present: Topics of the Day in the Victorian Novel* (Columbus: Ohio State University Press, 1991), p. 435.

14 Ibid., p. 435.

15 Vega, V. de la, *Cartas familiars inéditas* (Madrid, 1873), pp. 25–6.

16 Sala, G.A., *Twice Round the Clock*, first published in 1859 (Leicester: Leicester University Press, 1971), p. 293. It had first appeared as essays in magazines in the 1840s.

17 Altick, R., *The Shows of London* (Cambridge, Mass: Harvard University Press, 1976), pp. 323–31.

18 Nowrojee, J. and Merwangee, H., *Journal of a Residence of Two Years and a half in Great Britain* (London: W.H. Allen, 1841), pp. 102–3.

19 Dickens, C., *Dickens's Journalism*, ed. M. Slater, 4 volumes (London: Dent, 1996), vol. 2 'The Amusements of the People and Other Papers 1834–1851', p. 171.

20 Ibid., p. 59.

21 Weightman, G., *Bright Lights: Big City* (London: Collins & Brown, 1992), pp. 51–2, offers an animated description of the popular London theatre.

22 Dickens, C., *Dickens's Journalism*, ed. M. Slater, 4 volumes (London: Dent, 1996), vol. 2 'The Amusements of the People and Other Papers 1834–1851', pp. 193–201.

23 Leigh, P., *Manners and Customs of the Englyshe, Drawn from ye Quick by Rychard Doyle, To which be added some extracts from Mr Pips hys Diary* (London: Bradbury and Evans, 1850).

24 Altick, R., *The Shows of London* (Cambridge, Mass: Harvard University Press, 1976), p. 454.

CHAPTER 8

Outsiders

'The Pope and his Cardinals have learnt nothing from the teachings of adversity'

Tractarians, so long as they did not 'go over to Rome', and evangelicals were two sides of the same Anglican coin. Methodists and other Non-conformists might be seen as overexcited, disrespectful of the proper ordering of society and even vulgar, but Roman Catholics were a different matter altogether, for they had the taint of the foreign about them; not the old Catholic families, of course, but the newcomers, the streams of poverty-stricken Irish immigrants, as well as some high-profile Tractarians who went over to Rome.

Anti-Catholicism was part of being English. Foxe's *Book of Martyrs*, with its gruesome details of the torture and burning of heretics by the Catholic Queen Mary in the 1550s, was regular Sunday afternoon reading in many households and had only recently been issued in a fine new edition.[1] People who had the taste for it could go to Exeter Hall and hear a 'serious' clergyman rant for an hour and a half against Catholicism. One Essex curate even claimed in his sermon that there was a connection between the 'advance of Popery' and the cholera epidemics.[2]

Nothing, save her foreignness, indicated that Maria Manning was a Catholic. Indeed, her father's position as postmaster in Protestant Geneva suggests the opposite. Nevertheless, Robert Huish's lengthy and imaginative account of her early life claims that she had a Catholic convent education, and suggests that this was the origin of her murderous character. Readers of *The Times* in today's ecumenical age would be horrified to see the comment, shortly after the Mannings' execution, of the Northumberland vicar who, while protesting because the prison chaplain gave Holy Communion to the Mannings, added that it might have been expected from a Catholic priest, who would have been satisfied with a cursory expression of remorse for their sins. To its credit, *The Times* published a retort from a Catholic priest. Neither he nor any of his colleagues, he wrote, would have given the Mannings communion without being convinced that their repentance was genuine.

Hostility towards Catholics explains the huge petitions which were signed in 1845 against Sir Robert Peel's proposal to make a substantial increase in the annual grant to Maynooth College for the training of Irish priests. The protests were shortsighted, however, because Maynooth had been founded, in 1795, precisely to remove the need for seminarists to study on the Continent and be imbued there with what many considered the politically reactionary stance of Continental Catholicism. This latter had seemed to be approaching its nemesis when, in November 1848, Pope Pius IX fled from the Vatican and the Italian liberator Giuseppe Mazzini proclaimed the Roman Republic. The Republic was short-lived, however, for Louis Napoleon, President of France, soon to declare himself Emperor, suppressed it and allowed the Pope to return to Rome in March 1850.

In Britain, however, things had changed in a more tolerant direction. The old repressive laws against Catholics had been repealed in 1829. Catholics could now hold State or municipal office. Furthermore, the 'Oxford Movement', as the Tractarians were known, had encouraged a significant number of the socially distinguished to go further and become Catholics.[3] Recognising the Catholic revival, on 29 September 1850 the Pope restored the Catholic hierarchy in England, officially appointing bishops rather than the administrators who had supervised Catholic dioceses until then. Nicholas Wiseman was appointed Cardinal-Archbishop of London.

Popular animosity towards Catholics surged. 'The Pope and his Cardinals have learnt nothing from the lessons of adversity!' thundered the *Illustrated London News*. Primitive fears of the alien and of Jesuitical plots against Protestant England were revived. 'Papal Aggression' became the vogue term. Lord John Russell, the Prime Minister, wrote to the Bishop of Durham in terms which seem to come from a much earlier age, one in which the Spanish Armada and Guy Fawkes were in recent memory:

> *No foreign prince [. . .] will be at liberty to fasten his fetters upon a nation which has so long and so nobly vindicated its right to freedom of opinion [. . .] a nation which looks with contempt on the mummeries of superstition.*[4]

In August 1851, almost in a panic, Parliament passed the Ecclesiastical Titles Bill, forbidding Catholic bishops to adopt the same place names in their titles as their Anglican equivalents. The law, however, was never enforced and was later repealed.

Charles Dickens reacted to 'Papal Aggression' in characteristically fierce and vivid style. On 23 November 1850 he published an attack on the Anglican bishop of London, the Rev. Charles James Blomfield, for his pro-Tractarian instructions to clergy under his control. Dickens's essay takes the form of a story about Mr and Mrs Bull, representing England. They reprove Master C.J. London (Bishop Blomfield)

> *'Hadn't you had warning for playing about with candles and candlesticks? You were told often enough that [. . .] when they got to candlesticks, they'd get to candles; and when they got to candles, they'd get to lighting 'em; and when they began to put their shirts on outside, and to play at monks and friars, it was as natural that Master Wiseman should be encouraged to put on a pair of red stockings, and a red hat, and to commit I don't know what other Tom-fooleries and make a perfect Guy Fawkes of himself [. . .] Is it because you are a Bull, that you are not to be roused till they shake the scarlet close to your very eyes?'*

This last sentence was very clever, linking 'John Bull' with the cruel bullfights of ultra-Catholic Spain, England's traditional enemy since Elizabethan times, and the scarlet of the bullfighter's cape with the colour of Cardinals' robes.

Mr and Mrs Bull are the English, while what Dickens calls 'the Bulls of Rome', meaning the Catholic Church in general, 'perpetuate misery, oppression, darkness and ignorance'. This can be seen, writes Dickens, in the 'horrible condition' of Mr Bull's Catholic sister, Miss Eringobragh (sic), symbolising Ireland, who 'presented a most lamentable spectacle of disease, dirt, rags, superstition and degradation'.[5]

'The wail of distress and sickness that comes from the roadside, or from the miserable cabins of the interior' (*Illustrated London News*, 4 August 1849)

The most noticeable and numerous Catholics in London were indeed the very poor Irish immigrants. Patrick O'Connor, the Mannings' victim, belonged in contrast to the Irish Catholic middle class. Rumour said that he had obtained his easy and well-paid job in the docks through some influential Protestants who thought he would be able to proselytise among Irish Catholic dockers and turn them away from Rome. The story comes from Robert Huish's imaginative account of the Manning case, but Huish names O'Connor's patrons, among them the Bishop of Llandaff, so the story may well be true. If it is, it might explain why O'Connor obtained his job independently of his own patron, the well-known defender of Catholic causes, the Irish barrister Richard Sheil, Member of Parliament and later Master of the Royal Mint.

It was evictions from their farms and the terrible famine caused by the potato blight of 1846–1847 which brought so many people across the sea from Ireland. By 1841 there were already 74,000 Irish-born people living in London, about 4 per cent of the total population of the city. By 1851, however, the Irish-born population of London was 108,548, still only 4.6 per cent of a much larger total, and a far lower percentage than in some other British cities such as Liverpool or Glasgow. The census, how-ever, recorded only place of birth, and while many Irish-born people might well have been Protestants, or English born in Ireland, there was an increasing number of Catholic Irish who had been born in England. The Irish population of London was thus larger than the figures sug-gested. Furthermore, given the transient and rough-living nature of many Irish labourers' lives, some, particularly 'navvies' away 'on the tramp' in search of work, may have been missed by the enumerators.

The vast majority of Irish were in semi-skilled or unskilled employ-ment. In London, the poor Irish, agricultural labourers back home, worked in the docks and on building sites. Their improvidence, their hard drinking, their slatternly wives and the dirty habits of some of them, encouraged by low-quality housing, with concomitant high death rates, were highly visible, particularly on both sides of the Commercial Road in London's East End. 'The worst quarters of all the large towns are inhabited by Irishmen', wrote Friedrich Engels, the factory owner who subsidised Karl Marx.[6] Many Irish women had no domestic skills at all. They could not work for the needle trades and were not employable in domestic service. Selling fruit from stalls or walking the streets with a heavy basket was a typical Irish woman's occupation. Irish women bought oranges, lemons, walnuts and chestnuts, or greens according to the season, in Covent Garden or Duke's Place market near Aldgate and sold them, as one told the investigative journalist Henry Mayhew, 'for a ha'pinny the three apples which cost a farruthing' either from door to door or in the poorer markets. The profits were, however, very low: five shillings a week at best, from which a room had to be rented. Even the poorest room could hardly cost less than a couple of shillings. One woman whom Mayhew spoke to gathered old walnuts, dried them and used them for fuel. She and her children had no bedspread; just a flock bed in the corner of the room on the floor, with a sheet, blanket and quilt, quite insufficient for the winter. The room had neither chair nor table; just a stool with two pieces of board for a table and a narrow tea-canister to hold a stump of candle. Yet the Irish women were known to be chaste, the adolescent girls were not allowed to frequent the Penny Gaffs and the children were brought up to be pious.[7]

The arrival of immigrants who occupy scarce housing among the native working class, and also work for lower wages, is usually a cause of social tension, which often explodes into violence. It was remarkable that there was so little conflict between Irish and English. Perhaps the Camden Town riot of summer 1846 was the exception to the rule.

On Monday afternoon 9 August 1846, a mile along the railway line out of Euston, where Chalk Farm Road is now, a fight broke out between a large crowd of Irish navvies and the English labourers working inside the gate at the entrance to the building site at the Round House, where the engines were turned round. Shovels, pick-handles and brickbats were freely used as weapons. After an hour the fighting had spread all over the wide extent of railway land at Camden Town. Even large forces of police brought in from local stations were unable to stop the fighting until the equivalent of modern 'snatch squads' managed to seize about twenty men and take them to Albany Street police station. The next day, the leaders of the Irish navvies, John Duggan and David Glory, tried to explain to the magistrate that they had been provoked, that the English labourers swore foully at them and refused to let them on to the building site to work. When the accused appeared at the Old Bailey they had been advised to plead guilty, so no detailed account of the reason for their attack on the building site was ever given.[8]

The large Irish immigration was a source of future strength for the Church, but at the time created serious problems for it, given that in 1840 there were only 26 Catholic churches in the whole of London. Henry Mayhew vividly describes the powerful influence of the priest as he walked from door to door in the Irish streets of London, and the respect in which he was held even by drunken wife-beaters. Archbishop Wiseman strove to meet the religious and social needs of the poor Irish arrivals. In coming years, many more churches, religious houses, fee-charging and charity schools and orphanages would be established.[9]

'England is the only home of the exile – the only safe refuge of the distressed' (*Illustrated London News*, 8 September 1849)

London had always had a small population of foreigners. They lived near Leicester Square, in Soho or, if they were poor, in the slums of St Giles and the East End. There were Italians fleeing from the earlier failure of the *Risorgimento* in the 1820s and 1830s, including the distinguished Giuseppe Mazzini, who arrived in January 1837, returned to Italy in 1848 and sought refuge again in London after the overthrow of the Roman Republic. Poles came to London fleeing the Russian repression of their independence movement in 1831. Another small group were the Liberal Spaniards, who had fled their country when the reactionary Ferdinand VII was restored to his throne by the Duke of Wellington in 1813. They were recalled by Thomas Carlyle in 1851:

> In those years a visible section of the London population [. . .] was
> a small knot of Spaniards who had sought shelter here as political
> refugees [. . .] Six and twenty years ago when I first saw London,
> I remember those Spaniards among the new phenomena. Daily in the
> cold spring air, under skies so unlike their own, you could see a

group of fifty to one hundred stately figures in proud threadbare cloaks
perambulating [. . .] Euston Square and the region about St. Pancras
New Church [. . .][10]

By 1849, however, most of those Spaniards had gone home, but a few, who had become domiciled and found prosperity or academic appointments, remained.

Perhaps the only foreigners, except the Irish who were not really considered such, that Maria and Frederick Manning were likely to see in the streets, were the ubiquitous Italian street entertainers.

The Italian colony in London lived in Hatton Garden, Leather Lane, Saffron Hill and the streets leading northward off Holborn. The area, known as 'Little Italy', was one of dilapidated lodging houses which had probably attracted the Italians because of its closeness to Clerkenwell, where the long-established clock and instrument trades interrelated with the repair of the barrel organs that the Italians played in the streets. St Peter's church was built in 1864 in the heart of the district, in order to protect the Catholic Italians from the missionary campaigns of evangelical Protestants.[11]

The Italians seen in London's streets were mainly organ-grinders or street vendors of plaster statuettes, looking-glasses and picture frames. Among the street entertainers competing for the pennies of passers-by was an Italian man who had dolls which he made dance by a string attached to his knee as he played the pipe and drum.[12] There were other Italian men and boys with dancing dogs and mechanical figures. Organ-grinders, however, were so common that banning or protecting them became a significant point of political difference. Members of the House of Lords, cocooned in their gated estates with long front gardens, could get away from the noise of the streets, so they were tolerant, but the upper middle class of London's more prosperous streets were exasperated in the summer by the endless din of street organs.[13] Italian boys exhibiting white mice aroused pathos, especially since one had been murdered in 1831.[14]

An Italian name, incidentally, had its uses in certain fields, particularly millinery and dressmaking. In Chapter 10 of *Nicholas Nickleby*, Dickens's character Muntle has changed his name and his wife's to Mantalini:

[. . .] the lady rightly considering that an English appellation would be of serious injury to the business.

London sheltered Continental lawyers and military officers of Liberal leanings, or republicans and socialists. London also had a foreign artistic population. The wealth of the city could support a number of French painters, hairdressers, actors, singers and chefs, Italian musicians, and German nursemaids. Greek merchants had settled in Finsbury, Moroccan Jews in Whitechapel, German bakers and Swiss watchmakers in Clerkenwell. The centre of London's foreign district was an island bounded by Soho Square, Leicester Square, Golden Square and Lincoln's Inn Fields. The streets of this area were dreary, with multi-occupied houses. When Charles Dickens placed Ralph Nickleby's office in Golden Square, in the Soho district, he remarked that:

It is a great resort of foreigners [. . .] On a summer's night, windows are thrown open, and groups of swarthy mustachioed men are seen by the passer-by lounging at the casements, and smoking fearfully.[15]

The British attitude to foreigners, while officially tolerant, was notoriously unfriendly and superior. The two Parsee marine engineers, Nowrojee and Merwanjee, who spent a long time studying in London's shipyards, advised theatregoers to avoid the rowdiness of the gallery and pit, and concluded that:

The majority of the lower orders in England are very rude [. . .] towards strangers, whom they do not like to see in their own country.[16]

Political refugees, however, were tolerated, often welcomed and sometimes lionised, especially if they were anti-Catholic, as was the case with the Italians, some of them ex-priests, who arrived after the failed revolutions of 1848–1849.[17] Louis Kossuth, the Hungarian revolutionary against Austrian domination, reached London in 1851, to be acclaimed at a public reception in the Guildhall, while in contrast the Austrian General Baron Julius Haynau, who had ordered the flogging of women revolutionaries, was chased out of Barclay and Perkins' brewery on Bankside in September 1850 by draymen flourishing their cart whips and mispronouncing his name as 'Hyena'. Those years saw the arrival in London of Karl Marx, of the French socialist Louis Blanc, French ex-minister Ledru-Rollin, the Russian intellectual Alexander Herzen, the Italian revolutionary Orsini, and of Mazzini, ex-King Louis Philippe, and Louis Napoleon, soon to be President and then Emperor of France.

Land of freedom

The restrictions on immigrants entering Britain, which had begun in 1793 with the Napoleonic Wars, came to a delayed end in 1826. From 1826 onwards, until the Aliens Act of 1905, nobody was refused entry or expelled from Britain on political grounds.

The 1851 census revealed that there were 50,289 foreigners in England and Wales, though in London there were 25,500 out of the total population of 2,362,000, a percentage of only 1.08. The percentage was really even smaller, because many foreigners, particularly seamen, were here only on the date the census was taken.

British foreign policy under Lord Palmerston, Foreign Secretary from 1846 to 1851, was largely pragmatic. The main intention was to avoid major European war. The 1848 revolutions in Paris, Berlin, Vienna, Budapest, Prague, Milan, Venice, Naples and Rome created a potentially explosive situation. However, the French Republican regime of 1848, which replaced King Louis Philippe, assured London that it envisaged no changes to the international settlement of 1815. The suppression by Austria of revolution in Piedmont restored the status quo. When the Hungarian aristocracy rose against Austro-Hungary, Palmerston approved of Russian intervention to crush the revolt. Only after the situation had returned to what it had been did Palmerston protest against Russian and Austrian severity. He lectured Continental autocrats about their tyranny but believed in maintaining the international balance of power undisturbed.

In 1848 Chancellor Metternich of Austria arrived in London hurriedly, as did ex-King Louis Philippe, under the alias of 'Mr Smith'. For safe, self-confident England, of course, what these excitable for-eigners got up to was rather funny. *Punch* caught the mood. On 25 March 1848 it published a poem by Thackeray about the fleeing French monarch, who was reputed to have arrived with only the clothes he stood up in:

A veteran gent, just stepped out of a boat, In a tattered old hat and a ragged pea-coat [. . .][18]

The poet suggested that Louis-Philippe should be advised to get himself immediately outfitted at E. Moses and Son.

Revolutions on the Continent were seen as the usual state of things, so much so that, in its *Almanack* for 1849, *Punch* suggested that:

If any complaint is made [about overstaying leave of absence from work] you have a capital excuse, by declaring that you were stopt (sic) by a revolution on the Continent.

In 1848, perhaps as many as 7,000 French, Austrian, Polish, Hungarian, Italian and German refugees entered the country. The largest individual numbers were Germans, Poles, French and Hungarians fleeing from the Austrian and Russian suppression of their revolutions.[19] An echo of today is heard in the complaint from the Channel port of Dover to the Home Secretary on 18 July 1849 when a shipload of refugees applied for relief, which had caused '[. . .] a great burthen on the rates of the town'.[20]

Most of the fugitives lived in financial straits, earning their living by teaching languages or music. For most of them London was dirty, cold and unwelcoming. They were overcharged for rent and swindled by dishonest money-changers. Many had no employment and, though in general law-abiding, some went in for petty crime. The important political exiles usually had enough money and friends to live in modest comfort. One rotten apple, such as the swindler who called himself 'Colonel Count Sarcie Dumbicki', who begged money as a political refugee and lived in high style between spells in gaol in 1849 and 1850, led people to consider all refugees to be scroungers. Foreign refugees were associated with immorality, atheism and not paying their rent.[21] Perhaps this was because they were frequently bearded, or perhaps beards were associated with immorality because foreigners wore them.

Their nightly gatherings in London 'cafés' – a new word – were seen by the journalist George Augustus Sala as exotic:

[. . .] rings of fantastic fashion, marvellous gestures, Babel-like tongues [. . .] the smoke as of a thousand brick-kilns; the clatter as of a thousand spoons.[22]

Refugees, dressed in what was, in English eyes, outlandish and picturesque style, met in political clubs, smoky rooms over a Soho café or perhaps in a hired schoolroom where they heard a lecture, had a discussion and often a row over principles, personalities or money. Whatever information came to the ears of the authorities about foreigners' activities would have underlined that they were intensely schismatic. Karl Marx, who was in London, could not even get his 'Universal League of Revolutionary Communists' off the drawing board.

Foreign governments of course protested about the tolerance shown to revolutionaries in England, but lordly British conceit led public opinion to take a superior view towards these fears. Let other regimes govern properly and they would have nothing to fear. The foreigners should behave themselves here in England, of course, but State interference was so disliked that spying on them was thought to be intolerable. Britain's lack of centralised and expensive State police machinery and snoopers in comparison with Continental Europe was a favourite subject for self-congratulation. Austrian Government agents, in particular, were suspected of watching the refugees, so much so that Jane Carlyle wrote that a particularly nosey servant whom she caught reading the family letters was like 'an Austrian spy'.[23]

Chartists

In England, people feared the ideals of the French Revolution. Some even thought that advocating democracy and the mass franchise was treasonable, while many were out of sympathy with the revolutionary despair of the Luddites, who destroyed factory machines because they threw men out of work. Charles Dickens, who for all his liberal sentiments feared the mob and scorned demagoguery, had published *Barnaby Rudge* in 1841. This novel described the London mob raging and pillaging in 1780, a time still in the common memory. In particular, the fifteen years after Waterloo had seen an epoch of extreme reaction in England, typified by the 'Peterloo massacre' of 1819 when troops ran down a protesting Manchester crowd.

The Mannings had grown up, however, in the midst of a drive for progress. They had seen parliamentary reform, the struggle for the right to join trade unions, Factory Acts to protect workers, agitation against the harshness of the Poor Law, the growth of secularism, the struggle for a tax-free press, the Anti-Corn Law League and the anti-slavery movement. It was not surprising that these reforms and movements of the 1830s and 1840s led to demands for even greater changes. Socialism, the extension of the right to vote, greater protection for workers, and many more issues were in the air, especially in the 1840s, called the 'Hungry Forties', most of which had been years of economic depression, unemployment, bad harvests and now, in 1849, cholera.

'Slowly comes a hungry people, as a lion creeping nigher,' wrote Tennyson in 1842 in *Locksley Hall*. The Chartist movement, so-called because it advocated the *People's Charter*, was a sustained working-class movement. Its demands for all men to have the right to vote, the secret ballot, pay for Members of Parliament to allow men without private means to be elected, equal-sized electoral districts and annual Parliaments, were rejected by the Home Office in 1839, 1842 and 1848.

Chartism was not a focused movement. It consisted of a variety of radical groups presenting a range of grievances, including men whose skills had been made redundant by machines, others on short time, pro-testers against the iniquities of the Poor Law, as well as middle-class members campaigning to remove the property qualification for MPs.

The poor harvests of 1846 and 1847, the bad winter that followed with its toll of deaths from influenza, bronchitis, pneumonia, measles and typhus, and the examples of the fall of the French monarchy, the humi-liation of Metternich, forced to escape Vienna in a laundry basket, the Hungarian uprising and the other rebellions on the Continent, all encour-aged the advocates of the Charter to try again.

In February 1848 it was learned that a republic was imminent in France. The audience in the pit and the gallery at Sadler's Wells sang 'La Marseillaise', still a revolutionary rather than a national anthem. On 6 March 1848, a meeting of middle-class people in Trafalgar Square, called to protest about the income tax, was taken over by Chartists chaired by G.W.M. Reynolds, taking valuable time from his weekly several thousand words for the *Mysteries of London*. Since Parliament was sitting, the assembly of 10,000 people was told by the police that it was illegal. Refusing to disperse, the acompanying mob tore down the palings around the still incomplete Nelson's Column. Shouts of '*Vive la République!*' were heard, coming either from Frenchmen or from Englishmen pretend-ing to know how to shout the fashionable slogan. Police dispersed the crowd with some difficulty. Later that evening, a mob smashed street lamps and windows, and looted shops. The Queen and the Government were alarmed. Would London be another Paris or Vienna?

The authorities were preoccupied by the fear that foreign revolutionaries might make common cause with home-grown ones. Despite their small number, the concentration and high visibility of foreigners made people think they were many. 'We need only walk from Temple Bar to Charing Cross [about three-quarters of a mile along a major thoroughfare of London] to satisfy ourselves that London contains an unusual number of citizens from a powerful military republic within sight of these shores,' wrote *The Times* coyly on 12 April 1848. Did this mean that the few thousand Frenchmen here were the vanguard of an invasion? It had been feared that the French were here to teach Londoners how to revolt. Apprehension that foreigners would cooperate with native revolutionaries led to the Aliens Act of 1848, which allowed deportation. In the event, it was not found necessary to deport anyone and so the fears of an influx of bearded revolutionaries that were expressed by the Commissioner of the Metropolitan Police, Sir Richard Mayne, as the Great Exhibition of 1851 approached, were shared neither by the Foreign nor the Home Office. It had been feared that foreigners would play a leading part in the Chartist demonstration on 10 April. They did not, as *The Times* congratulated itself on 15 April. This was probably fortunate, as police constables had orders to beat up bewhiskered rioters in particular.[24]

The mass demonstration was to be followed by a march from Kennington to Westminster and then by the presentation of an immense petition to Parliament. The plan was that if the Commons rejected the petition, the meeting would elect a National Assembly and call on the Queen to dissolve Parliament. The assembly would remain in permanent session until the Government agreed to accept the Charter. Alarm ran through the London middle class. Was the capital about to experience the revolution that so many Continental cities had seen?

The Mannings' political opinions did not come up at their trial, but Maria probably shared the conservative views of the aristocratic ladies she had served, while Frederick Manning, as tenant of a house worth over £10 a year, had the right to vote. As a churchgoer and a one-time pub landlord, a cut above his rowdy customers, he might be supposed to take a rather hostile attitude to reform movements.

Waterloo Station was cordoned off for hours by troops while Queen Victoria left for the Isle of Wight. But if the military were called on to fire on revolutionaries advancing on Parliament, would they obey their orders, or would they fire over people's heads? It was feared that the revolutionaries might board a warship in Portsmouth, sail it into the Solent and fire on the Queen's place of refuge, Osborne House. The Duke of Wellington, victor of Waterloo, was appointed to oversee the capital's defence. Close to 150,000 special constables were sworn in and 1,500 Chelsea Pensioners were brought out of retirement to put their old soldiers' training to work. Government offices, the General Post Office, the British Museum, Somerset House, Buckingham Palace, the Customs House, Guildhall and the Bank of England were barricaded with sandbags and provided with loopholes and the occasional cannon, while students at King's and University Colleges were armed with staves.

The Chartist convention assembled as planned in John Street, just north of Gray's Inn. They marched down Gray's Inn Road, then along Holborn to Farringdon Street, and over Blackfriars Bridge to Kennington. Another group marched from Stepney Green and another from Russell Square.[25]

In all, about 150,000 people attended the demonstration, far fewer than the up to half a million hopefully forecast by the Chartists themselves.[26] Their leaders decided not to resist when the police refused them permission to cross Westminster Bridge. The petition, reputedly containing 5 million signatures, bore just under 2 million, but many were forgeries or facetious, such as 'Queen Victoria', 'Old Cheese' and 'Punch'. It was taken to the Commons in cabs over Blackfriars Bridge and by the back streets to Westminster, but once again rejected.

The Chartist movement was not violent. The 8,500 troops which had been put on alert were not called in; the 4,000 police remained unarmed. Neither Bronterre O'Brien nor Feargus O'Connor, the Chartist leaders, wanted to risk the consequences of violence. In the spring rain O'Connor shook hands with the Commissioner of Police and by early afternoon the great day was over.

Nevertheless, there was still life in the revolutionary movement. On 29 May 1848, 80,000 people marched silently through the city. On 4 June the Home Office ordered the police to disperse meetings of Chartists in the East End. A day of protest was planned for 12 June, prevented by the arrest of the London Chartist leaders. An uprising was planned for 15 August 1848. Its leadership, penetrated by agents, was arrested by armed police at the Orange Tree pub in Orange Street, off the Haymarket. They had a few rusty pikes and swords. There nearly was a barricade in the Continental style when a man was seen to prise a cobblestone from the road in the semi-criminal district of the Seven Dials, but the police warned off the participants.[27] About a thousand Chartists who used violence were arrested and given long prison sentences.

The Prime Minister announced in the Commons on 3 July 1849 that he could not support the adoption of the Chartist demands, given 'the state of France and the results congruent upon universal suffrage there'. It was obvious that the aims of the Chartists would not be achieved by purely working-class agitation. Middle-class supporters were, however, rare. Conservative-minded citizens in the 1840s feared the paraphernalia of Continental-style revolution, the Phrygian cap stuck on a pole and waved beneath the windows of magistrates and manufacturers, anti-clericalism, violent rhetoric at torchlit meetings, marches, banners and shouted slogans. In any case, London's population was too large to be efficiently organised. Its complicated social structure and the large numbers of working-class occupations meant that no sustained single effort would be able to concentrate on a particular end. London's great size (it was twice the extent of Paris), its inertia and its efficient police contrasted with the provocative use of troops elsewhere. London was not ripe for revolution.

As it collapsed, however, Chartism left in its wake over a hundred working men's clubs.[28] More importantly perhaps, the radical tailor Francis Place called a meeting on 29 January 1849 to form the National Association for Parliamentary and Financial Reform. His aim was to try to unite radicals and moderate Chartists. The Association proposed a 'Little Charter', demanding the suffrage for all male householders, the secret ballot, Parliamentary elections every three years and more equal distribution of seats. But the impossibility at the time of combining a working-class with a middle-class movement led to the Association's dissolution in 1855. Its leader, the Chartist Bronterre O'Brien, went on to form the National Reform League, which would meet at 18 Denmark Street, Soho, for another 24 years. A crowded meeting on 16 March 1850 demanded the humane reform of the Poor Law, purchase of land by the Government to occupy the unemployed, and sweeping nationalisation. Land should not be exclusively owned by individuals; there should be a national credit system and shops to sell essential items at cost price.

English reform would, however, move in the direction of trade unions rather than revolutionary movements. Once again, the Mannings lived just before a new phenomenon: the appearance of skilled workers' unions in the modern sense, concerned with protecting their sectional interests. The Amalgamated Society of Engineers was formed in 1851. Its members paid the quite high membership fee – only possible for skilled men in regular employment – of one shilling per week, while the Union had salaried officials and a London headquarters.[29]

Ol' Clo'!

The Irish were the largest identifiable minority in London. All the Continental refugees, if counted together, probably constituted the next largest group of outsiders. The third group were London's Jews, totalling about 20,000 out of about 35,000 who lived in the country as a whole.

If Frederick had ever met a Jew it would have been a pedlar in Taunton, or one who was travelling on a train where Frederick was a guard. A shabbily dressed Jewish man might have offered Maria a price for some of her mistresses' old clothes. In parts of London which were better-off than Bermondsey, bearded Jews with sacks on their shoulders and wearing several hats on their heads to keep their shape, might be seen tramping the streets crying 'Ol' Clo'!'. They bought used and unwanted clothing, which was later cleaned, altered and resold, until the spread of firms such as the also Jewish E. Moses and Sons enabled ordinary people to buy new clothes rather than wear others' cast-offs.

Most Jews in London were English-born, though Henry Mayhew describes a Moroccan Jewish street vendor of rhubarb and spices, who had come to England via Gibraltar and Lisbon. This man used to be a pedlar roaming all over England. He used to stay in a lodging house for Jews in Taunton.[30] Who knows if Frederick had not see him there? Yet, though most Jews were native-born, they were seen as a foreign element, not really because of their religion, which concerned hardly anybody save the well-meaning but resented groups which had appointed themselves to try to convert Jews to Christianity, but more because of what was considered their clannishness. Consequently, though most 'sweaters', for example, were not Jews, Charles Kingsley's pamphlet 'Cheap Clothes and Nasty', describing the starvation earnings of the sweaters' victims, indulges in an anti-Jewish diatribe. In *Oliver Twist*, Charles Dickens depicts the Jew Fagin, who keeps a team of boys at work stealing, because there were such people earning their livings as fences of stolen goods, though whether Jews ever ran schools for pickpockets is doubtful. Dickens never suggests that Fagin's criminality is religiously or racially determined. Indeed, Fagin is kind to Oliver and hardly as nasty as Mr Bumble, the parish beadle. Nor is Fagin a violent murderer like Bill Sikes. This was the upshot of Dickens's reply to a protest about Fagin which he received from a Jewish correspondent, but to redress the balance he introduced a group of Jews into *Our Mutual Friend*, one of whom is the gentle Mr Riah, who is in the harsh hands of a Gentile moneylender. Certainly there is no proof that Jewish moneylenders were more usurious than their non-Jewish counterparts. Charles Reade indicated thus in his novel of 1856, *It's Never too Late to Mend*, where Isaac Levi is clever and good. He forgives his enemy at the end of the novel when the latter begs his pardon. Levi is portrayed as a mysterious, dignified, Oriental Jew as opposed to the ubiquitous, humble old clothes man that people saw in London. Most London Jews in fact were rather poor; some very much so. One-third of the capital's 20,000 Jews were receiving poor relief at the end of the 1840s.[31]

Down the Lane

Living in Houndsditch, the Minories and Aldgate, Jews roamed over the City hawking walking sticks, jewellery and 'fancy goods' such as pencils, sealing-wax, penknives and razors, though the coming of the railway had put an end to their market among travellers leaving by coach from La Belle Sauvage on Ludgate Hill or the Saracen's Head on Snow Hill. In Duke's Place, near Aldgate, they had run the orange, lemon and nut market until they were undercut by the Irish. There were 'superior' retail Jewish fruiterers in Covent Garden, Cheapside and the West End. Mayhew describes Jewish fried-fish vendors whose product was more expensive but had a better flavour because the Jews used salad oil rather than linseed and dipped the fish in egg.[32]

'Down the Lane', that is in Middlesex Street, known as Petticoat Lane, and in the streets leading off it, wrote the investigative journalist Henry Mayhew:

> *Gowns of every shade and every pattern are hanging up, but none,*
> *perhaps, look either bright or white; it is a vista of dinginess, but*
> *many-coloured dinginess as regards female attire. Dress coats, frock*
> *coats, great coats, livery and gamekeepers' coats, paletots, tunics,*
> *trousers, knee-breeches, waistcoats, capes, pilot coats, working jackets,*
> *plaids, hats, dressing-gowns, shirts, Guernsey frocks, [. . .] present a*
> *scene which cannot be beheld in any other part of the greatest city*
> *of the world [. . .].*[33]

On a winter's night, with flaring gaslights, a multiplicity of shadows was cast over the Lane, causing the clothes swinging in the wind to assume ghostly forms and, 'if the wind be high, make them, as they are blown to and fro, look more mysterious still'.[34] Boys and women pushed their way through the teeming crowd with trays of sweetmeats, ginger beer, lemonade, fried fish, sponge cakes, dates, figs and coconuts. Mayhew considered that the Jews of 'the Lane' gave the best value, as did those who bought old clothes at people's doors. Mayhew writes that the Jewish old-clothes men were good husbands and fathers. The Jewish girls were 'pert and ignorant' but chaste.[35]

Most opposition to giving Jews the civil rights that Nonconformists and Catholics had received was based on the view that to excuse Jews who were elected to Parliament, for instance, from swearing the oath '[. . .] on the true faith of a Christian' was tantamount to removing the Christian basis of English life. One did not hear fears expressed, as on the Continent, of the mysterious powers of the Jews, that they were both extremely rich and, contradictorily, planning to overthrow bourgeois society at the same time. References to Jews were often joking, contemptuous even, but not vicious, and rarely reasoned. Does Mr Caudle, for instance, in Douglas Jerrold's *Mrs. Caudle's Curtain Lectures*, object to having Lazarus Goldman as a godfather for the latest addition to his family because Goldman is 'a usurer and a hunks' (slang for a miser) rather than for the reason – which would surely have been valid in this case – that Goldman must have been Jewish? Actually, says Mrs Caudle, it's a good thing that there are some people who save their money, considering that others (she would glance meaningfully at her husband if they were not in bed in the dark) would spend it foolishly. As for the Christian name, since it was apparently the custom to give the child the godparent's name, she concedes that Lazarus is not a genteel name but, after all, says she, the little boy can always change it to Laurence later.[36]

Until 1832 Jews were not allowed to engage in retail trade in the City of London. Until 1835 they might be challenged to swear an oath 'on the true faith of a Christian' if they tried to vote at local elections. Nevertheless, by the late 1830s prominent Jews in the City had held the office of Sheriff. Yet at the time of the Manning murder, Lionel de Rothschild, repeatedly elected MP for the City, was being refused permission time after time to take his seat, because he would not take the oath. Sir David Salamons, elected for Greenwich and later the first Jewish Lord Mayor of London, was expelled after taking his seat, because he had not sworn the oath in the form prescribed. While the House of Commons had voted annually to alter the oath, the Lords had not consented. On 14 July 1849 *Punch* sneered at the Lords in a cartoon showing the peers jumping on the benches and holding the skirts of their robes away from creepy-crawlies labelled *Jewish Disabilities Bill*. Finally, in 1858, a compromise was reached: each House would determine its own form of the oath. Jewish Members at last took their seats in the Commons, but not in the Lords until a Rothschild was granted a peerage in 1885.

Notes

1 Altick, R., *The English Common Reader: a Social History of the Mass Reading Public 1800–1900* (Chicago: University of Chicago Press, 1957), p. 116.

2 Hoppen, K.T., *The Mid-Victorian Generation 1846–1886* (Oxford: Oxford University Press, 1998), p. 445.

3 Lytton Strachey's essay on Cardinal Manning in his *Eminent Victorians* (first published 1918) is vivid on this.

4 Quoted in Hoppen, K.T., *The Mid-Victorian Generation 1846–1886* (Oxford: Oxford University Press, 1998), p. 145.

5 Dickens, C., *Dickens's Journalism*, ed. M. Slater, 4 volumes (London: Dent, 1996), vol. 2 'The Amusements of the People and Other Papers 1834–1851', pp. 297–305.

6 Engels, F. *The Condition of the Working Class in England*, eds W. Henderson and W. Challoner (Oxford: Oxford University Press, 1958), p. 123. See also Swift, R. and Gilley, S., *The Irish in Britain 1815–1939* (London: Pinter, 1989).

7 Mayhew, H., *Life and Labour of the London Poor*, 3 volumes, first published 1851 (London: Charles Griffin & Co., 1861–1862), vol. 1, pp. 108 and ff.

8 Thomson, D., *In Camden Town* (1983), quoted in Wilson, A.N. (ed.) *The Faber Book of London* (London: Faber & Faber, 1993), pp. 290–3.

9 See Jackson, J., 'The Irish in London' (London University MA thesis, 1958).

10 Carlyle, T., *Collected Works* (London: Chapman & Hall, 1857), vol. 1, p. 67.

11 Sponza, L., *Italian Immigrants in Nineteenth Century Britain: Realities and Images* (Leicester: Leicester University Press, 1988), pp. 21–2.

12 Ibid., p. 62.

13 See Sala, G.A., *Twice Round the Clock*, first published in 1859 (Leicester: Leicester University Press, 1971), pp. 106–7. It had first appeared as essays in magazines in the 1840s. See also Sponza, L., *Italian Immigrants in Nineteenth Century Britain: Realities and Images* (Leicester: Leicester University Press, 1988), Chapters 5 and 6.

14 Altick, R., *The Presence of the Present: Topics of the Day in the Victorian Novel* (Columbus: Ohio State University Press, 1991), pp. 527–8.

15 Dickens, C., *Nicholas Nickleby* (1838–1839), Chapter 2.

16 Nowrojee, J. and Merwangee, H., *Journal of a Residence of Two Years and a half in Great Britain* (London: W.H. Allen, 1841), p. 110.

17 Sponza, L., *Italian Immigrants in Nineteenth Century Britain: Realities and Images* (Leicester: Leicester University Press, 1988), p. 133. My thanks to Professor Sponza for guiding me around London's 'Little Italy'.

18 'Mr Smith and Moses', *Punch*, 25 March 1838 and the *Oxford Thackeray* (1908), vol. 7, pp. 199–201. My thanks to Donald Hawes for this last reference.

19 Porter, R., *London: a Social History* (Harmondsworth: Penguin, 1996), p. 16.

20 Quoted in Porter, B., *The Refugee Question in Mid-Victorian Politics* (Cambridge: Cambridge University Press, 1979), p. 42.

21 Ibid., p. 765.

22 Quoted in ibid., p. 25.

23 Holme, T., *The Carlyles at Home*, first published 1965 (London: Persephone Books, 2002), p. 83.

24 Porter, B., *The Refugee Question in Mid-Victorian Politics* (Cambridge: Cambridge University Press, 1979), p. 92, quoting from a private diary.

25 Wilson, A.N., *The Victorians* (London: Hutchinson, 2002), p. 118.

26 Goodway, D., *London Chartism 1838–1840* (Cambridge: Cambridge University Press, 1982), p. 72.

27 Royle, E., *Chartism* (Harlow: Longman, 1980 and 1986), Document 36.

28 Seaman, L.C.B., *Life in Victorian London* (London: Batsford, 1973), p. 44.

29 Sheppard, F., *London 1808–1870: The Infernal Wen* (Berkeley: University of California Press, 1971), p. 332.

30 Quennell, P. (ed.) *Mayhew's Characters* (London: Spring Books, 1967), pp. 139–45.

31 Finestein, I., *Anglo-Jewry in Changing Times* (London:Vallentine, Mitchell, 1999), p. 31.

32 Mayhew, H., *The Morning Chronicle Survey of Labour and the Poor: the Metropolitan Districts* (Horsham: Caliban Press, 1982), vol. 2, p. 112.

33 Ibid., p. 44.

34 Ibid., p. 45.

35 Ibid., p. 135.

36 Jerrold, D., *Mrs. Caudle's Curtain Lectures* (P. Harvill, 1974), p. 64.

CHAPTER 9

· · · · · · · · · · · · · · ·

Communications

Cab!

You cannot conceive, if 'tis not pointed out,
How quickly in London you travel about [. . .]
So I'll tell you, all fabulous narratives scorning,
The various places we saw in one morning.

So wrote a young lady in 1842 to her friend living in the country.[1]
The really fast method of getting around London, the Metropolitan underground railway, the first in the world, would not draw crowds into its smoky tunnels and stations for another twenty-one years. The Mannings, had they escaped the hangman, would have seen the Metropolitan platforms at Baker Street. Now imaginatively rebuilt and with much of the advertising excrescence stripped away, they eerily resemble the newspaper illustrations of them in the 1860s.

The only way the young lady could travel so fast around London was by cab. The rich could buy or hire broughams, barouches and phaetons, listed in order of stylishness, but when others needed urgent transport they had to make do with a hansom cab, named after Joseph Aloysius Hansom, who had patented his vehicle in 1834. The hansom kept out bad weather and allowed the passenger to speak to the driver through a trap in the roof. It was a cut above the cabriolet, with its two wheels and an uncomfortable ledge for the driver alongside the passengers. The hansom was better also than the old-style hackney coach. This was usually a shabby and lumbering carriage, which had once belonged to a noble family. Now it had dirty straw on the floor and was driven by a foul-mouthed and well-wrapped up Jehu, as the driver was known from the furiously driving scriptural character.[2] Young Pip, in Chapter 20 of Charles Dickens's *Great Expectations*, arrives from Kent at the Cross Keys coaching inn in Cheapside and takes a hackney to Mr Jaggers's office near Smithfield:

> [. . .] *a hackney-coachman, who seemed to have as many capes to his greasy great-coat as he was years old, packed me up in his coach [. . .] His getting on his box, which I remember to have been decorated with an old weather-stained pea-green [. . .] cloth, moth-eaten into rags, was quite a work of time. It was a wonderful equipage, with six great coronets outside, and ragged things behind for I don't know how many footmen to hold on by, and a harrow behind them to prevent amateur footmen from yielding to the temptation. I had scarcely had time to enjoy the coach and to think how like a straw-yard it was, and yet how like a rag-shop [. . .] when I observed the coachman beginning to get down [. . .]*

The fare was a shilling, quite substantial, although the carriage could take four people. In Pip's case the coachman does not dare to demand any more, confessing that he does not want any trouble from the lawyer Jaggers, who would know that the correct fare was indeed one shilling for the first mile and then six pence per half mile or less. The hackney could also be hired by the clock. A shilling would buy thirty minutes, which suggests that the full mile in London would take half an hour. Hackneys had to have a licence plate issued by the Excise Office at Somerset House so that annoyed passengers would know who to complain about.

If you wanted to go further afield, there were short-stage coaches which were not allowed to infringe the monopoly of the London cabs by plying for hire in the central streets. The short-stages would take excursionists or prosperous City men out to semi-rural suburbs such as Paddington, Clapham, Clapton, Hammersmith, and as far as Richmond-on-Thames.

Really wealthy people, who needed to get around London comfortably and in style, such as distinguished physicians, could hire a complete equipage and driver for £2 a day or, if they intended to use it every day, they could commute the cost for £300 a year. A very comfortable arrangement for those who liked to get out of town at the weekend was to arrange to have a coach and driver at their disposal every Sunday for £60 a year. Of course, here we are talking of the seriously well-off, with incomes of perhaps £1,500 a year.

Hurry along there, please!

Since 4 July 1829, however, getting around London had been revolu-
tionised by the omnibus, very soon known and spelled as 'the buss' with
two s's. George Shillibeer, who took the name from the French and Latin
voiture omnibus or 'carriage for all', which was already on the streets of
Paris, started a route which went from the Yorkshire Stingo pub, which
was quite near where its namesake stands today next to the Edgware
Road Underground station, to the Bank of England along the New Road
(today's Marylebone and Euston Roads). The fare was high, probably
because the omnibus used three horses. It cost one shilling to go all the
way, but if you wanted to go only as far as Islington it cost sixpence. It
was at the start of this route that 'Pretty Little Polly Perkins of Paddington
Green' lived, in Harry Clifton's song, published in 1863. Polly Perkins was
'as proud as a queen' and turned down the simple milkman, who loved
her, in the unreal hope of ensnaring a baron or a viscount. In the end,
however, she had to settle for 'the bow-legged conductor of a twopenny
bus'. Fares had gone down by the time Clifton composed 'Polly Perkins',
but London's bus conductors have always stood bow-legged while the
bus stops, starts and jerks along the city's often ill-surfaced streets.

At the beginning, Shillibeer ran five daily services each way. His route
was outside the area of the cab monopoly, so he could pick up and
set down his passengers anywhere. There were no regular stops and no
regulation to prevent the driver turning his horses in response to a
summons from the other side of the road.

Cabbies' noses were put out of joint when omnibuses were allowed
into the centre of London in 1832 and when the tax on them, originally
the same as that paid by cabs, was reduced. Shillibeer now ran his
omnibuses through profitable Oxford Street instead of along the heavily
competitive New Road. Fares halved; it now cost sixpence 'all the way'
or threepence to travel halfway along the route.

Buses did not start until well after 8 a.m. so they were of no use and
in any case far too expensive for labouring men who had to be on the spot
at 6 in the morning for whatever work was going. The first journey of
the day from Paddington carried prosperous clerks to their offices; the
second their employers, who appeared at their desks round about ten
o'clock. Later, ladies took the omnibus to go shopping.

Buses were for chief clerks who had reached the heights of £150 a year, up the scale as far as senior officials on £600. These latter were men who did not have to be at their desks until late or give an account to anybody if the bus made them late for work, unlike Bob Cratchit in *A Christmas Carol* who had to run all the way from Camden Town to the City where Mr Scrooge was waiting with his watch in his hand. Running was quicker than the bus, which Cratchit did not earn enough to take in any case.

The *omnibus*, whose Latin name brought back memories of school-days to the gentlemen who used it, encouraged the quotation of Latin tags heavy-handedly playing on the two meanings of the word ('for everyone' and 'the bus'). Two of the best known were '*Impendet omnibus periculum*' or 'Danger hangs over all of us' and '*Mors omnibus est communis*' or 'Death is common to all of us.'[3] The joke went on into the twentieth century: 'What is it that roarest thus? Can it be a motor bus?' A.D. Godley continued by declining 'motor bus' in its various Latin cases, concluding with the heartfelt appeal:

> *Domine, defende nos*
> *Contra hos motores Bos!*[4]

Although the Latin word *omnibus* means 'for all', the bus was not only expensive but also slow. So, though Maria Manning must have been in a hurry to get to Patrick O'Connor's lodgings in Mile End to take his money and shares after murdering him, she probably walked the two miles rather than wait for a bus coming from Deptford, which would then have had to negotiate the blocked traffic over London Bridge. Next she would have had to wait for another going east through Aldgate and Whitechapel towards Mile End. And in Chapter 1 of Wilkie Collins's *The Woman in White*, Walter Hartwright, as a matter of course, walks three miles uphill from Clement's Inn in the Strand to see his mother and sister who live in Hampstead.

The 3,000 omnibuses, able to carry 22 passengers each, which were negotiating the narrow and crowded streets of central London by 1850, were seen as the up-to-date mode of travel. Their routes as yet unnumbered, the vehicles were painted in different colours, red, green or blue, according to their companies, Paragon, Atlas, Waterloo, Camberwell and many others, some running only two or three vehicles. They were rectangular boxes, with windows at the sides and a door with a window at the back. Though they were upholstered with bright scarlet or green plush velvet cushions, the crews had to put down straw, which soon became dirty, in order to try to absorb the mud that passengers brought in with them.

Working on the buses was a hard job. Driver and conductor were exposed to the weather. They were harshly treated by the omnibus owners. The crews worked every day, with only two hours off every alternate Sunday. They had to start early and get the omnibus and its horses ready to be out on the road by half past eight. Often they could not go home until after eleven at night. The long day was broken up by a number of intervals, but none long enough for having a proper meal. Conductors could be sacked without notice. Drivers, who were not so easily replaceable, had to keep to the timetable or be fined. Nevertheless, like their equivalents a century later, the conductors were often in high spirits, singing out 'Hurry along there, please!' and banging on the floor to signal the driver to move off.

Passengers tugged a strap, running above their heads and fixed to the driver's arm, when they wanted him to stop. There were no fixed stops but at certain places drivers were in the habit of delaying for a long time, to the irritation of passengers, in order to fill their buses.

The financial arrangements at first required the conductor to pay a certain amount over to the owner. The conductor or 'cad' (perhaps because he 'cadged' passengers) shared what was left over with the driver. Later the conductor handed in all his takings and received a wage, augmented by commission. There were no tickets, so owners could not check on their conductors' honesty. The conductors had to be careful, however, because the owners used what they called 'respectables' or 'lady-likes', who were women, sometimes for better cover accompanied by children, who estimated the number of passengers carried for 6d and 3d. This must have been one of the first middle-class women's professions. Nevertheless, the 'respectables' could be bribed if the conductor spotted them, or even handed off the bus straight into puddles or a pile of dung. Conversely, owners could sack conductors on mere suspicion of pocketing the fares. The 24s per week wage that the best routes paid – drivers could get up to 34s – was not one which could easily be found elsewhere.

Some drivers were well-known characters who sported a white top-hat, a rose in their buttonhole and a cigar given to them by their favourite passengers who expected to have the seat next to the driver reserved for them as they drove down, say, from Highgate to the City. These passengers, fantasising perhaps that they were like Regency bucks posting down to Brighton in the old days, would show off by tipping the driver generously.

Ladies travelled 'inside'. They could not ride 'outside' ('inside' and 'outside' were the terms used until recently by London bus conductors) because it would mean climbing the iron rungs up the back of the vehicle, immodestly exposing their ankles to loiterers in the street. Later, stairs which were easier to climb were built to reach the clerestory or 'knifeboard' upper deck, where one sat facing outwards against a back-board and rested one's feet against destination boards which also served to protect the modesty of the occasional woman who preferred the fresh air 'outside' to the stuffiness, dirty straw and excessive proximity of people 'inside'. Nevertheless, the wide skirts and especially the crino-lines of the 1850s made it hard to climb the stairs and indeed to get inside the narrow bus itself.

There were soon many complaints to the authorities about conductors' rudeness. The rows usually happened when the passengers got off the omnibus. People tried to get away without paying while others were irritatingly slow to extract their money from their pockets or purses. Conductors, especially if they were on commission, wanted as many pas-sengers as possible but sometimes ran short of change or were stubborn about providing it. One of Dickens's *Sketches by Boz* describes a con-ductor, pictured standing on a step at the left of the door holding on to a strap for safety, who went in for pulling hesitating elderly gentlemen into his bus even if they were not sure they wanted to travel in it. On 30 June, 1849 the clerk at the Mansion House court reported that more than 4,000 summonses had been issued in the previous year to bus conductors for rudeness and even for manhandling passengers.[5] The 'cads' were fined so often that they got together and collected a fund. Things got so bad that one irritated magistrate sent a bus conductor to prison for two months for deliberately delaying his bus in order to collect more passengers and then for refusing to give change. 1849 seems to have been a bad year for bus passengers. *Punch* was running a campaign against the behaviour of the conductors. In one case, where there was a notice on the bus saying that the fare was sixpence 'ALL THE WAY' but only 3d TO CHARING CROSS, an argument arose about whether the conductor deliberately stood in front of the words 'TO CHARING CROSS' in order to attract customers to what they thought was a cut-price service. In another case, there had been an argument about exactly which point constituted the location of Charing Cross. Still, if bus conductors were offensive, *Punch* published a letter on 13 January 1849 (perhaps it was a spoof) from a conductor complaining about old ladies who took ages to extract three pennies from their purses.

Omnibuses could be extraordinarily convenient as Thackeray's eponymous hero Pendennis found in Chapter 28 when 'A City omnibus would put him down at the gate'. But they could sometimes be dangerous as well. *Punch*'s *Almanack* for 1849 advised readers who found they had to stand out in the road to attract the driver's attention and to climb into the bus:

> *If two omnibuses are racing, never hail the first, unless you have a particular fancy to be run over by the second.*

Heigh ho, the wind and the rain

Rather than squelch through the mud and dung of London streets or squash into a crawling and packed bus where everybody was bad-tempered, one could travel by one of the 69 steamboats whose paddle-wheels churned up the malodorous Thames westwards to Battersea or eastwards to Greenwich. Steamboats, costing 4d, plied for hire from London Bridge, past Southwark, Westminster, Vauxhall, as far as Chelsea. Some short trips cost only a penny. Cutting prices to the bone could go too far, nevertheless. Soon after the Mannings were married, in summer 1847, the boiler of the *Cricket*, with 150 passengers who had just embarked at Hungerford Pier, hoping to go down to London Bridge, blew up, killing five people and seriously injuring fifty others. The fare was only a half-penny, but the ship had already been declared unsafe.[6]

The river steamboat was a pleasant, if slow, alternative to the train. You could reach Margate in six hours for eight or nine shillings, or go down to Greenwich on a 'Diamond' line steamboat for 1s 2d in the main cabin or 2s in the ladies' saloon. There was a boat every half-hour in the winter and every fifteen minutes in summer. If the Mannings travelled downriver they would use the wharf just west of London Bridge on the north side of the Thames.

Travelling on these boats was not always pleasant. Sometimes they were grossly overloaded and in the winter you had to cope with the wind and the rain. When you got to your destination you still had to take another conveyance or walk to where you wanted to go. Perhaps this is why the Thames, although it is often declared to be the natural route from one side of London to the other, is not really convenient unless one both lives and works near one of the piers. However, when Thomas Carlyle went to Scotland he preferred to take the river steamer from where he lived in Chelsea, as far as the London docks and to continue his voyage north by coastal steamer. This was in 1852, but Maria Manning had taken the train, though it wasn't yet a direct service, from London to Edinburgh three years earlier.

'A risk of folly'

As early as 1844, John Turner exhibited his railway picture, *Rain, Steam and Speed*, at the Royal Academy. By 1845 hundreds of railway lines had been planned and scores of speculative companies had been set up. The speculators would rent an office, put a noble name, sometimes without permission, on a fancy prospectus and tout shares to the public. This is what the financier Melmotte does in Trollope's 1874 novel *The Way We Live Now*. In one week alone in 1845 there were 89 new schemes seeking £84 million from investors. Lawyers, Members of Parliament and bankers, but even less financially acute clergymen, tradesmen, landladies, widows and even servants and potboys at taverns sold shares before they had even paid for them. In the *Yellowplush Correspondence*, Thackeray's character Jeames de la Pluche, really the footman James who wore yellow plush, makes £30,000 in share dealings after starting out with a £20 loan. People who applied for an allocation of shares and sold them at once for a profit before they had paid for them were called 'stags', so Dickens chose 'Stagg's Gardens' as the name for the slum district destroyed to make way for Euston Station in *Dombey and Son*. In 1846, 4,538 new lines were proposed, making it the peak year. Parliament authorised the raising of £60 million of railway capital. But by 1848 only 1,182 miles of new track had been laid. In the intermediate year, 1847, the bubble had burst when investors were called on to pay for their shares. In April 1847 the Bank of England raised the discount rate to 5 per cent and in August to 5.5 per cent. There were many business failures. Thousands of people were ruined in the railway mania. On 28 July 1847, commiserating with the anxious parsons and half-pay officers who had sunk their all in railway shares, *Punch* wrote, in imitation of Cowper's 'Wreck of the Royal George':

Toll for a knave!
A Knave whose day is o'er.
All sunk – with those who gave
Their cash, till they'd no more.

The 'knave' in this case was George Hudson, who controlled a sizeable proportion of the 5,000 miles of railway in the country. He was Chairman of the Eastern Counties Railway, the Midland, the York and North Midland, and the York, Newcastle and Berwick. When the price of railway stock fell in 1848 as a result of the Continental revolutions, Hudson did some manoeuvring to try to keep up the price of his stock, including paying dividends out of capital. At the time, Company Law was not sufficiently developed to make this illegal. Hudson was never prosecuted even though the shareholders of the Newcastle and Berwick Railway tried to sue him for applying £189,204 of the Company's funds to his own use.

Hudson was a semi-literate linen-draper from York. While his shares were riding high, elegant society flattered him, inviting him to receptions at Carlton House Terrace while from behind kid gloves and perfumed fans, ladies and gentlemen sneered at his uncouth manners and Yorkshire accent. Mrs Hudson, who is caricatured as 'Mrs Hodge-Podson' in Thackeray's *Pendennis*, was jeered at behind her back. She asked once if a bust of Marcus Aurelius was of 'the last Markiss', the father of her host the Marquess of Westminster. She once returned a pair of magnificent globes to the famous James Wyld, exhibitor of the Great Globe in Leicester Square, because they did not match the decor. The Hudsons owned a mansion in Albert Gate, today the French embassy, which they had bought from Thomas Cubitt the builder for £15,000 (over thirty times what the Mannings' house had cost), and spent another £14,000 on it.[7] In his day, Hudson was compared, unfavourably, with Thomas Brassey, an articled surveyor's clerk who by 1845 had contracts out for 800 miles of railways in England and France. He, however, produced a return for his investors of 3 per cent and lived modestly.

Patrick O'Connor, the Mannings' victim, had railway shares, but they were mostly in French lines. Perhaps he had been clever and sold his British shares before they collapsed. In the 1845–1846 mania he might have earned 10 per cent on the London to Birmingham line, and as much as 20 per cent on the Stockton and Darlington.

By 1849, London was connected by rail from the newly opened Waterloo Station to Southampton, where Frederick Manning went to flee to Jersey, and one could travel from the capital by rail to Bristol, Birmingham, Manchester, Liverpool, Leicester, Sheffield, Norwich, Hull, Newcastle and Edinburgh, though not always directly. From where the Mannings lived in Bermondsey, they would have heard and perhaps gone to see the huge five feet six inches driving wheels, the bright brass and the green and red paint of the locomotives pulling the trains along the viaduct carrying the London, Deptford and Greenwich Railway since December 1836. Trains ran at fifteen-minute intervals. From 1839 the Croydon Railway, from 1841 the Brighton line and from 1849 the Gravesend line brought their trains into London Bridge. The fare to Greenwich was cut to 4d single in 1844. Understandably, the numbers travelling rose to 2 million.[8]

Since 1844 there had been excursions to Brighton, leaving London Bridge at 8.30 a.m. The first one, on Whit Monday 1844, used four engines to haul 45 carriages. At New Cross six more carriages and another engine were added. In an age without motor transport, the train took two thousand trippers to the coast that day. On the same day, trains took 35,000 to Greenwich and back, charging just the single fare. Fares were going down all the time. The year after the Mannings were hanged, 3/6d bought a day trip to Brighton, and a shilling bought an excursion ticket to Hampton Court.[9] The following year, Londoners would not, of course, need to use the railway for the greatest excursion of the century: the trip, taken by tens of thousands from all over the country, to see the Great Exhibition in Hyde Park in 1851.

How travel had changed in barely a decade! Even youngish people could recall

'[. . .] a life which has passed away [. . .] and only lives in fond memory. Eight miles an hour for twenty or five and twenty hours [160 or 200 miles], a tight mail coach, a hard seat [. . .] who has not borne these evils in the jolly old times?'[10]

Coaching inns like the White Horse Cellars in Piccadilly and the Saracen's Head in Snow Hill, where Wackford Squeers interviews Nicholas Nickleby, had given way to railway 'termini' with proper hotels.

The Mannings were children of the railway age. In 1830, when they were still of school age, only 100 miles of line had been constructed. By 1852, only three years after their lives had been taken by the hangman, there were 6,600 miles of railway open. Yet the expansion was very recent. As late as 1845 there had been only 2,200 miles of track. It was the 1845–1848 period that saw the most ambitious laying of railway tracks in the century. Frederick Manning himself had been part of the railway revolution, for though his father ran a coaching inn, he had been a guard on trains from the West of England to London. Maria had come up to London regularly with her employers by train in the season and had probably travelled with them on trains on the Continent. The rails had reached London between 1837 and 1847, and London Bridge and Euston, the two termini that figure in the Mannings' case, had been opened. The Mannings, however, mounted the scaffold before the railways were allowed into central London. Twenty years later, when they would have been about fifty years old, not only had the Metropolitan underground railway opened from Paddington to Farringdon Street, but the overground lines had crossed the river to Victoria, Charing Cross and the cavernous Cannon Street Station. The view looking up Ludgate Hill to St Paul's had been blocked by the railway bridge over the road. Along the Euston Road, not only Euston itself but also King's Cross was open. When Frederick Manning had been a guard, his train from Bristol had reached a temporary terminus on the other side of Bishop's Bridge Road, but in 1855 Brunel's soaring station was opened in Paddington itself.

Time and speed

Speed was the dominant impression:

> [. . .] Whizz! Dust heaps, market-gardens and waste grounds.
> Rattle! New Cross Station. Shock! There we were in Croydon.[11]

The railway even changed ideas of time. The guard's watch replaced the sun. In 1847 Manchester adjusted all its clocks to read the same as London's 'railway time'. 'Greenwich Mean Time' became standard in Britain in the 1850s, and when 25 countries agreed on Greenwich as the zero meridian, British 'railway time' became the standard against which other times were measured.

The noise . . . and the people

Despite the careful separation of travellers into three classes, with very different standards of comfort, the cheapening of travel would have, as Lord de Mowbray in Disraeli's *Sybil* feared, 'a very dangerous tendency to equality'.[12] This was somewhat exaggerated for, although more people than ever before could travel, entire trains were of one class, and third-class trains were very uncomfortable, even the 'Parliamentary Trains' which were obliged to have roofed-in carriages and to cover the whole route at least once a day for one penny a mile and at a minimum speed of 12 miles per hour. For quite a long time the wealthy could travel by train yet still in their own carriage on a flat wagon, or have their private coaches carried on an earlier train and be waiting for them when they arrived, as the Spanish visitor Ventura de la Vega found when he went with the embassy staff to see a royal military review near Chertsey on 21 June 1853.[13]

Perhaps Disraeli's Lord de Mowbray was worried about the tone of 'mutual frankness and civility – so new in the English character' that was noticed among railway passengers by a writer in the *Quarterly Review*,[14] or by the comment of Thomas Arnold, Headmaster of Rugby, who said of the London and Birmingham Railway:

> I rejoice to see it, and to think that Feudality is gone for ever.[15]

Arnold seems in this case to have been a prophet before his time. Nevertheless, the railway allowed the middle classes to get around much more and, perhaps more significantly, the railway allowed the cheap circulation of books and letters.

There were three times as many railway passengers in 1849 as in 1842. One of them had been Maria Manning, though nobody reported having spoken to *her* on her journey to Scotland.

'Away with a shriek, and a roar and a rattle'
(Charles Dickens, *Dombey and Son*, Chapter 20)

Four days after the murder of O'Connor, Maria Manning took a cab to London Bridge Station, deposited a trunk in the left-luggage office, then continued to the Euston Square Station of the London and Birmingham Railway. She stayed overnight in a hotel and began her long journey to Edinburgh at 6.15 a.m. on Tuesday 14 August 1849.

Even someone as blasé as Maria could hardly fail to have caught her breath at the magnificence of the entrance to Euston, just north of the as yet undeveloped Euston Road.

Passing through a gateway, wrote the *Penny Magazine*,

> [. . .] we feel at once that as the mode of conveyance is different, so is
> the place. We are not within the narrow precincts of an inn-yard, jostled
> by porters and ostlers, and incommoded by luggage; everything is on
> a large scale [. . .] 'First' and 'Second' class passengers have their
> different entrances and their separate booking desks; and on passing
> through the building have to produce their tickets as passports into
> the covered yard where the trains lie.[16]

It was rather like the change that would be experienced by travellers when they enjoyed air travel for the first time: the sheer 'modernity' of it all.

From the outside of Euston, one's eye was drawn to the screen of seven stone blocks (two of which still stand, inscribed with the names of the places to which the railway would take you) linked by iron railings, in the middle of which stood the Euston Arch, more properly the

Propyleum. Behind the portico was the station yard, and at its end Maria entered the just completed outer vestibule with its mosaic pavement and passed through one of the five entrances to the Roman Great Hall. A 'regal apartment in its style and size' as the *Illustrated London News* wrote on 15 September 1849, it was a double cube, 125 feet long and a towering 62 feet high, its ceiling lit by high windows. A grand double staircase led up to a central flight of steps to an even longer vestibule and thence to the Shareholders' Room. At the foot of the staircase stood a statue of George Stephenson. Eight bas-reliefs depicted the towns one could reach by rail. Passing again through glass doors Maria reached the booking offices where, never one to economise, she paid £3s 17 6d for a first-class ticket to Edinburgh. She could hardly have been expected to travel third class in a carriage letting in rain. In the circumstances, the police also were allowed to travel first class when they brought her back to London. It was quite a change for them to sit comfortably rather than on hard seats, getting steadily covered with smuts from the engine.

After seeing that her luggage was properly stowed in the luggage van, and paying the extra charge for its huge volume, Maria settled in one of the three comfortably upholstered seats on either side of the compartment. There was no corridor and no lavatory accommodation, so we may assume that she made precautionary arrangements, given that the first brief stop was at Tring in Hertfordshire.

The London and Birmingham, which by now was part of the thousand miles of track of the London and North Western Railway, together with the Grand Junction, the Manchester and Birmingham, and the Liverpool and Manchester, was probably the largest public work ever to be undertaken in the history of mankind, leaving aside the Great Wall of China. It had been finished in a record five years, by 20,000 'navvies'. It cost over £6 million. New techniques of surveying and engineering and particularly management had been required. Yet, despite the expenditure, the London and North Western was still paying a dividend of 7 per cent.

For the first few years the carriages were hauled up the incline outside Euston by cable for about a mile until the ground levelled at Camden, where there was a goods station with a warehouse of colossal dimensions, equipped with steam cranes and capstans to deal with thousands of tons of goods every day. Then the traveller would have felt the bump as an engine was connected to the train after chuffing over from the turntable in the Round House, still there today on the east side of the tracks at Primrose Hill. Then the train steamed off, descending into the Primrose Hill tunnel and emerging at speed to rush past the few houses being built at the three-mile post around the recently opened commuter stop at Kilburn. A few trains stopped there every day, but railways were not much used yet by commuters. In 1849, only 1,500 season tickets, for example, were issued to Waterloo.[17]

Did Maria have to fight her way to the bar at the station restaurant when the train stopped? And what about the queue in the ladies' lavatory? When Mr. Pips and his wife travelled to Bath they had to use their elbows in the bar at Swindon. Mrs Pips spilled her scalding soup over her dress and Mr Pips had managed to finish only half his glass of stout before he had to run for the train holding his half-eaten ham and veal pie.[18]

Maria had to change at Birmingham, 112 miles from London, and at Newcastle, on to trains belonging to other companies, and she did not arrive at Edinburgh until the next day. Still, twenty-four hours was a fraction of the time the coach would have taken.

Maria came back to Euston at 4.45 a.m. on Wednesday 22 August accompanied by Superintendent Moxey of the Edinburgh police. In the summer dawn the passengers yawned, stretched and prepared to leave the train after their all-night journey.

By now the last few hundred yards as the train coasted down the incline to Euston were no longer as they had been in the late 1830s, when in Chapter 6 of *Dombey and Son* Dickens described them during construction:

> *Houses were knocked down; streets broken through and stopped; deep*
> *pits and trenches dug in the ground; enormous heaps of earth and clay*
> *thrown up.[. . .] here a chaos of carts, overthrown and jumbled together*
> *[. . .] Everywhere were bridges that led nowhere, thoroughfares that*
> *were wholly impassable [. . .] There were a hundred thousand shapes*
> *and substances of incompleteness, wildly mingled out of their places,*
> *upside down, burrowing in the earth [. . .].*

But by the time the railway was built, in Chapter 15:

There was no such place as Staggs's Gardens. It had vanished from the earth. Where the old rotten summer-houses once had stood, palaces now reared their heads, and granite columns of gigantic girth opened a vista to the Railway world beyond. The miserable waste grounds, where the refuse-matter had been heaped of yore, was swallowed up and gone; and in its frowsty stead were tiers of warehouses, crammed with rich goods and costly merchandise. The old by-streets now swarmed with passengers and vehicles of every kind; the new streets that had stopped disheartened in the mud and waggon-ruts, formed towns within themselves [. . .] Bridges that had led to nothing led to villas, gardens, churches [. . .].

At Euston terminus, four minutes after the train had been authorised by electric telegraph to descend the gradient from Camden, a guard listening for its approach waved a flag. Porters hastened to their allotted posts and a few seconds later the train was seen emerging from the tunnel 'like a serpent from its hole'.[19]

The electric spark

The semaphores, with their multi-armed posts, still commemorated by places called 'Telegraph Hill', were quickly outdated when Euston Square terminus was connected by electric telegraph to Camden in 1837. At first, the telegraph was used only on the railways as a device to warn of an approaching train. But when the wires were strung between Paddington and Slough the new immediate mode of communication was soon used for another purpose as well. Mrs Manning was not the first murderer to be caught by the magic spark. In January 1845, John Tawell committed a murder in Slough. He was seen; the Slough stationmaster telegraphed to Paddington, where police were waiting when Tawell's train arrived. Within three years, 1,800 miles of track had been wired for the telegraph. People went to the railway station to 'send a wire', as they said. However, by the 1860s, telegraph companies had offices, employing women, in several parts of London, and the streets were beginning to be festooned with the wires which, with the later telephone wires and tram cables, would be backdrops as characteristic of London streets as mobile telephone masts and dish television aerials are today.

It was expensive to send a telegram, as the telegraphic message came to be called: eight or nine shillings for twenty words from London to Manchester and fourteen shillings to Glasgow.[20] The telegraph was used primarily by the railways themselves in their running operations, and by businessmen. The telegraph was a useful tool for stock exchange dealers and for bookmakers, who needed immediate informtion about racing results. The stationmaster at Slough had used his telegraph to trap the murderer Tawell, but the police would use it to catch Maria Manning.

Once Maria was known to have taken a train at Euston, Inspector Haynes of Scotland Yard wired her description to the Edinburgh police. On Tuesday 21 August, Superintendent Moxey wired London that he had arrested Maria only one hour after he had received Hayne's telegraph message. It was a stunning result, though *Punch*'s reaction to the news was somewhat overwrought:[21]

> [. . .] the inexorable lightning – the electric pulse – thrills in the wires – and in a moment idiot Murder stammers and grows white in the face of Justice.

The Mannings just missed the inauguration of the London to Paris cable. Between 1851, when it began service, and 1855, the number of messages surged from 99,000 to 745,000.[22] And when Professor John Pepper, of 'Pepper's Ghost' fame,[23] organised a banquet, the second Duke of Wellington cabled a goodwill message to United States President Andrew Johnson. It took nine and a half minutes to reach Washington and a reply came in 29 minutes.[24]

Postman's knock

What a wonderful man the postman is,
As he hastens from door to door.
What a medley of news his hands contain
For high, low, rich and poor;
In many a face he joy doth trace,
In as many he grief can see,
As the door is ope'd to his loud rat-tat,

And his quick delivery.
Ev'ry morn, as true as the clock,
Somebody hears the postman's knock.

Although this song was chanted by street urchins and ground out by every barrel-organ in London, L.M. Thornton, its composer, sold his copyright to music publishers for a mere one guinea and died a pauper in the workhouse.[25] True enough, it was the penny post, carried by the railway, which made the greatest difference to the lives of ordinary people, by enabling them to communicate with their families if they were away or, if they were in trade, with their salesmen, agents and customers. By 1849 all letters were going by the railway, which travelled at least twice as fast as the old mail coaches. The last daily mail coach from London to Norwich ran in 1846.

After a polemical debate about the new postal system, during which 40,000 copies of a favourable pamphlet were sewn into the twelfth number of *Nicholas Nickleby* in March 1839,[26] the new penny post was approved by Parliament.

What an enormous change occurred on 10 January 1840 when the cost of sending a letter – just one sheet folded and sealed with a wax 'wafer' and with the address written on the outside – from London to Edinburgh fell from 1s 1d to one single penny, one-thirteenth of the previous charge! If you had sent three sheets to Brighton before, it would have cost two shillings. It was like the introduction of electronic mail at the end of the twentieth century: a message anywhere for a penny. Previously the envelope had been charged for as well as each sheet enclosed. Now the envelope was free, and whatever it contained, up to half an ounce in weight, went for a penny. Although it was not yet necessary to buy an adhesive stamp, for you could prepay at the Post Office, 600,000 of the famous Penny Blacks were bought at once and there was an immediate increase in the volume of post. In the first year of the penny post 169 million letters were sent, over twice the number as in the year before. Some of these were nuisances, though nineteenth-century 'junkmail' consisted mostly of begging letters. Six deliveries came to one's door every day, rising later to twelve, so when David Copperfield met his friend Traddles in town he could post a note to his wife Dora to say he would bring Traddles home that evening for dinner and expect it to arrive in time.[27]

Like today's electronic mail and mobile telephones, the postal revolution created a need to communicate which had not been felt previously. So great was the volume of London post that the capital was divided into twelve districts. On some old street nameplates, the letters indicating the district can still be seen without the number, which was added because the temporary postmen and postwomen during the First World War did not know the streets as well as the old sorters, and because of the vast increase of mail from the Front.

Maria and Frederick would expect the double knock, rat-tat, of the postman – or the letter-carrier as he was still known then. He wore a scarlet uniform with blue lapels, blue cuffs and a blue waistcoat. If he was bringing a registered letter, his knock was the exciting double rat-tat. Previous to the penny post, the letter-carrier had to wait at the door for the person receiving the letter to pay the fee. Many a woman did not have the shilling to pay for the letter and had to do without any news of her long-gone son or husband. Now, in 1849, people were recommended to have a slit opened in their front doors for the postman to put the letters in without wasting time waiting for the door to be opened. The elaborate frames around the slits had knockers incorporated in them for the post-man's knock. But how would you know that letters had been delivered? In some big houses, perhaps, the knock would not be heard, but there was a solution: Dean's Postal Alarum and Letter Box. 'Without it, communications of the utmost importance often remain for hours unnoticed,' said the advertisement.[28] Was it an instance of a product invented and sold to solve a non-existent problem?

In 1847, in their first year of marriage, the Mannings would have received and sent Christmas cards, introduced in 1843. The first of these depicted three generations of an ideal family eating Christmas dinner.[29] And Maria would be able now to write to her relations in Switzerland for as little as 1s 2d, according to the weight of the letter, instead of the several shillings it had cost before. Letters from abroad came surprisingly quickly. On 18 June 1853, Ventura de la Vega, the Spanish visitor to London, received a letter sent from Madrid a week earlier. He commented that it usually took only five days.[30]

To send a letter you went to the Post Office, although in the early years of the penny post in London 'bellmen' walked around busy parts of town ringing a bell and holding a bag with a slit in it in which you could post letters. There were no letter boxes until 1852 when the first one was placed in Jersey, recommended by the novelist Anthony Trollope, then an official at the Post Office, who had seen similar boxes in France. The first London pillar box was placed on the corner of Fleet Street and Farringdon Street in 1855.[31]

Omnibuses in London, trains all over the country, letters anywhere in the British Isles for a penny and the telegraph, if you had to send urgent messages, were ubiquitous by 1849. Maria and Frederick Manning had grown to adulthood and marriage in the age of the railway and the cheap letter. However, their execution at the age of about thirty meant that they would never know the underground railway in London, nor the really cheap telegram, nor the telephone of the late 1870s, nor the tram of the 1890s.

Notes

1 *Comic Almanack*, 1842, in Altick, R., *The Shows of London* (Cambridge, Mass: Harvard University Press, 1976), p. 181.

2 2 Kings, 9:20.

3 Altick, R., *The Presence of the Present: Topics of the Day in the Victorian Novel* (Columbus: Ohio State University Press, 1991), pp. 439–40.

4 'Lord, defend us against these motor buses!' *The Penguin Book of Comic and Curious Verse* (Harmondsworth: Penguin, 1952), p. 239.

5 Day, J., *The Story of the London Bus* (London: London Transport, 1973), p. 9.

6 Hayward, A.L., *The Days of Dickens* (London: Routledge, 1926), pp. 7–8.

7 Altick, R., *The Presence of the Present: Topics of the Day in the Victorian Novel* (Columbus: Ohio State University Press, 1991), p. 608.

8 Barker, T.C. and Robbins, M., *A History of London Transport*, 2 volumes (London: Allen & Unwin), 1963, vol. 1, p. 46.

9 Burnett, J., *A History of the Cost of Living* (Harmondsworth: Penguin, 1969), p. 216.

10 Thackeray, W.M., *Pendennis*, Chapter 8.

11 Dickens, C., 'A Flight', in *The Uncommercial Traveller* (1851), cited in Hoppen, K.T., *The Mid-Victorian Generation 1846–1886* (Oxford: Oxford University Press, 1998), p. 290.

12 Quoted in Cruickshank, D. and Burton, N., *Life in the Georgian City* (London: Viking, 1990), p. 97.

13 Vega, V. de la, *Cartas familiars inéditas* (Madrid, 1873), pp. 20–1.

14 *Quarterly Review*, vol. 74, p. 250, cited in House, H., *The Dickens World* (Oxford University Press, 1941), p. 151.

15 Quoted in Cruickshank, D. and Burton, N., *Life in the Georgian City* (London: Viking, 1990), p. 95.

16 Cited in House, H., *The Dickens World* (Oxford University Press, 1941), p. 140.

17 Sheppard, F., *London 1808–1870: The Infernal Wen* (Berkeley: University of California Press, 1971), p. 135.

18 *Punch*, 31 July 1849.

19 Sir Francis Bond Head, quoted by Freeman, M., *Railways and the Victorian Imagination* (New Haven and London: Yale University Press, 1999), p. 42.

20 The word 'telegram' was strongly contested by purists. See Altick, R., *The Presence of the Present: Topics of the Day in the Victorian Novel* (Columbus: Ohio State University Press, 1991), p. 212.

21 *Punch*, 1 September 1849, p. 83.

22 Briggs, A., *Victorian Things*, first published 1968 (Harmondsworth: Penguin, 1990), p. 377.

23 See Chapter 7.

24 Cane, R.F., 'John H. Pepper – Analyst and Rainmaker', *Journal of the Royal Historical Society of Queensland* (Brisbane, 1974–1975), vol. IX, no. 6, pp. 116–33.

25 Hayward, A.L., *The Days of Dickens* (London: Routledge, 1926), p. 209. I have changed 'Ran-Tan' to 'rat-tat'.

26 Altick, R., *The Presence of the Present: Topics of the Day in the Victorian Novel* (Columbus: Ohio State University Press, 1991), p. 203.

27 Dickens, C., *David Copperfield*, Chapter 44.

28 *Illustrated London News*, 15 September 1849, p. 191.

29 See the picture in Briggs, A., *Victorian Things*, first published 1968 (Harmondsworth: Penguin, 1990), p. 364.

30 Vega, V. de la, *Cartas familiars inéditas* (Madrid, 1873), pp. 17 and 42.

31 For details about the post, see James, A., *The Post* (London: Batsford, 1970).

CHAPTER 10

Crime and punishment

If you want to know the time, ask a policeman

It was Police Constable Henry Barnes who spotted that the basement kitchen of 3 Miniver Place was exceptionally clean and scrubbed in comparison with the disorder of the rest of the house, and that the mortar around one of the flagstones was new and still soft. He and his colleague PC James Burton lifted the flagstone and dug up the putrefying body of Patrick O'Connor.

Friday 17 August 1849 was a sultry day. The two policemen had removed their uncomfortable, if protective, steel-reinforced leather 'pot' hats, their heavy, brass-buttoned, stiff-collared blue coats in whose tails they concealed truncheons, and their black-varnished belts, on which hung their bulls-eye lamps for the night patrols and the rattles which they 'sprang' to call for aid.

The word 'police', in the sense of a body of men who kept public order, had hardly been known in England before the end of the eighteenth century. The body instituted by Sir Robert Peel in 1829 was so unfamiliar that it was known for quite some time as the 'new police'. The word itself was unpopular, redolent of authoritarian regimes in foreign countries. While it was obviously a civilian body and quite unlike the quasi-military police of some European countries, Peel's force was suspected of being a standing army in all but name, headed as it was by a retired officer, Colonel Rowan, and with its hierarchy of ranks, its uniform and its rigorous discipline.

People who were against the creation of the police force commonly believed that only Irish or 'Popish' labourers would become police constables, given the Irish flavour about the force. Colonel Rowan was a magistrate in Ireland. The 'civilian' Commissioner, the barrister Richard Mayne, was the son of an Irish judge. Those who were hostile to the police also claimed to be satisfied with the corrupt and inefficient system of parish watchmen and constables, known as 'Charlies', and the 'Bow Street Runners' who, like a detective agency, pursued malefactors on behalf of the magistrates but also acted on behalf of private individuals. The 'Bow Street Runners' were accused of neglecting their duties to the public and being too closely associated with the murkier parts of the criminal world. The 1820s was a decade of political and criminal disorder. Peel succeeded in defusing prejudice against an official and disciplined force and created the London, or Metropolitan, Police in 1829. By 1849, there were police forces all over Britain. Their value was generally accepted when the perceived threat of revolution in London in 1848 was met by the police and the special constables, rather than by the army. The Spanish dramatist Ventura de la Vega, who visited London in 1853, was struck by the absence of soldiers in the capital's streets. He was amazed that, in contrast with Madrid, policemen went unarmed and that there were no rules in force requiring visitors to register with the authorities, display one's passport or other bureaucratic controls. Nobody asked anyone their business in London. He certainly saw the downside of this – that it was hard to keep track of criminals – but he thought that there were few malefactors and that they were soon caught.[1]

The first five divisions of the 'Met' were sworn in and went on duty at 6 p.m. on Tuesday 19 September 1829. Known affectionately as 'bobbies' or 'peelers' after Sir Robert Peel, the neutral word for them was and still is 'coppers' (because they 'copped' criminals). Twenty years later the police were well accepted and had begun to establish a measure of control. Those who disliked them called the constables 'bluebottles', because of their uniform, while Londoners' backward slang reversed the word 'police' and pronounced the result 'ecilop' or 'slop', a word still around in the 1860s as the educational pioneer Quintin Hogg recalled. He had tried to recruit a couple of crossing sweepers to teach them to read. Spotting a policeman, the boys shouted 'kool ecilop!' and ran away.[2]

The Met was independent of the local vestries. It was the only body that covered all London directly under the Home Office for 7 miles around Charing Cross, extended in 1837 to 15 miles. From 1840 onwards, the City of London had its own separate force, as it still does. Under two Commissioners, the Met consisted of an inspecting superintendent, 17 superintendents of divisions, 77 inspectors, 354 sergeants and 3,000 police constables.

Perhaps the nature of the complaints which were now being made about the police reflected just how much they were valued. Rather than accusing them of being an authoritarian arm of interfering or tyrannical government, the complaint now was that they were not doing their crime-prevention job properly. On 27 January 1849, *Punch* complained that the police were never to be seen when they were wanted because they were courting servant girls down in the areas by the basement kitchens of London houses. They ought, wrote the anonymous wit, to put a sign on the railings with an arrow to say 'Police-Constable B96 is here'. 'What adds to the audacity of this crime,' pronounced the *Illustrated London News* on 4 August 1849, 'is that it was committed within a stone's throw of the police station for this district.' After a series of crimes in South London, *The Times* asked on 26 October 1849: 'Where are the police in Lambeth?'

When Patrick O'Connor, the future victim of the Mannings, arrived in England, he was given a letter of recommendation from the Irish barrister Richard Lalor Sheil, addressed to his erstwhile and likewise Irish colleague at the Bar, Commissioner of Metropolitan Police Mayne. O'Connor probably hoped for an important position in the force. However, the two Commissioners shared the view that the police service was not to be a comfortable berth for the well connected, and that promotion was to be from the ranks. Probably they told O'Connor that they could not offer him anything but a post as a mere constable, beginning at 17s a week, rising to 19s and then to £1. If he worked hard and stood out from the others he might become a sergeant at 21s 6d per week. Even an inspector earned only £2 5s a week, hardly enough for more than a lowish middle-class lifestyle. Not unless at some time in the future he reached the exalted status of a superintendent could he hope for £5 a week. The ordinary policeman's wages were low, though regular, for a twelve-hour day or night, risking limb and perhaps life in London's roughest areas. Policemen who reached the exacting standards demanded by the Commissioners, and there were not many in the first years, could also look forward to a pension. But an ambitious man like O'Connor would not be satisfied to be a mere copper, strictly disciplined, wearing an uncomfortable uniform, out at all hours of the night without even proper meal breaks and at risk from every Bill Sikes in London, capable of murder to avoid penal servitude or transportation as a convict to Australia.

Catch me if you can

Keeping public order was one thing; detecting and arresting criminals after they had robbed or murdered their victim was another. In the early years of the police service, detective work was carried out by police constables in plain clothes. Some magistrates still retained their own officers for crime detection and thief-taking. Even as late as the mid-1860s the Metropolitan Police employed only fifteen detectives, and they were widely suspected of being police spies whom the Government used to infiltrate potentially threatening political organisations.

In 1842, after Daniel Good murdered his wife at Roehampton and had to be tracked down to Tunbridge, Kent, there was such widespread criticism of the system for catching criminals that the detective department was set up with two inspectors and two sergeants. Its office was in Scotland Yard, giving rise to the world-famous title of the Metropolitan Police's criminal investigation department.[3]

'Intelligent men have been recently selected to form a body called "the detective police" [. . .] at times the detective policeman attires himself in the dress of ordinary individuals,' wrote *Chamber's Journal*.[4] Later, two detectives were attached to each division of the Met. They hunted down some notorious criminals, culminating in the dramatic Manning case.

Detective Sergeant Shaw searched for a week for the cab driver who had driven Maria Manning to London Bridge Station. When he found William Kirk he took him to see if he could recognise 3 Miniver Place as the spot where he had collected Maria, and questioned him at length about her actions. It probably never occurred to Maria that detectives would interrogate the cabbie. She had made the foolish mistake of engaging the same man to take her from London Bridge to Euston Square, which gave the detectives further clues to her whereabouts.

Detective Inspector Haynes persuaded the railway officials at London Bridge – he had no power of compulsion – to allow him to search the trunks that Maria had left to be collected. Haynes knew, from Shaw's careful questioning of the cab driver, that Maria had marked the trunks 'Mrs Smith, passenger to Paris. To be left till called for'. Haynes also knew from the interrogation of the cabbie that Maria had gone to Euston, as well as from her foolishness in marking her Euston trunks with the same name that she had fixed to the luggage she had left at London Bridge. The porters who had loaded her large pile of boxes into the luggage van at Euston identified the owner as a female and gave a description which matched Maria's and which Haynes was enterprising enough to telegraph to the Edinburgh police. The expensive telegraph was not a device which had been much used by the police, though it had been famously employed to catch the murderer Tawell four years before. Usually, the Commissioners of the Met sent 'route papers' by a courier on a horse to the various London divisional headquarters with information on recent crimes, lists and descriptions of stolen property and of wanted men. Each division added its own information and passed the details on.[5] But it would take twenty-four hours to send Maria's description by train to Edinburgh and she might well have moved on by then.

Edinburgh had an alert Superintendent of Police, Richard Moxey. When he received Haynes's telegraph message with Maria Manning's description, he realised that it corresponded to the woman who had been brought to his notice that same morning, Tuesday 21 August, by the Edinburgh stockbrokers to whom Maria had tried to sell some of O'Connor's shares. Apparently also unaware of the efficiency of the mails, Maria did not know that, on the morning of the day she visited the stock-brokers, they had received a printed circular advising them not to deal in certain railway shares which had been stolen in London. Maria was arrested and brought back to London.

It was probably the triumphant tracking down and arrests of the Mannings that impelled Charles Dickens to publish a series of pieces in *Household Words* in high praise of the Metropolitan Police detectives.[6] The first article was by W.H. Wills, Dickens's subeditor, who called it 'The Modern Science of Thief-taking'. Appearing on 13 July 1850, it com-pared the detective to an art critic, who knows who has painted the picture by the manner of its execution. In the same way, the detective could identify the criminal by the nature of the crime.

Dickens's own first and second articles, called 'A Detective Police Party (1) and (2)',[7] were written after Scotland Yard, recognising the value of good publicity, had accepted Dickens's invitation to send a number of its detectives to the offices of *Household Words* in Wellington Street off the Strand, where they sat smoking cigars and drinking brandy (very abstemiously, Dickens points out), and discussing their activities. Dickens gave the detectives barely concealed names, but present were the famous Inspector Field and a number of detective sergeants, including Thornton and Shaw, who had been involved in the Manning case.

Dickens, who idolised the detective force, noted that every man quietly took in the room and the editorial staff at a glance. Each detective was an expert at pursuing a different kind of crime, from housebreaking to selling stolen goods ('fencing'), and from safebreaking to juvenile delinquency. Each deferred to the other's superior knowledge and experience.

Detective Sergeant Thornton, who had boarded the *Victoria* when the Mannings were suspected of getting away to America, described going below to the dark steerage in the hold, accompanied by the captain with his lamp in his hand, and speaking to the Mrs Manning who was on board, making her turn her head towards the light so that he could see that she was not the Maria Manning for whom he was searching. Sergeant 'Witchem' (really Whicher), the original of Wilkie Collins's Sergeant Cuff, gave a long account of his detective work in running a noted horse thief to ground. The skill of the detectives often lay in their pretending to be what they were not, in playing dangerous roles, in one case for ten weeks. The detectives were keen, knowing and perceptive, professional, courageous and competent at their jobs, with the appearance of living lives of 'strong mental excitement', wrote Dickens.

Dickens's great hero was Inspector Field, since 1846 Chief of the Detective Department at Scotland Yard. A man five foot ten in height, tall for the time, of imposing presence and ebullient personality and who had acted on the stage in his youth, which particularly endeared him to Dickens, who loved amateur theatricals, Field had been one of the first recruits to the new police, which he joined in 1829 at the age of 25. On his first night on patrol in the dangerous St Giles's High Street, Field arrested a notorious robber. Within four years, probably because of the high turnover of the first men to be recruited, Field became an inspector, based in L Division in Lambeth.[8] Inspector Bucket in Dickens's *Bleak House* is modelled on Field. Introduced in Chapter 12 on a sultry evening in Mr Tulkinghorn's house in Lincoln's Inn Fields, Bucket is described as attentive, composed and a good listener; 'He is a stoutly built, steady-looking, sharp-eyed man in black, of about the middle age.' Bucket and Mr Snagsby, the stationer, go in search of Jo the crossing sweeper. As they walk towards Tom All-Alone's rookery, Bucket pretends not to know any policeman he passes in case an observant criminal realises that he is a plain-clothes detective. In the rookery, people know him; there is no need for concealment, so for additional protection he recruits a constable at the beginning of the fetid street that leads into the slum. Armed with lanterns, they walk through the mud and foul puddles, keeping well away from the houses where people are known to be dying of fever. Bucket speaks to men and women of all kinds with absolute self-confidence, in a jocular and patronising tone, just as Dickens portrays Inspector Field doing in a piece in *Household Words* published on 14 June 1851 in which the novelist describes a tour he made of the slums accompanied by the famous inspector.[9] From the St Giles rookery they went south of the Thames to Southwark, near where the Mannings lived, then crossed the river again to visit the Ratcliff Highway, with its sailors' taverns and brothels. According to Dickens's account, the brutal roughs of the district slunk off when warned to make way by the detectives and the burly constables who accompanied them. Self-possession and aplomb seems to have been the quality that most struck Dickens in his description of the detectives. Inspector Field, whose hand 'is the well-known hand that has collared half the people here' is evidently feared. All the common thieves, local bullies and whores seek to propitiate him. Nobody would lift a finger to protect anyone from arrest by him.

Back in the fictional portrayal of Field, in *Bleak House*, Mademoiselle Hortense, the French maid, is now introduced. Dickens based her on Maria Manning. He presents her as 'sufficiently good-looking' with an intense expression on her face, and a harsh tone to her voice:

> '*My Lady's maid is a Frenchwoman of two-and-thirty, from somewhere in the southern country between Avignon and Marseilles – a large-eyed brown woman with black hair; who would be handsome but for a certain feline mouth [. . .].*'

Dickens describes Mademoiselle Hortense as proud, imperious and violent, like Maria Manning. She shoots the lawyer Tulkinghorn because he refuses to pay her money she claims is due to her. In Hortense's violent gestures and slightly imperfect English, Dickens, who may have attended the Manning trial, perhaps left posterity a record of Maria Manning's voice.[10] Yet it is strange that he did not use the notorious trial and the execution of the Mannings, which he attended, as raw material for his novel.

They swung for it

By the 1840s, hanging, imposed for a range of crimes in the early part of the century, was restricted to treason, piracy and murder. Even so, in 1845 49 men and women were sentenced to death for murder in England and Wales, though only 12 were executed.

Between 1847 and 1852, however, there was an epidemic of murder by women. Thirteen were executed for murder, and nine more were reprieved.[11] In particular, 1849 was an outstanding year for women murderers: Sarah Thomas, Mary Ball, Charlotte Harris, Rebecca Smith, Hannah Sandler and Mary Ann Geering, described as 'of masculine and forbidding appearance',[12] had all been tried before the Manning case. Sarah Thomas had murdered her employer; Charlotte Harris had killed her husband with arsenic. She wanted another man and she married him, rather foolishly, on the very day of her husband's funeral. Since she was pregnant the death sentence was commuted to transportation for life. Hannah Sandler, like so many women, desperate with hunger, killed her child and had her death sentence commuted. Mary Ball killed her husband, whom she caught spying on her and her lover. Rebecca Smith poisoned eight of her children; there was no mercy for her. Sarah Jackson was found to be insane. Catherine Cork was said to have murdered her husband in a fit of jealousy but the evidence was doubtful and she was acquitted. Mary Furley was sentenced to hang for attempted suicide and the murder of her child. She had been in the workhouse and had toiled in the sweated trades. Starving and homeless, she threw herself and her baby into the Thames. After a public outcry, the sentence was reduced to seven years' transportation.

There could be no mercy for Maria Manning. She had not murdered a brutal husband or employer in desperation. In such cases public opinion sometimes demanded a reprieve. She was not starving, hopelessly unable to look after a child. Despite the admiration aroused by her self-possession and the fascination of her evident sexual attraction, her perceived unfeminine cold rationality, her lack of tears or fainting or remorse, and her preoccupation with her appearance, all prejudiced public opinion against her. Most people thought that it was she who had killed O'Connor. Even those who thought the verdict had not taken everything into account accepted that she at least knew that her husband had planned the crime. Nobody who saw her could believe that she was under the thumb of the shambling drunkard Frederick. There was no resemblance between her and the often mentally deficient and illiterate single mothers who had drowned their newborn infants and were usually treated by the courts with mercy.

Maria was bracketed with the women poisoners who seemed to have proliferated in recent years. Wives poisoned their husbands, and mothers their grown-up sons and daughters in order to claim the burial insurance money, which would yield a small profit after the interment.[13] On 28 April 1849, *Punch*, which was against capital punishment, remarked that there had been six hangings of female poisoners in the last six weeks alone. Women murderers were especially loathed because they appeared to betray the very nature of Victorian womanhood. A murderess was seen as an unsexed monster. She could not be a real woman because no woman who had the sentiments and emotions thought proper to her sex could bring herself to murder, especially in the premeditated way that was characteristic of poisoning.

Hanging did not seem to be much of a deterrent, but making it harder to buy poison would be. Arsenic was far too easy to buy. *Punch* published a cartoon on 8 September 1849 with the title 'Fatal Facility; or, Poisons for the Asking'. A lisping child asks the chemist:

> *'Please, mithter, will you be so good as to fill this bottle again with Lod'num, and let Mother have another pound and a half of arsenic for the rats?'*

Arsenic was cheap, colourless, odourless and soluble. Its symptoms were abdominal pain and diarrhoea, so death from poison could appear to have been caused by cholera. It might have been a better idea, indeed, for the Mannings to have poisoned O'Connor and to have called the doctor who might well have assumed that he had been struck down by cholera during that hot summer. All the same, if murder were suspected, an autopsy could often reveal the presence of arsenic, so perhaps the Mannings had not wanted to take the risk.

In the dock

Maria Manning's case was, however, unique. To begin with, she did not use poison, the premeditating murderess's usual weapon. Second, she was not charged with firing the shot that wounded Patrick O'Connor and would have killed him even if Frederick had not beaten him to death. Nevertheless, the jury found her guilty of murder by being an accessory before the deed. She had known about or participated in the plan to kill her lover for his money, which was also an original circumstance, for if a woman killed her lover it was normally because of his infidelity.

The Mannings were tried at the Old Bailey on Thursday and Friday, 25 and 26 October 1849.[14] Such was the notoriety of the circumstances and the fascination aroused by the press descriptions of Maria that seats were reserved for the ambassadors of several foreign countries. The Attorney-General prosecuted, while the Mannings were each defended by a leading lawyer. All eyes were on Maria as she was led into the dock. She wore a close-fitting black dress, offset by a multi-coloured shawl in which blue predominated, set off by primrose gloves and a white lace veil. The details of her clothes were carefully listed by the reporters, but Maria also wanted to have her dignified and modest though elegant appearance noted by all as she stood motionless in the dock during all that day. Frederick Manning was charged with the murder of O'Connor; Maria only with having been present and aiding and abetting her husband.

A jury of her peers

Maria's counsel had realised that Frederick was going to throw as much of the blame as possible on his wife. Her barrister also had to deal with the embarrassing issue of Maria's relations with O'Connor. It would be difficult to endear a foreign adulteress to the jury. Defence counsel hit on the idea of dredging up a statute of Edward III, dating from 1355, referred to as *de medietate linguae*. This provided for a foreign defendant to be judged by a jury half composed of foreigners.

The Attorney-General seems to have been prepared for this defence ploy. He cited a statute which had become law only the previous year. It stated that a woman married to a British subject was to be considered for all purposes as British. The judge had to decide whether the recent statute removed the right to a jury *de medietate linguae* in this case. Yes, it did, said Lord Chief Baron Pollock. Maria was to be considered as a British subject and judged as such, even though she was still obviously foreign. If the 1355 statute had been intended to protect aliens against prejudicial decisions by English juries, this protection had now been removed from Maria Manning. What is more, she would now be judged by the same twelve male property-owning Londoners who would hear how when Frederick was arrested he had accused her of killing O'Connor, even though they had been instructed to ignore his words.

The Attorney-General made a point of explaining to the jury that, even if they thought that only one of the pair had actually committed the murder, if the other was present and participated, or even absent but had prior knowledge of the intention to murder, the jury could convict both defendants. As for a married woman, the prosecution forestalled any suggestion that the law considered her as under her husband's control. In matters of murder a wife was responsible for her own actions.

The Attorney-General went through the case in detail, suggesting that Maria had been on intimate terms with Patrick O'Connor. What fantasies went through the jurymen's minds as they gazed at the immobile, self-possessed and attractive woman in the dock? After detailing all the points in the evidence which pointed to the guilt of both Mannings, the Attorney-General reminded the jury that Frederick, while throwing the blame on Maria, had not explained who had battered in O'Connor's skull so cruelly. The suggestion was that it must have been him. On the other hand, while it might have been possible for only one person to have lifted the flagstone, as Constable Barnes averred when questioned by the defence, he was a strong young man. The jury must have found it difficult to accept that Frederick and only he shot O'Connor, bashed in his skull, then bound his body and manhandled it into the grave, having lifted the stone. Both Maria and Frederick were guilty.

The real conflict of evidence, never clarified, centred on the precise time that Maria had reached O'Connor's lodgings in Mile End. Her defence counsel claimed that she could not have been at 3 Miniver

Place when the murder occurred. Even so, the jury believed that Maria must have had prior knowledge, given the purchases and deliveries at 3 Miniver Place of the crowbar and of the lime.

Charles Wilkins, appearing for Frederick, dismissed the medical student William Massey's account of Frederick's questions about how to drug a man. He claimed they were disjointed and an inconsequential issue. But Wilkins was unable to plant in the jury's mind the unlikely idea that the tools which the prosecution claimed had been bought to lift the flagstone and conceal the corpse had actually been used quite innocuously to install a chimney-piece in the front parlour. Wilkins had the difficult job of defending Frederick in the only possible way: by throwing all the blame on Maria and on the irresponsibility of the sensationalist press. Moreover, he had to do it without prejudicing his case by arousing the chivalrous sentiments of the jurymen. He suggested that Manning was weak; Maria had duped him. According to Wilkins, Maria could have inflicted the wounds on O'Connor's head and buried him. Nor was Manning a jealous man who would have intended his rival's death. Had he not already tolerated his wife's adultery? Wilkins tried to suggest that Maria had acted quite independently of Frederick, though Bainbridge, the second-hand furniture dealer, insisted that Frederick had told him that he himself had sent Maria away after the murder. No, said Wilkins, Manning had shown great surprise when he did not find his wife at home and indeed Maria herself had told Superintendent Moxey at Edinburgh that she had left London without his knowledge. Wilkins cleverly reminded the jury how Frederick had told the detective who had arrested him that Maria had shot O'Connor. This fact could not have been given in evidence, but apparently Frederick's counsel was entitled to use it in the way he did.

Nor did the jury seem to have been impressed by Maria's counsel, William Ballantyne, when he tried to destroy the evidence of Hannah Firman, who testified that Maria had hired her to clean up a mess in the downstairs kitchen two days after the murder. Hannah had stolen a number of articles, but this evidence of dishonesty did not alter the facts. Ballantyne did, however, successfully demolish evidence of bloodstains on Maria's clothes. These were inconclusive in the absence of forensic proof that they were indeed blood. He also managed to imply that the lime, the spade and the crowbar were purchased either for reasons unconnected with the murder, or without Maria's knowledge. As for O'Connor's shares that had been found in Maria's possession, she had asked him to invest money for her and in the haste of the moment might have taken away documents which she thought belonged to her. Ballantyne spoke with contempt of Frederick, who 'ought to have cherished and protected' his wife but accused her of total responsibility in O'Connor's murder. Given the strength of the evidence against Maria, Ballantyne continued by attacking Frederick's counsel for defending his own client by attacking Maria.

Ballantyne's main point was that Maria was not guilty of murder unless she was there. The vagueness of O'Connor's landlady, Miss Armes, about the time Maria arrived at her house, allowed Ballantyne to do this, but even so, the jury could hardly forget that Maria might well have planned the murder. Anticipating this reaction, Ballantyne asked, 'But why would she? Did she not love O'Connor?' Here Ballantyne had to be careful not to prejudice Maria by reminding the jury of her adultery, so he suggested that Frederick had mistreated her, though there was no evidence of this. Ballantyne grasped at straws when he claimed that, as mistress of a man twenty years older than herself, Maria did not need to kill O'Connor in order to get all the money she wanted out of him. Hard-headed jurymen, indeed, might have reflected that O'Connor was as clever as her and, contrary to what her counsel was suggesting, had no intention of indulging a young mistress.

The Attorney-General rebutted the defence's arguments. He told the jury, who must have been thinking along similar lines, that Maria alone could not have shot O'Connor, struck him seventeen violent blows on the head, raised the kitchen flagstone, dug the grave, stripped and bound O'Connor's corpse and forced it into the small grave, and then filled the hole, replaced the stone and cemented it in place. On the other hand, he asked, why would Frederick have committed the murder alone? For what purpose? After all, unlike Maria, who had free access, he could not go into O'Connor's rooms and take his shares and the money. She must be guilty and he must at least have helped her.

Summing up, the judge pointed out that nobody had suggested that anybody but one or both of the prisoners had committed the murder. Since defendants in murder cases did not give evidence in those days, Maria and Frederick were completely in the hands of their counsel. Maria would later claim that her defence had not called favourable witnesses. She mentioned a 'young man from Jersey'. Perhaps she had tried to suggest that another person had been present and her counsel had told her that this was a blind alley. Yet no evidence from the police suggested that she had ever previously claimed that anybody but Frederick had killed O'Connor.

Manning had said that his wife Maria had shot O'Connor. This was not acceptable evidence against her but, paradoxically, it did establish that he had been present at the murder. So did he know anything about its planning? He had said nothing about the head wounds or the burial of the corpse. If it had been Maria who had struck the dying O'Connor's head seventeen violent blows, why had Frederick not tried to stop her? As for Maria, it was clear, said the judge, that she had taken O'Connor's keys. The deed certainly suggested premeditation. In any case, did the jury believe that the murder had been planned and perpetrated by one of the Mannings without the knowledge and the cooperation of the other? The judge's question was clearly rhetorical and invited a negative answer.

Within three-quarters of an hour the jury returned with a verdict. Both Mannings were guilty.

It was at this point that Maria spoke. Vehemently she made an uninvited speech:

> There is no justice and no right for a foreign subject in this country. There is no law for me. I have had no protection, neither from the judges, nor from the prosecutors, nor from my husband. I am unjustly condemned by this Court. If I were in my own country I could prove that I had money sent from abroad, which is now in the Bank of England. My solicitors and counsel could have called witnesses to identify shares that were bought with my own money.
>
> Mr O'Connor was more to me than my husband. He was a friend and brother to me ever since I came to this country. I knew him for seven years. He wanted to marry me, and I ought to have been married to him. I have letters which would prove his respect and regard for me; and I think, considering that I am a woman and alone, that I have to fight against my husband's statements, that I have to fight against the prosecutors, and that even the Judge himself is against me – I think that I am not treated like a Christian, but like a wild beast of the forest;

*and the Judges and Jury will have it upon their consciences for giving
a verdict against me.*

*I am not guilty of the murder of Mr O'Connor. If I had wished to
commit murder, I would not have attempted the life of the only friend I
had in the world – a man who would have made me his wife in a week,
if I had been a widow. I have lived in respectable families, and can
produce testimonials of character for probity in every respect, if inquiry
is made. I can account for more money than was equal to the trifling
shares that were found upon me. If my husband, through jealousy and
a revengeful feeling against O'Connor, chose to murder him, I don't see
why I should be punished for it. I wish I could have expressed myself
better in the English language. That is all I have to say.*

If this speech was in fact spontaneous or reported just as she said it,
her English was extremely good. Her case was that she loved O'Connor
and that Frederick had killed him out of jealousy. She had a good point,
if it could be believed that she knew nothing about the planning of the
murder and if she could have proved that everything she took from
O'Connor's rooms was in fact her own property.

As for Manning, the jury evidently believed that only he could have
struck the series of frenzied blows that finished O'Connor off. The police
also found a dealer in the New Cut who had sold a pair of small pistols to
a man looking like Manning. After the murder, Frederick, giving a false
name, pawned a pair of pistols in a pawnshop. He did not have a leg to
stand on. As for Maria, she gave an impression of strength and determina-
tion which inclined the jury to believe Frederick's allegations against her.
Had Maria been tried separately from her husband, his allegations would
not have been mentioned and her counsel might have been able to
shift enough blame on to Frederick to reduce her guilt and thus help her
escape the rope.

As the judge, black silk on his head, began to pronounce the death
sentence, Maria shouted:

*No! No! I won't stand it. You are to be ashamed of yourselves. There is
neither law nor justice here!*

As she was being turned and led away she seized a handful of the rue
which by tradition lay along the ledges of the dock, and which had once

helped to disguise the stench of the prisoners, and threw it into the well of the court, shouting, 'Base and shameful England!' As she was led away she was heard to 'pour dreadful imprecations upon all around her', crying, 'Damnation seize you all!'

By bus and cab to see the Mannings hanged

The Mannings were due to be hanged at 9 a.m. on Tuesday 13 November. During the previous three weeks the press and the rumour mills had been full of reports about how Maria and Frederick were facing the end of their lives. Many people applied for permission to enter the prison, hoping to catch a glimpse of the exotic and striking woman.

By the Friday before the Tuesday appointed for the hanging, it was becoming apparent that the event would attract a huge crowd as well as an unruly mob, anxious to see the spectacle of the suffering of the self-possessed and dominant Mrs Manning. There was little interest in Frederick.

Since December 1783, hangings had no longer taken place at Tyburn, where Marble Arch stands today, but outside Newgate, the gaol where most prisoners sentenced at the Old Bailey were incarcerated. Hanging criminals at Newgate or, in the case of the Mannings, at Horsemonger Lane Gaol in Southwark, avoided the scandal and disorder of the long ride in the tumbrel through the main streets of central London, Holborn and Oxford Street, before arrival at Tyburn.

At public executions flashy men-about-town, the type who liked bare-knuckle fighting or watching dogs set upon each other, would make up parties. When James Rush was 'turned off' at Norwich in 1849, one very large group chartered a special train, as if for a day at the races.

The Manning case was, however, quite exceptional, because of Maria's strange fascination and her intriguing aplomb. Did people want to see whether she died proud and remote, or were they secretly looking forward, with sadistic curiosity, to the moral collapse, the shrieking and begging for mercy of a woman who had at last lost her icy self-possession?

Most of the string of murders by women in 1849 had taken place outside the capital. Rarely had there been a murder with so much drama and so magnetic an interest for Londoners, a murder by a seemingly ordinary lower-middle-class London couple who lived in an ordinary street. The penny parts of Robert Huish's fictionalised biography of Maria were being snatched eagerly, hot off the press. Newspaper supplements and hastily published copies of the trial proceedings repeatedly covered every single aspect of the murder, the house at 3 Miniver Place, the gruesome details of how the policemen had dug up O'Connor's corpse, the depositions of the witnesses and the fascinating details of how the condemned were behaving in prison. Journalists interrogated the wardresses who were with Maria in her cell. They recounted, or the journalists invented, juicy items such as that Maria had made a new pair of drawers to be hanged in and that she insisted on donning a new pair of silk stockings for the great event.

Windows and roofs in the streets facing the prison entrance were being expensively let to spectators. Enterprising men rented the gardens from the landlords of the houses and kept carpenters busy erecting tiered platforms with seats at five shillings, irrespective of the wishes of the tenants of the houses, although the latter also let places by their upstairs windows. Stands of a dangerous nature were built to accommodate everybody willing to pay. The authorities did their best, using inadequate legislation, to pull down scaffolding and seats. Observation spots on the first-floor terraces of two pubs which had a good view were on sale at £2 each. The spectators varied from the dregs of the criminal population to the cream of Mayfair men-about-town. In one place the arrangements made for the entertainment included a champagne breakfast.

Probably a large proportion of the crowd which congregated on Monday 12 November 1849 to see the Mannings hang next morning had walked to Horsemonger Lane Gaol, close by the present Newington Sessions House and appropriately only half a mile or so from where the crime had been committed. Nevertheless, many would have come by bus and others would have come into London Bridge by train, while the better-off class of spectators had arrived in hansom cabs.

Outside the prison that night, a vast crowd assembled, barely controlled by hundreds of police who had the task of keeping the mob away from the prison building itself. There was no law to prevent such assemblies. The *Examiner* reported on 17 November 1849 that even if the area before the gaol had been as large as Hyde Park, it could have been filled at high prices. Stallholders, fast-food vendors and all sorts of peddlers got ready to make hay while the sun shone, as did the pick-pockets and cheap whores for whom a public hanging offered an unequalled opportunity.

In the meantime, Maria and Frederick were contemplating their approaching death. Frederick was reading Psalms, but the chaplain could find no way of persuading Maria to make a full confession. Nevertheless, he administered the Sacrament to her, perhaps because when she met her husband for the last time in the prison chapel she told Frederick that she no longer bore any animosity towards him.

By early morning on Tuesday 13 November, the crowd before the prison was enormous. Stalls with flaring naphtha lamps that cold November night sold sausages, kidneys and porter, while ambulant vendors offered biscuits and peppermints which they had morbidly baptised as 'Mrs Manning's'. The crowd included 'the dregs and offscourings of the population', wrote *The Times*, as well as labourers and clerks taking time off work, urchins and the mixed multitude of the curious and the prurient. They had been there all night, drinking, smoking, fornicating, dancing, singing obscene songs and, every now and then, 'Oh, Mrs Manning, don't you cry for me!' to the tune of Stephen Foster's latest hit, 'Oh, Susanna!' Broadsides and ballads were hawked at the execution itself, including the following:

> *At length they planned their friend to murder,*
> *And for his company did crave,*
> *The dreadful weapons they prepared,*
> *And in the kitchen dug his grave.*
> *And, as they fondly did caress him*
> *They slew him – what a dreadful sight,*
> *First they mangled, after robbed him,*
> *Frederick Manning and his wife.*
> *Old and young, pray take a warning,*
> *Females, lead a virtuous life.*
> *Think upon that fateful morning*
> *Frederick Manning and his wife.*[15]

'I believe,' wrote Charles Dickens to *The Times* just after the executions, 'that a sight so inconceivably awful as the wickedness and levity of the immense crowd . . . could be presented in no heathen land under the sun.' The already famous novelist shuddered at the 'atrocious bearing, looks and language' of the spectators, the shrill cries and howls, screeching and laughter of boys and girls, together with 'every variety of foul and offensive behaviour' from the thieves, whores, vagabonds and ruffians who swarmed in front of the prison and in the streets around. Dickens continued:

> When the sun rose . . . it gilded thousands upon thousands of upturned faces, so inexpressibly odious in their brutal mirth or callousness, that a man had cause to be ashamed of the shape he wore, and to shrink from himself, as fashioned in the image of the Devil. When the two miserable creatures who attracted all this ghastly sight about them were turned quivering into the air, there was no more emotion, no more pity, no more thought that two immortal souls had gone to judgment, no more restraint in any of the previous obscenities, than if the name of Christ had never been heard in this world, and there were no beliefs among men but that they perished like the beasts.[16]

The hangman was William Calcraft, who had been doing the job up and down the country since 1829. He still used the short drop, so a slow death by strangulation was Calcraft's trademark. This was despite the introduction of the high gallows and the long drop. Calcraft never mastered the skill of adjusting the length of the rope to the weight of the victim, nor of fitting the knot in the right place so that the drop produced the instant separation of the upper vertebrae and the swift unconsciousness of the condemned person, even though the heart might continue to beat for some while.

In the Mannings' case, when they were cut down, the hoods removed and the bodies examined by the doctors, Frederick appeared to have died instantly, but Maria's face was distorted and showed signs of a struggle for life.[17] Probably, Calcraft's calculations had been accurate in Frederick's case, but perhaps he had not lengthened his rope sufficiently to take account of Maria's lighter body.

Maria appeared for her execution in a black satin dress with a large white collar. She died, wrote The Times with some degree of admiration even for this woman who had behaved in a way so inappropriate to her sex, 'exhibiting an amount of courage and nerve which contrasted strangely with the terror-stricken aspect of her husband'.[18] The Chronicle wrote that 'even the distortion consequent upon the mode of death she suffered could not destroy the remarkable fine contour of her figure as it swayed to and fro [. . .].'[19]

Dickens himself recalled Maria's body as 'a fine shape, so elaborately corsetted and artfully dressed, that it was quite unchanged in its trim appearance as it slowly swung from side to side.'[20]

Both men and women perhaps, as Judith Knelman has pointed out, achieved a sense of sexual satisfaction: the former from seeing a dominant, aggressive woman being made to suffer; the latter from seeing the punishment of a woman who had transgressed against the approved way for her sex to behave.[21] In this case, the spectators had the treat, as it were, of a double hanging, though it was Maria whose death they came to see and about whom they talked and sang. The issues were, however, more complicated. At a public meeting reported by the *Illustrated London News* on 24 November 1849, while all agreed that the behaviour of the mob at the Manning execution should never be repeated, numerous voices argued that hangings carried out in private were simply official assassinations and that 'the punishment of death ought to be immediately and totally abolished'. Abolition would not come for over another century. Even public hangings continued. That particular amusement for Londoners ended with the execution of an Irish Fenian, Michael Barrett, hanged outside Newgate on 26 May 1868. The drama of the execution, the crowds outside the prison waiting for the bell to toll and the warder to fix the notice that the execution had taken place, ended, as far as women were concerned, with Ruth Ellis's hanging at Holloway on 13 July 1955, while the last man to drop through the heavy oak trapdoor of a London execution chamber was Ronald Marwood in 1959.[22]

Notes

1 Vega, V. de la, *Cartas familiars inéditas* (Madrid, 1873), p. 21.

2 *Polytechnic Magazine*, 28 January 1903. Quintin Hogg added that the word 'slop' was still the slang word for the police.

3 Lock, J., *Dreadful Deeds and Awful Murders; Scotland Yard's First Detectives 1829–1878* (Taunton: Barn Owl Books, 1990), p. 70.

4 *Chamber's Journal*, no. XIII, p. 54.

5 Lock, J., *Dreadful Deeds and Awful Murders; Scotland Yard's First Detectives 1829–1878* (Taunton: Barn Owl Books, 1990), p. 36.

6 Most of the following is drawn from Michael Slater's introduction and notes to Dickens's two articles about detectives. See Dickens, C., *Dickens's Journalism*, ed. M. Slater, 4 volumes (London: Dent, 1996), vol. 2 'The Amusements of the People and Other Papers 1834–1851', pp. 265–82.

7 Ibid., p. 266 and ff. The article appeared in *Household Words* on 27 July 1850.

8 Lock, J., *Dreadful Deeds and Awful Murders; Scotland Yard's First Detectives 1829–1878* (Taunton: Barn Owl Books, 1990), p. 34.

9 Dickens, C., *Dickens's Journalism*, ed. M. Slater, 4 volumes (London: Dent, 1996), vol. 2 'The Amusements of the People and Other Papers 1834–1851', pp. 356–69.

10 This is Eugene Borowitz's suggestion, although Maria did not speak except for her outburst at the end of the trial. See Borowitz, E., *The Bermondsey Horror* (London: Robson Books, 1989), p. 306.

11 On the subject of the attitude to women who murdered, see Knelman, J., *Twisting in the Wind: the Murderess and the English Press* (Toronto: University of Toronto Press, 1998).

12 Ibid., p. 65.

13 Ibid., p. 50.

14 I have made heavy use of Borowitz's account, see Borowitz, E., *The Bermondsey Horror* (London: Robson Books, 1989), occasionally referring to the trial record, in the Public Record Office, DPP 4/2.

15 Quoted by Diamond, M., *Victorian Sensation* (London: Anthem Press, 2003), p. 163.

16 Quoted in Borowitz, E., *The Bermondsey Horror* (London: Robson Books, 1989), p. 261.

17 Ibid., p. 253.

18 *The Times*, 14 November 1849, quoted in Knelman, J., *Twisting in the Wind; the Murderess and the English Press* (Toronto: University of Toronto Press, 1998), p. 253.

19 Quoted in Knelman, J., *Twisting in the Wind; the Murderess and the English Press* (Toronto: University of Toronto Press, 1998), p. 262.

20 Dickens, C., 'Lying Awake at Night', in *Household Words*, 30 October 1852, as quoted in Knelman, J., *Twisting in the Wind; the Murderess and the English Press* (Toronto: University of Toronto Press, 1998), p. 262. Unless

Dickens had a privileged view, the artists' impressions must be wrong, because they suggest that the drop was concealed from public eyes.

21 Knelman, J., *Twisting in the Wind; the Murderess and the English Press* (Toronto: University of Toronto Press, 1998), pp. 261–2.

22 For details of hanging, I have consulted Bailey, B., *Hangmen of England* (London: W.H. Allen, 1989).

Epilogue

One of the pioneers of the penny post, Henry Cole, who had worked with Rowland Hill in 1838 and was now a civil servant employed at the Public Record Office, conceived the idea of a great national exhibition of arts and manufactures. He talked about it to the London builder Thomas Cubitt and to Richard Cobden, one of the leaders of the Free Trade movement.

During the course of his work Cole met Prince Albert and mentioned his idea. Albert was enthusiastic, drew up a plan and on 30 June 1848 proposed it to the Royal Society of Arts at Buckingham Palace. Another meeting was held later that summer at the royal holiday home at Osborne, Isle of Wight. Faced with an unenthusiastic Government, the Royal Society of Arts enrolled 5,000 'promoters' in 65 manufacturing districts, who succeeded in persuading ministers. On 3 January 1850, a few weeks after the Mannings were hanged, a Royal Commission to plan the Great Exhibition of Arts and Manufactures of All Nations was appointed, consisting of Prince Albert, Lord John Russell, Sir Robert Peel, Lord Stanley the Opposition Leader, Gladstone, Charles Lyell the geologist and others. Plans were invited for constructing the exhibition on the site opposite Kensington Gore in Hyde Park. Joseph Paxton submitted his designs in July 1850, which were accepted at a tender of £79,800. Schweppes obtained the contract for refreshments (non-alcoholic only). The classes were completely separated, the prices for admission varying between one shilling from Mondays to Thursdays, half a crown on Fridays and a substantial five shillings on Saturdays. The average daily attendance from May to October 1851 was 43,311.[1]

It is not too hard to imagine Maria Manning employed as a French interpreter for the large numbers of French, Swiss and Belgian visitors who came to London for the Great Exhibition. Maria was a native speaker of French who spoke English well and was highly presentable and particularly suitable for attending to women visitors.

The Great Exhibition might have offered another possibility. Some of the Mannings' capital belonged to Maria personally, so even if she had decided to leave the alcoholic Frederick, it is feasible to imagine her starting up a little business of her own, an agency for rooms perhaps. She might even have taken a lease, spent some money on a house and offered apartments for French and Swiss visitors that summer of 1851, with Continental breakfast and an evening meal acceptable to her guests. What a tragedy that her talents were devoted to greed and murder, that she, who after all was only thirty years old, more or less the same age as Queen Victoria, and could easily have lived another forty years, did not grow old like her sovereign and see the immense progress that took place in all aspects of life in London.

Note

1   Harrison, J.F., *Early Victorian Britain 1832–1851* (Fontana, 1979); Mottram, R.H., 'Town Life', in G.M. Young (ed.) *Early Victorian England 1830–1865*, 2 volumes (Oxford University Press, 1934), vol. 1, pp. 155–223, specifically pp. 212 and ff; Wilson, A.N., *The Victorians* (London: Hutchinson, 2002), p. 128; Margetson, S., *Leisure and Pleasure in the Nineteenth Century* (London: Cassell, 1969), Chapter 7.

Bibliography

Ackroyd, P., *Dickens* (London: Sinclair-Stevenson, 1990).

Ackroyd, P., *London: The Biography* (London: Vintage Press, 2001).

Adburgham, A., *Shops and Shopping 1800–1914* (London: Allen & Unwin, 1964).

Altick, R., *The English Common Reader: a Social History of the Mass Reading Public 1800–1900* (Chicago: University of Chicago Press, 1957).

Altick, R., *Victorian People and Ideas*, first published 1973 (London: Dent, 1974).

Altick, R., *The Shows of London* (Cambridge, Mass: Harvard University Press, 1976).

Altick, R., *The Presence of the Present: Topics of the Day in the Victorian Novel* (Columbus: Ohio State University Press, 1991).

Bailey, B., *Hangmen of England* (London: W.H. Allen, 1989).

Barker, T.C. and Robbins, M., *A History of London Transport*, 2 volumes (London: Allen & Unwin, 1963).

Barret-Ducrocq, F., *Love in the Time of Victoria* (London: Verso, 1991).

Bennett, A., *London and Londoners in the 1850s and 1860s* (London: Fisher Unwin, 1924).

Bentley, N., *The Victorian Scene* (London: Weidenfeld & Nicolson, 1968).

Borowitz, E., *The Bermondsey Horror* (London: Robson Books, 1989).

Briggs, A., *Marx in London, an Illustrated Guide* (London: BBC, 1982).

Briggs, A., *Victorian Things*, first published 1968 (Harmondsworth: Penguin, 1990).

Brightfield, M., *Victorian England and its Novels* (Los Angeles: University of California Press, 1968).

Brockway, A.F., *Bermondsey Story* (London: Allen & Unwin, 1949).

Burnett, J., *A History of the Cost of Living* (Harmondsworth: Penguin, 1969).

Burnett, J., *Plenty and Want: A Social History of Diet in England from 1815 to the Present Day*, first published 1966 (London: Scolar Press, 1979).

Burnett, J., *A Social History of Housing 1815–1870* (London: Methuen, 1980).

Bynum, W. and Porter, R. (eds), 'Living and Dying in London', in *Medical History*, Supplement 11, 1991.

Calder, J. *The Victorian Home* (London: Batsford, 1977).

Carlyle, T., *Collected Works* (London: Chapman & Hall, 1857).

Cane, R.F., 'John H. Pepper – Analyst and Rainmaker', *Journal of the Royal Historical Society of Queensland* (Brisbane, 1974–1975), vol. IX, no. 6.

Chamber's Journal, no. XIII.

Chancellor, E. *Pleasure Haunts of London During Four Centuries* (London: Constable, 1925).

Chesney, K., *The Victorian Underworld* (London: Temple Smith, 1970).

Colman, H., *European Life and Manners in Familiar Letters to Friends*, 2 volumes (Boston and London, 1850).

Connan, D., *A History of the Public Health Department in Bermondsey* (London: Bermondsey Borough Council, 1935).

Cruickshank, D. and Burton, N., *Life in the Georgian City* (London: Viking, 1990).

Cruickshank, R.J., *Charles Dickens and Early Victorian England* (London: Pitman, 1949).

Davis, D., *A History of Shopping* (London: Routledge, 1966).

Day, J., *The Story of the London Bus* (London: London Transport, 1973).

Diamond, M., *Victorian Sensation* (London: Anthem Press, 2003).

Dickens, C., *The Chimes* (1844).

Dickens, C., *Dickens's Journalism*, ed. M. Slater, 4 volumes (London: Dent, 1996), vol. 2 'The Amusements of the People and Other Papers 1834–1851'.

Dickens, C., *Nicholas Nickelby* (1838–1839); *Dombey and Son* (1846–1848); *David Copperfield* (1849–1850); *Bleak House* (1852–1853); *Little Dorrit* (1855–1857).

Dickens, C., *Sketches by Boz* (1836 and 1839).

Dodd, G., *The Food of London* (London: Longman, Brown, 1856).

Dodds, J.W., *The Age of Paradox: A Biography of England 1814–1851* (London: Gollancz, 1953).

Dyos, H. and Wolff, M., *The Victorian City: Images and Realities*, 2 volumes (London: Routledge, 1973).

Engels, F. *The Condition of the Working Class in England*, eds W. Henderson and W. Challoner (Oxford: Oxford University Press, 1958).

Finestein, I., *Anglo-Jewry in Changing Times* (London: Vallentine, Mitchell, 1999).

Freeman, M., *Railways and the Victorian Imagination* (New Haven and London: Yale University Press, 1999).

Goodway, D., *London Chartism 1838–1840* (Cambridge: Cambridge University Press, 1982).

Grant, J., 'Penny Theatres', from *Sketches in London* (1838) (1950–1951).

Greer, G., *Sex and Destiny* (London: Secker and Warburg, 1984).

Hamlin, C., *Public Health and Social Justice in the Age of Chadwick* (Cambridge, UK: Cambridge University Press, 1998).

Hardyment, C., *From Mangle to Microwave: The Mechanization of Household Work* (Cambridge: Polity Press, 1988).

Harrison, J.F., *Early Victorian Britain 1832–1851* (Fontana, 1979).

Hayward, A.L., *The Days of Dickens* (London: Routledge, 1926).

Holme, T., *The Carlyles at Home*, first published 1965 (London: Persephone Books, 2002).

Hoppen, K.T., *The Mid-Victorian Generation 1846–1886* (Oxford: Oxford University Press, 1998).

House, H., *The Dickens World* (Oxford University Press, 1941).

Huish, R., *The Progress of Crime: or, Authentic Memoirs of Maria Manning [a Romance]* (London: Huish, 1849).

Illustrated London News (1849).

Inwood, S., *A History of London* (London: Macmillan, 1998).

Jackson, J., 'The Irish in London' (London University MA thesis, 1958).

James, A., *The Post* (London: Batsford, 1970).

Jerrold, D., *Mrs. Caudle's Curtain Lectures* (P. Harvill, 1974).

Johnson, E., *Charles Dickens, his Tragedy and Triumph* (Harmondsworth: Penguin, revised edition 1986).

Kingsley, C., *Two Years Ago* (London: Macmillan, 1882).

Knelman, J., *Twisting in the Wind: the Murderess and the English Press* (Toronto: University of Toronto Press,1998).

Knight, P., 'Women and abortion in Victorian and Edwardian England', *History Workshop Journal* (1977), 4.

Lane, J., *A Social History of Medicine, Health, Healing and Disease in England 1750–1950* (London: Routledge, 2001).

Laver, J., *Taste and Fashion from the French Revolution until Today* (London: Harrap, 1937).

Laver, J., *Manners and Morals in the Age of Optimism 1848–1914* (London: Weidenfeld & Nicolson, 1966).

Laver, J., *A Concise History of Costume* (London: Thames & Hudson, 1969).

Leigh, P., *Manners and Customs of the Englyshe, Drawn from ye Quick by Rychard Doyle, To which be added some extracts from Mr Pips hys Diary* (London: Bradbury and Evans, 1850).

Levitt, S., *Victorians Unbuttoned* (London: Allen & Unwin, 1986).

Lock, J., *Dreadful Deeds and Awful Murders; Scotland Yard's First Detectives 1829–1878* (Taunton: Barn Owl Books, 1990).

Longmate, N., *King Cholera, the Biography of a Disease* (London: Hamish Hamilton, 1966).

Margetson, S., *Leisure and Pleasure in the Nineteenth Century* (London: Cassell, 1969).

Mayhew, H., *Life and Labour of the London Poor*, 3 volumes, first published 1851 (London: Charles Griffin & Co., 1861–1862).

Mayhew, H., *The Morning Chronicle Survey of Labour and the Poor: the Metropolitan Districts* (Horsham: Caliban Press, 1982).

Mayhew, H. and Binney, J., *The Criminal Prisons of London and Scenes of Prison Life*, first published 1862 (London: Frank Cass, 1968).

Moses, E. and Son, *The Growth of an Important Branch of British Industry* (London: E. Moses and Son, 1860).

Murray's Handbook to London (London: John Murray, 1851).

Nowrojee, J. and Merwangee, H., *Journal of a Residence of Two Years and a half in Great Britain* (London: W.H. Allen, 1841).

Olsen, D.J., *The Growth of Victorian London* (London; Batsford, 1976).

Pearsall, R., *The Worm in the Bud: The World of Victorian Sexuality*, first published 1969 (Harmondsworth: Penguin, 1971).

The Penguin Book of Comic and Curious Verse (Harmondsworth: Penguin, 1952).

Perkin, J., *Women and Marriage in Nineteenth Century England* (London: Routledge, 1989).

Peterson, M., *The Medical Profession in Mid-Victorian London* (Los Angeles: University of California Press, 1978).

Polytechnic Magazine, 28 January 1903.

Porter, B., *The Refugee Question in Mid-Victorian Politics* (Cambridge: Cambridge University Press, 1979).

Porter G.R., *The Progress of the Nation* (London: John Murray, 1847).

Porter, R., *London: a Social History* (Harmondsworth: Penguin, 1996).

Porter, R., *A History of Medicine* (Cambridge, UK: Cambridge University Press, 1966).

Porter, R., *The Greatest Benefit to Mankind* (London: Harper Collins, 1997).

Pratt, J., *A report on the Trial of Maria Manning and George Frederick Manning for the Wilful Murder of Patrick O'Connor at Miniver Place, Bermondsey, London on Thursday the 9th of August, 1849.*

Priestley, H., *The What it Cost the Day before Yesterday Book* (Havant: Kenneth Mason, 1979).

Public Record Office, DPP 4/2.

Public Record Office, Metropolitan Police, MEPO 3/54.

Punch (1849).

Quennell, P. (ed.), *Mayhew's London* (London: Pilot Press, 1949).

Quennell, P. (ed.) *Mayhew's Characters* (London: Spring Books, 1967).

Rawlings, P., *Crime and Power: a History of Criminal Justice 1688–1998* (London: Longman, 1999).

Reade, C., *It's Never Too Late to Mend* (London; Richard Bentley, 1856).

Reynolds, G.W.M., *The Mysteries of London*, ed. T. Thomas (Keele University Press, 1996).

Reynolds, G.W.M., *The Mysteries of the Court of London*, 8 volumes (London: John Dicks, 1849–1856).

Royle, E., *Chartism* (Harlow: Longman, 1980 and 1986).

Sala, G.A., *Gaslight and Daylight* (London: Chapman & Hall, 1859).

Sala, G.A., *Twice Round the Clock*, first published in 1859 (Leicester: Leicester University Press, 1971).

Seaman, L.B.C., *Life in Victorian London* (London: Batsford, 1973).

Seymour, B., *Lola Montez* (New Haven: Yale University Press, 1996).

Sheppard, F., *London 1808–1870; the Infernal Wen* (Berkeley: University of California Press, 1971).

Shipley, S., *Club Life and Socialism in Mid-Victorian London* (Oxford History Workshop, 1972).

Slater, M., *An Intelligent Person's Guide to Dickens* (London: Duckworth, 1999).

Sponza, L., *Italian Immigrants in Nineteenth Century Britain: Realities and Images* (Leicester: Leicester University Press, 1988).

Strachey, L., *Eminent Victorians* (London: Chatto and Windus, 1918).

Stamp, G., *The Changing Metropolis: Earliest Photographs of London 1839–1879* (Harmondsworth: Viking, 1984).

Stanley, M.L., *Marriage and the Law in Victorian England 1850–1895* (London: I.B. Tauris, 1989).

Sutherland, J., *Is Heathcliff a Murderer? Puzzles in 19th-Century Fiction* (Oxford: Oxford University Press, 1996).

Swift, R. and Gilley, S., *The Irish in Britain 1815–1939* (London: Pinter, 1989).

Taine, H., *Notes on England* (1872).

Thackeray, W.M., *Pendennis* (London: Bradbury and Evans, 1849).

Thomas, R., *London's First Railway: the London and Greenwich* (London: Batsford, 1972).

Thomson, B., *The Story of Scotland Yard* (London: Grayson & Grayson, 1935).

Trudgill, E., *Madonnas and Magdalens* (London: Heinemann, 1976).

Vega, V. de la, *Cartas Familiars inéditas* (Madrid, 1873).

Walker, G.A., *Gatherings from Graveyards, particularly those of London* (London: Longman, 1839).

Weightman, G. *Bright Lights: Big City* (London: Collins & Brown, 1992).

Weindling, D. and Colloms, M., *Kilburn and West Hampstead Past* (London: Historical Publications, 1999).

Weinreb, B. and Hibbert, C., *The London Encyclopaedia* (London: Macmillan, 1983).

Wigley, J., *Rise and Fall of the Victorian Sunday* (Manchester: Manchester University Press, 1980).

Wilkes, J., *The London Police in the 19th Century* (Cambridge, UK: Cambridge University Press, 1977).

Wilson, A.N. (ed.) *The Faber Book of London* (London: Faber & Faber, 1993).

Wilson, A.N., *The Victorians* (London: Hutchinson, 2002).

Young, G.M. (ed.) *Early Victorian England 1830–1865*, 2 volumes (Oxford University Press, 1934).

Index

Acton, Dr. William, 32
Adelaide Gallery, 57, 138–9
Agar Town, 16, 20
Albert, Prince, 75, 85, 219
Aldgate, 6, 62, 171, 179
Amalgamated Society
of Engineers, 170
Anaesthetics, 1, 72
Anti-Catholicism, 129, 155, 156–7, 162
Antiseptics, 1, 71
Areas, 95
Armes, Ann, 2, 209
Arnold, Thomas, 187
Arsenic, 69, 205–6
Astley's Amphitheatre, 142–3, 145
Austria, 162, 163, 164, 165

Bainbridge (furniture dealer), 7, 10, 98,
208
Baker Street Station, 176
Ballantyne, William, 208, 209
Balloonist, 144
Bank of England, 168, 178
Bankruptcy, 91
Barnes, PC, 197, 207
Barrett, Michael, 216
Bathrooms, 93, 96
Battersea, 182
Beards and moustaches, 64–5, 164
Belle Sauvage, La, 171
Bazalgette, Joseph, 85
Beer-drinking, 30, 133
Blantyre, Lady, 26, 28
Bermondsey, 4, 11, 17, 23, 51, 79, 100,
185
sanitary condition of, 75, 80, 82, 95
Birth and death rates, 73

Bishop's Bridge Road, 186
'Black-Eyed Susan', 149
Blackwall, 56
Blanc, Louis, 163
Blood analysis, 71
Bloomer, Amelia, 1, 33
Bond Street, 40
Boulogne, 20, 29, 132, 133
Bow Street Runners, 198
Brassey, Thomas, 185
Bread, 45
British Museum, 16, 115, 123, 152, 168
Reading Room, 114
Broad Street, Soho, 83
Brougham, Henry, 113, 114
Buckingham Palace, 168
Burial Grounds, 78
Burlington Arcade, 38
Burton, PC, 197

Cabs, 176–7
Calcraft, William, 215
Californian gold, 87–8
Camden Town, 16, 45, 189, 191
riot of 1846, 159–60
Cannon Street Station, 186
Canterbury Music Hall, 151
Capital Punishment, 216
Carlyle, Jane and Thomas, 19
and Austrian spies, 165
Count D'Orsay, 91
diet, 48
eating out, 53–4
house, 93
kitchen range, 97
river steamer, 165
Spaniards, 160

Carlyle, Jane and Thomas (*continued*)
taxes, 104
use of coal, 97
use of gas, 99
Cassell's *Popular Educator*, 115
Catholics, 155
churches, 160
relief of disabilities, 156
restoration of Hierarchy, 156
Catnach Press, 115
Caudle, Mr. and Mrs.
hat, 61
holidays, 132
Jews, 172–3
Chadwick, Edwin, 74, 84
'Champagne Charlie is my Name',
151
Charing Cross, 17, 45, 182, 198
Charing Cross Station, 186
Chartism, 1, 165–70
Cheapside, 171, 177
Chelsea, 18, 93, 182, 183
Chinese junk, 29, 139
Chinese pagoda, 139
Cholera, 1, 23, 74, 78–85, 155
Christmas cards, 194
Church of England, 122, 129
attendance at, 125
Clapham, 177
'Clapham Sect', 127
Clapton, 177
Clement's Inn, 179
Clerkenwell, 162
Class, 100–101, 104
Clothes
women's, 58–60
men's, 61–4
Coal, 97, 98
Coal Hole, The, 88, 151
Cobden, Richard, 219
Cockney Rhyming Slang, 107
Cole, Henry, 219
Collins, Wilkie
and sanctimoniousness, 127
Sergeant Cluff, 202
stays, 60
walking in London, 179

Colman, Henry, 19–20
churches, 122
clothes, 61
cost of dining, 54
Regent Street, 58
'Consols', 89
Contraception, 1, 34–5
Cooking, 46, 48, 97
Copenhagen Market, 78
Copper, kitchen, 93
Covent Garden, 171
Covent Garden Theatre, 37, 141, 148,
149
Coventry Street, 37, 55
Cremorne Gardens, 38, 88, 144–5
Cross-Keys Inn, 177
Cubitt, Thomas, 92, 185, 219
Currency, 2
Custom House, 12, 168
Customs and Excise Service, 14
Cyder Cellars, 87, 151

Daguerrotype, 138
'De Medietate Lingue', trial, 207
Debtors' Prison, 92
Denmark Street, 169
Department Stores, 57
Dickens
and anti-Catholicism, 157–8
Astley's, 142
bailiffs, 90–1
Britannia Saloon, 150
centralisation, 52
class, 100–101
debtors' prison, 92
detectives, 201–4
education, 112
English Sunday, 121,122, 123
Examiner, The, 118
food, 44–5
foreigners, 162
Greenwich Fair, 146
Hackney Carriages, 177
Jews, 171
Household Words, 118
incomes, 102–3
literacy, 110

Dickens (*continued*)
 magazines, 114
 Manning executions, 214–15,
  216
 Marylebone workhouse, 105–6
 men's clothes, 61–2
 moneylending, 90
 Old Vic, 149–50
 omnibuses, 181
 Penny Post, 193
 philanthropy, 127
 railways, 183, 188, 190–1
 revolution, 165
 Royal Marylebone Theatre, 149
 Sadler's Wells
 Theatre, 148
 shellfish, 55
 'Slap-bang' restaurants, 54
 Smithfield, 77
 Stock Exchange, 89–90
 Tooting scandal, 80–1
 United States, 20
 Vauxhall Gardens, 143
 Women, 33
Diseases, 74
Disraeli
 and railways, 186
 sabbatarianism, 123
 'seriousness', 126
 Sybil, 104–5
Divorce, 31
Docks, 13, 183
 Prostitutes in, 38
Dockers, 15
Doctors, 69
Domestic management,
 Books on, 95
 See also under Soyer, A.
D'Orsay, Count, 91
Drury Lane Theatre, 37, 40, 148,
 149
 concerts at, 148
Dry-Cleaning, 65
Ducrow, Andrew, 142–3
Duke's Place, 171
Dumbicki, Count, 164
Dupin, Baron, 13

Ecclesiastical Titles Act, 157
Edgware Road, 38, 178
Edinburgh, 9, 183, 190, 208
Education, public funding of,
 111–12
Egyptian Hall, 134, 139
Ellis, Ruth, 216
Ether, *See* under Anaesthetics
Euston Road, *See* under New Road
Euston Square, 161
Euston (Square) Station, 9, 16, 18,
 159, 186, 188–9, 190, 191, 200,
 201
Evangelism, 126–7, 128, 133, 156
Evan's Supper Rooms, 151
Examiner The, 213
Excrement, 75
 Disposal of, 96
Exeter Hall, 126–7, 147, 155

Farringdon Street, 186, 195
Field, Inspector, 202–3
Firman, Hannah, 100, 208
Fish, 55, 171
Fleet Street, 195
Food
 adulteration of, 30, 51–2
 budgets, 47–8
 high class, 56
 in *David Copperfield*, 44–5
 middle class, 49
 supply, 50
 working class, 44
Foreigners, 160–5
 attitude towards, 162
 cafés, 165
 fear of, 167
 numbers of, 163
 restrictions on, 163, 167
Fortnum and Mason's, 50
Foxe's *Book of Martyrs*, 155
France
 excursions to, 132–3
 1848 revolution in, 166, 169
Frith, William, RA, 137
Fruit, 50
Furniture, cost of, 98

Gas, 98–9
General Post Office, 168
Gin Palaces, 30, 133
Golden Square, 162
Good, Daniel, 200
Gore House, 91
Government interference, hostility
    towards, 52
Gravesend, 132, 185
Great Exhibition, 1, 13, 123, 167, 185,
    219–20
Greenwich, 4, 55, 145, 152, 173, 182,
    185
Greenwich Mean Time, 187
Guildhall, 168
Gunter's, 56–7

Hackney coaches, 176–7
Hammersmith, 50, 177
Hampstead, 16, 84, 179
Hanging, 204–5, 212, 215, 216
Hansom, Joseph, 176
Hansom cabs, 176, 213
'Happy Families', 145
Hatton Garden, 161
Haymarket, 37, 38, 39, 55
Haynau, Baron, 162
Haynes, Det-Insp., 200, 201
Her Majesty's Theatre, 148
Herzen, Alexander, 163
Highgate, 181
Hill, Rowland, 219
Hogg, Quintin, 198
Holborn, 168, 212
Holloway Prison, 216
Holywell Street, 40, 119
Horsemonger Lane Gaol, 212, 213
Hospitals, 72
'Hottentot Venus', 139
Houndsditch, 171
Houses of Parliament, 136
Housing, 92–3
Hudson, George and Mrs., 18
Huish, Robert, 25, 93, 155, 158,
    213
Hungerford Bridge, 17, 44
Hungerford Pier, 182

Illiteracy, 110–11
'Inspector Bucket', 202–3
Irish
    Camden Town riot, 159–60
    immigrants, 155, 158–9, 160
    in police, 197–8
Islington, 178
Italians, 145, 160–2

Jacob's Island, 75–6
Jerrold, Douglas, 149
    See under 'Black-Eyed Susan' and
      Caudle. Mr. and Mrs.
Jersey, 10, 11
Jews, 162, 170–3
John Street, 168
Jullien, Louis-Antoine, 147

Keble, Professor John, 128
Kennington, 167, 168
Kilburn, 190
King John's Head, The, 29
King's Cross, 16, 186
Kingsley, Charles
    and church attendance, 126
    and sweating system, 170
Kirk, William, 8, 9, 200
Kitchens, 97–8
Knelman, Judith, 216
Kossuth, Louis, 162

Lambeth, 16, 199, 202
Laudanum, 69, 70
Laundry, 99
Lavatories, 96–7
    See under excrement and water-
      closets
Leather Lane, 161
Ledru-Rollin, 163
Leicester Square, 134, 142, 160, 162
Libraries, public, 118
    See under Mudie and W.H. Smith
Library of Entertaining Knowledge, The,
    115
Lighting, 91
Lincoln's Inn Fields, 162
Lind, Jenny, 123, 141, 148

Literature, 113
London, 16 and ff.,
  administration, 18–19
  dirtiness, 19
  industry, 17
  new building, 17
  noise, 19
  population, 17
  slums, 18, 20–2
  unlikelihood of revolution in, 169
London Bridge, 4, 6, 12, 14, 15, 18, 132,
    179, 182, 183, 186
London Bridge Station, 4, 8, 185, 200,
    201, 213
London, City of, 12
London & Greenwich Railway, 185
London & Birmingham Railway, 187,
    189
London & North-Western Railway, 16
  bookstalls on, 119, 189
Louis-Philippe, ex-King, 163
Lowther Arcade, 57, 138
Ludgate Hill, 171, 186

Macaulay, 120
Macready, William, 141, 148, 149
'Mlle. Hortense', 203–4
Mainzer, Joseph, 147
Manning, Frederick, 1, 5, 7, 28, 82, 87,
    91–2, 101, 111, 113, 137, 146, 167,
    186, 195, 205, 211, 213, 220
  marries Marie de Roux, 28
  loses job on railway, 29
  new job, 101
  visits Chamber of Horrors, 141
  murders O'Connor, 6
  arrested, 11, 192
  tried, 12, 206 and ff.
  takes sacrament, 125, 214
  hanged, 12, 124, 215
Manning, Maria, 25 and ff., 41, 91–2, 95,
    101, 111, 116, 119, 133, 137, 146,
    167, 179, 183, 188, 195, 200, 201,
    203–4, 219–20
  meets O'Connor, 26
  marries Manning, 28
  murders O'Connor, 6

  flees and is arrested, 188–90
  tried, 12, 206 and ff.
  clothes, 59–60
  books, 114
  religion, 155
  takes Sacrament, 125
  hanged, 12, 124, 215
  wax model of, 60
  property auctioned, 89
Mantalini, Mr. and Mrs., 162
Margate, 132, 182
Marie de Roux
  See Manning, Maria
Marwood, Ronald, 216
Marx, Karl, 114, 163, 165
Marylebone Road
  See under New Road
Massey, William, 5, 87, 94, 141, 208
Mayhew, Henry
  balloon ride over London, 15
  Catholics, 160
  costermongers' reading, 117
  costermongers' religious knowledge,
    126
  food of the poor, 44
  Jews, 170–1, 172
  Petticoat Lane, 172
Mayne, Richard, 14, 167, 198, 199
Mazzini, Giuseppe, 156, 160
Mealtimes, 43
Meat, 46
Mechanics' Institutes, 113, 114, 147
Medicine, Chapter Four passim
Melbourne, Lord, 27, 127
Metropolitan Board of Works, 85
Metropolitan Building Act, 94
Metropolitan Railway, 176, 186
Metropolitan Water Act, 84
Metropolitan Water Board, 85
Metternich, Prince, 163
Middlesex Street, 172
Mile End, 6, 179
Milk, 46
Miniver (Minver) Place, 5, 6, 7, 10,
    92–4, 197, 200
Minories, The, 171
Money supply, 88

Montes, Lola, 35–7
Morals, 27
Morton, Charles, 151
Moses E. and Son, 62–4, 164, 170
Moxey, Superintendent, 190, 192, 201, 208
Mudie's Library, 118–19
'Music for the Millions', 147
Music Hall, 151
Mysteries of London, The, 116

Napoleon, Louis, 156, 163
National Association for Parliamentary and Financial Reform, 169
National Gallery, 17, 123, 127, 137
National Reform League, 169
Natives, exhibitions of, 139–40
Nelson's Column, 17, 166
New Cross, 185, 187
New Cut, 11, 51, 149, 150, 211
New Oxford Street, 17, 21, 62
New Road, 16, 20, 62, 135, 178, 186
Newgate, 25, 212, 216
Newington Sessions House, 213
Newman, John Henry, Cardinal, 128
Newspapers and Magazines, 114, 117, 118
Nigger Minstrels, 146, 151
Nonconformist Churches, 122, 128, 155
Novels, 118, 119–20

O'Brien, Bronterre, 168, 169
O'Connor, Feargus, 168
O'Connor, Patrick, 1, 5, 6, 7, 8, 14–15, 26, 61, 70, 87, 88, 89, 103, 132, 133, 146, 158, 185, 197, 199
'Oh Susanna!', 135, 146, 214
Old Vic,
   See Royal Victoria Theatre
Omnibuses, 1, 178–82, 213
Orange Street, 169
Oratorio, 147
Orsini, 163
Oxford Movement,
   See under Tractarianism
Oxford Street, 16, 57, 178, 212

Paddington, 16, 177, 178, 186
Paddington Station, 29, 186, 191
   lending library, 119
Palmerston, Lord, 41, 141, 163
Panoramas and Dioramas, 134–6
Pantheon, The, 57
Patent medicines, 70
Patmore, Coventry, 40–1
Peel, Sir Robert, 141, 156, 197, 198, 219
Penny Gaffs, 150
Penny Post, 192–5
Pepper, Professor John, 138, 192
Petticoat Lane, 172
Phelps, Samuel, 148
Piccadilly, 37, 39, 186
Pickwick Papers, The, 116
Pius IX, Pope, 156
Place, Francis, 169
Poles in London, 160
Police, 197–204
   City of London, 198
   detective force, 200 and ff.
Pollock, Lord Chief Baron, 207, 209–10
Polytechnic, Regent Street, 137–9
Pool of London, 13, 14
Post, 1, 117, 194
   Sunday, 123–4
Primrose Hill, 190
'Pretty little Polly Perkins', 178
Prostitution, 37–9
Public Baths and Wash-houses, 96, 107
Punch
   and adulteration of milk, 52
   arrest of Mannings, 192
   Bermondsey murder, 23
   California gold rush, 88
   class, 101
   Continental revolutions, 164
   Gunter's, 56
   Jewish Disabilities, 173
   Louis-Philippe, 163–4
   omnibuses, 181–2
   poisoners, 205
   police, 199
   railway speculation, 184
   Tractarianism, 129
Vernon collection, 137

Rachael, Madame, 40
Railways, 183–91
  bookstalls, 119
  shares, 89, 91
  transport of food, 50
Ramsgate, 132
'The Ratcatcher's Daughter', 151
Ratcliff Highway, 38, 203
Reade, Charles, 90, 171
Reforms (political and social), 165–6
Regent Street, 16, 37, 58, 134, 135
  Quadrant arcade, 39
Regent's Park, 135
  Zoo, 152
Religion, questioning of, 121
Religious 'census', 125
Religious Tract Society, 120–1
Rent, 23, 93, 94
Restaurants, 53
  and women, 55
Revolutions, European, 33, 127, 163,
    165, 166
Reynolds, G.W.M., 43, 78, 116, 117, 166
Roman Republic, 156, 160
Rothschild, Lionel de, 173
Round House, 16, 159, 190
Rowan, Colonel, 197, 198
Rowland's Macassar Oil, 65
Royal Academy Exhibition, 127, 183
Royal Colosseum, *See* under Panoramas
    and Dioramas'
Royal Italian Opera House, *See* under
    Covent Garden Theatre
Royal Marylebone Theatre, 149
Royal Society of Arts, 219
Royal Victoria Theatre, 149
Rush, James, 140–1, 212
Russell, Lord John, 141, 156, 219
Russell Square, 168

Sabbatarianism, 122–4
Sadler's Wells Theatre, 148, 166
Saffron Hill, 161
St. Barnabas, Pimlico, 129
St. Giles rookery, 18, 21, 160, 202, 203
St. George's, Southwark, 129
St. Paul's Cathedral, 152, 186

Sala, George Augustus,
  and food, 44
  foreigners, 164
  oratorio, 147
  Poses plastiques, 142
  Regent Street, 58
  sabbatarianism, 124
  St. Giles' rookery, 21
Salomons, Sir David, 173
'Sam Hall, the chimney sweep', 151–2
Saracen's Head Inn, 71, 186
Schools, 111–12
Scotland Yard, 200, 201
Seven Dials, 169
Sewers, 74, 82, 85
Sewing machines, 59
Sex and contraception, 32, 34
Shaw, Det. Sgt., 200, 202
Sheil, Richard, 158, 199
Shillibeer, George, 178
Shop assistants, 57–8
Shopkeepers, attitude of, 58
Shopping, 57–8
Simon, Dr. John, 76
Smith, W.H., 119
Smithfield, 50, 76–8
Smithfield Fair, 140
Smoking and disease, 70
Snow Hill, 171
Snow, Dr. John, 83
Society for the Diffusion of Useful
    Knowledge, 115
Soho, 162
Somerset House, 168, 177
Southwark, 17, 79, 80, 82, 182, 203, 212
Southwark Bridge, 15
Southwark Bridge Road, 151
Southwark Market, 51
Southwark and Vauxhall Water
    Company, 84
Soyer, Alexis, 49
Spaniards in London, 160–1
Steamboats, 132, 182–3
Stepney Green, 168
Strand, 16, 38, 39, 179, 202
Stulz, George, 62
Sugar, 46

Surgeons and surgery, 71
Surrey Gardens, 147
Surrey Music Hall, 151
Swan and Edgar, 60
Sweating system, 1, 64, 171

Tableaux Vivants, 142
Taglioni, Madame, 148
Taine, Hippolyte
  and docks, 13
  prostitution, 38–9
  clothes, 58–9, 60–1
Taunton, 10, 28, 29, 170
Tawell, Jogn, 19, 201
Taxation, 103–4
Tea, 45–6
Telegraphs, 1, 9, 191–2
Thackeray, W. M.,
  and E. Moses and Son, 63
  Lady Blessington, 91
  Louis-Philippe, 163
  Pendennis, 120, 182, 184
  railways, 183, 184
  showers, 96
  Vauxhall Gardens, 143, 144
Thames, River, 12, 182, 183
  boats, See under Steamboats
Thornton, L.M., 193
Thornton, Det. Sgt., 202
Tom Thumb, 140
Tooting, Drouet's Home, 80–1
Tottenham Court Road, 16, 17, 62
Tower Bridge, 13
Tower of London, 12
Tractarianism, 128–9, 155, 156
Trafalgar Square, 17, 57, 166
Trial of Mannings, 206–12
Trollope, Anthony, 128, 183, 195
Tupper, Martin, 115
Turner, John, R.A., 183

Uncle Tom's Cabin, 120, 139
University College London, 113, 168
Utilitarianism, 126

Vauxhall, 182
Vauxhall Gardens, 38, 88, 143–4

Vauxhall Station, 11
Vestris, Madame, 143, 148
Victoria (ship), 8, 202
Victoria Park, 152
Victoria, Queen
  abandons river trip, 85
  anaesthesia, 72, 83
  fear of revolution, 166, 168
  respectability of Court, 126
  Tom Thumb, 140
Victoria Station, 186
Von Joel, yodeller, 145

Wages and salaries, 87, 99, 102–3,
  104–5
Warren's blacking factory, 65
Water closets, 74, 82, 97
  heating, 95
  storage, 97
  supply, 82–4, 95
Waterloo Road, 51
Waterloo Station, 10, 11, 18, 168, 185,
  190
Waxworks,
  Anatomical, 141
  Madame Tussaud's, 140–1
Wellington, Duke of, 17, 160, 168, 192
Wellington Street, 202
Westminster Abbey, 152
Westminster Bridge, 16, 168, 182
Westminster Bridge Road, 143, 151
Weston Street, 4, 75, 93
'What is it that roarest thus?, 179
White Horse Cellars, 186
Whitechapel, 6, 38, 78, 162, 179
Wilkins, Charles, 208
Wiseman, Cardinal Nicholas, 156
'Witchem,' (Wheeler), Sgt., 202
Women, murderers, 204, 205
  position of, 31 and ff.
  riding on buses, 181
Wordsworth, William, 143
Work, hours and conditions, 103,
  105
Workhouse, 105–7

Yorkshire Stingo, 178